the kid who missed the bus

Matt McCoy

central
avenue
publishing

2013

To my beautiful wife, Pauline, my daughter, Trinity,
and my son, Keegan.

You are my happy ending.

Although this book is based on some of the events that happened in my life, this is a work of fiction.

Names of people and places have been changed.

Craic:
(kræk)
a term for news, gossip,
fun, entertainment,
and enjoyable conversation.

Foreword

ONCE UPON A TIME, a soft, 250 pound guy walked into my exercise facility looking for a strength & conditioning program. When I asked him why, he looked at me evenly and replied, "My comeback."

Casually, I glanced around, convinced that there had to be a camera somewhere, certain that this must be some kind of joke, but it wasn't. His gaze was unblinking. Honest. Sincere. Ice hockey was his passion and he was going pro and no wasn't an option. He only had one question: "When can we start?"

Now, I've been a certified strength & conditioning specialist for twenty-eight years with an emphasis on hockey player development. I've seen every kind of person walk through my doors. I've trained, coached and mentored at both an amateur and a professional level. But this guy was a first. Some people come in here and they succeed and I mean really succeed but I've seen more fail and usually due to unrealistic expectations. Like mounting a professional comeback, for example.

I told this guy as much – that becoming an elite class of athlete was no small feat. That he'd need to be determined and dead serious and mentally strong. Completely committed. Confident. And that even then, he'd have to be naturally imbued with a level of genetic endowment matched only by his character and even then, I couldn't guarantee anything. And you know what he told me? He told me he wasn't afraid to take a gamble and he wasn't afraid to have a craic (whatever that is) and he wasn't afraid, full stop.

"I'm Danny Boy Doyle," he said, serious as a judge. "And I'm the real McCoy."

Boy, was he right.

~ Carlo Sferra, May 27, 2012

The Long Road to the NHL

This book was written for everyone. But not everyone knows hockey. This is a quick primer on the business of young people's hockey.

6-8 years old: Mighty Mites or Little Gretzkys

9-11 years old: Pup. There are two levels: House and Rep. The best players play Rep and the House league is purely for fun.

12-13 years old: Pee Wee: House and Rep leagues, and the separation in the players with talent.

14-15 years old: Bantam: House and Rep leagues. A good player will be selected by the Major Junior or the Tier 2 Junior leagues. Most kids will play two more years of minor hockey.

16-17 years old: Midget. House and Rep hockey. This is the make or break for kids aspiring to play at a higher level. Most kids will stay home two more years for growth and development. However, if the hockey program is weak where they live, they may leave for other towns. After this age bracket, kids are graduated from high school and they either quit hockey or just play for fun in adult leagues.

16-20 years old: Junior - Tier 1 & Tier 2.

Tier 1 (Major Junior): These teams own the rights to the player. It's the best players in that age group who aspire to make the NHL as fast as possible. Only a small minority of players get there. Players in the Major Junior hockey league are entitled to one year of Canadian university paid for every year played. However, a profesional game played anywhere will result in a loss of all education benefits. Players drafted higher into the league's teams entitle the team to more money.

Tier 2 (Junior A or Junior B): Players become eligible for a US scholarship or can use this league as a training ground for moving up to Major Junior. Players here can also get drafted to the NHL but it's more likely to happen in Major Junior. Many move onto get a US scholarship or play at a Canadian university.

In all Junior leagues, players are billeted out at host families. The season starts with training camp in mid August and goes until late May.

the kid who missed the bus

chapter 1

"How did you find out?"

"Accidentally. Went in with a wet cough, decreased energy, a forty-plus fever. Pancytopenic. That's the word they used. I'm learning lots of new words, actually. Another one is hepatosplenomegaly."

"And you knew it was serious then?"

"Not really. 'A few cells that were suspicious for blasts.' That's how they put it."

"I don't understand what that means."

"Neither did I. That's how they soften the blow. Gently break you in to the whole nightmare. Clinical euphemisms."

"Ah."

"So… This. What we're doing here. It's my first time."

"I'd gathered."

"I'm going to tell you right now, this isn't going to be easy for me."

"It's not supposed to be easy."

"Fair enough. How do we start?"

"Just start at the beginning and we'll address things as they arise. Think of it less as a chance to unload and more an opportunity to be reflective. To take stock. What do you think?"

"Sounds good."

"Good. When did it all start, then?"

SUMMER OF '73. I'M A breezy birth on a breezy Prince Peaks day, says Mum. In and out. They christen me Daniel Liam Doyle after Danny Doyle, the Irish folk singer who eventually achieved the dubious honour of knocking *Take a Chance on Me* off the top of the Irish charts with his hit, *The Rare Auld Times*. I'm their first boy and they treat me like the moon and stars spin around my cowlick. Catholic families love their firstborn sons. And with Nan and Granddad and the twin aunties, I'm never short on cuddles; nor should I be, I'm a lovely little fella. Mild mannered, easygoing, respectful. The whole lot.

MUM GETS PREGNANT AGAIN A year after I'm born—a little girl—but the baby isn't crying and the nurses are, and it all happens so, so fast.

They bury Kelly on a Friday, in a tiny plot in Seaview Cemetery at the base of Mount Jayne. Mum doesn't cry at the funeral. Not a tear. She's too busy being strong for everyone else. But two months later when she's scrubbing the kitchen floor, she breaks her heart on the cold linoleum. Every year on my little sister's birthday, we light a candle.

"Do you want to keep going?"

"Uh-huh."

"Why don't you tell me about your big sister."

ASHLYN. IT'S AN ADJUSTMENT FOR her, this little brother business, and she's dealing with the dethroning as any three-year-old would. But by the time I'm two, she's found my purpose as something between a plaything, an excuse and an alibi.

I'm lolling against the couch in the throes of mid-afternoon snot-nosed boredom when she grabs my hand.

"Come on, Danny," she says, leading me upstairs. The master bedroom is off limits, full stop, but I'm Ash's exception to most rules and an easy patsy when plans go awry. She's rummaging through Mum and Dad's closet: opening hatboxes, make-up boxes, pulling clothes off hangers with reckless abandon. Eventually, I'm covered in lipstick, stumbling about in a summer dress and we're gurgling so hard with glee we don't care if we're caught. Ash and I stay close through the years but that's the first and last time she convinces me to cross-dress.

"And your brother?"

HENRY'S BORN TWO YEARS LATER. The most grief he gives Mum his entire early life is the thirty-nine hours it takes to push him out. When the midwife finally deposits the little bundle into her exhausted arms, Henry looks up and smiles as if to say, "Don't worry, Mum. You won't have to do that again." He's her last child—her last baby—and like most youngest kids he more or less retains that status the rest of his life.

Ash and I are eventually granted an audience with the newest Doyle. The big sister gig's old hat for Ash by now and right from the get-go she's fussing and fawning with great confidence.

"He's lovely," she declares with authority as Henry wraps a pudgy purple fist around her finger. Me on the other hand? Underwhelmed. Ash already digs into my mum-time and this wrinkly little distraction isn't going to improve the situation. Besides, he smells like sour milk.

"Why's his face all scrunched up? Can't you give him back?" I ask. Everyone laughs. It's a serious question and why they'd all find it amusing is beyond me but intentionally or otherwise, I've won the room over.

Danny 1, Baby 0.

MONTHS PASS, AND HENRY MOVES from the crook of Mum's arm to her lap to the carpet and one day he's teetering across the room on his own and that's it. Ash is delighted with the title of de facto babysitter and Henry falls in behind me like a dogged, diapered shadow, tripping on my heels and tugging at my shirt and that's our default formation for the next little while, anyway.

Every few months, Mum measures us against the living room door frame. The shag carpet's as thick as grass and I can steal an unnoticed half-inch if I stand on my toes. There's something satisfying about stepping out from under the ruler and seeing that little line of lead penciled into the paint but nothing matches the thrill of writing on the wall. *Danny*, I carefully print next to the line and accompanying date (December 25) pleased to see that 'Ashlyn' is only a double-space above; much closer than our signatures from three months earlier. But as Christmas leads to summer leads to Christmas again (that's how kids tell time) it's not just our autographs that are inching away from Henry. Ash is growing up and I'm on my toes growing up right behind her and as we get taller our little brother's slowly and steadily becoming less a novelty and more a nuisance. That is, until the little guy develops a stutter…

Sibling sadism is a funny thing. We never mean Henry any *real* harm but suddenly our annoying little brother is an unwitting comedy routine every time he opens his mouth, which makes him more entertaining than cable TV. Ash and I, we torment him relentlessly of course. Day-in-day-out, which only makes his affliction worse.

We're leaving the house one day when Henry comes bounding up, bright-eyed, eager and undaunted.

"W-w-w-where ya going?"

"T-t-t-to HELL," I reply, flexing one of my latest adult words. He looks up at me, completely guileless.

"C-c-c… C-c-c… Can I come?"

Ash laughs so hard she pees herself a little bit. Poor Henry gets it like this for weeks and I'm not sure who's happier when I finally leave for kindergarten, me or Mum.

"Do you feel badly about teasing Henry?"

"No. Yeah. I don't know, a little. Should I?"

"Let's move on. Tell me about your parents."

NORTHERN IRELAND IN 1969 IS no place for a pretty Catholic girl. Not with the Apprentice Boys marching on Bogside, NICRA rallying in Belfast and the Royal Ulster Constabulary proving as useless as a chocolate teapot. Soon enough it will be raining bricks and petrol-bombs but right now, the clouds are just starting to gather.

Lily Gowan weaves unhurriedly through the barricades and barb-wire twists of College Street, passing Wadsworth's then Hoy's but stopping to fix her hair in the window of Temple Tailors. Beyond her reflection, a unit of British soldiers bear down and blow past like green sea spray, all boots and moustaches and lingering looks. But why wouldn't they stare? She's lovely, petite, put together, with dark hair tumbling to her shoulders and big brown eyes that almost tell her story on their own.

Shivering in her coat, she shakes off their gazes and tries to quell the unpleasant feeling in her stomach, tries to forget the cautionary clucking from the well-meaning women, whose business it most certainly was *not*. He *had* sounded strange on the telephone this morning, though.

If he's done with me, I won't cry, she tells herself.

NOLAN DOYLE CONTEMPLATES THE LAST inch of a cigarette as he leans in the entrance of the Bradford & Bingley Building Society. She's late, but he's not bothered. He'd wait a whole packet of fags if he had to.

She's not his first girl; and no surprise, with his square-jawed swagger and that Guinness-black hair. But she's the first to last longer than a fortnight. Lily's different than the rest, though: younger for starters and trusting. Not a jealous bone in her body, even with half of female Belfast owning stories about him and the other half wishing they did.

"Everyone deserves the benefit of the doubt," she'd stated matter-of-factly, punctuating her sincerity with a peck on his cheek. If she wasn't his fresh start, he didn't know what was.

They had met at a dance hall one rainy spring night when he spilled his Bushmills down her blouse.

"You're too pretty for your own good," he said.

"You're too clumsy an arse for anybody's," she replied but that's what love looks like sometimes.

Spring turned to summer and evenings out dancing gave way to afternoons rambling across the city. Lily would tell him about the girl who nannied for a rich Boston family to support her poor Irish one back home and Nolan would regale her with the exploits of the handsome pipe fitter who went to Chicago and conquered America. He wasn't afraid to take a gamble, he told her emphatically. And he wasn't afraid to have a *craic*. And he wasn't afraid, full stop.

"Good," she replied. "Because you're meeting my family this Sunday."

Lily's lot lived over on Arran Street in a narrow home that smelled of book glue and brass polish. Da Gowan was a butcher, and Ma Gowan was a ma and Lily's sisters were twins: shy, freckly kids who looked as though their lives' sole purpose was completing chores and combing each other's hair. As could be expected, Nolan was flawlessly charming the entire visit and when he and Lily left, her Da shook his hand twice.

But now, as he waits outside the Building Society, Nolan doesn't feel quite so invincible. Fishing in his pocket for the hundredth time, he checks for the ring. It's a tiny band with a diamond scarcely bigger than the gleam in his eye but it's the best he can do at the moment. No, she's not his first girl by a country mile, but he's hoping she'll agree to be his last.

Lily arrives and everything clever evaporates from Nolan's head. He's lost, completely lost in those big, beautiful eyes and he's digging in his coat and he's down on one knee and all he can hear is his heartbeat and the rumble of an approaching convoy. He tells her he adores her. Tells her he needs her and couldn't abide a life without her, and windowpanes start rattling in their frames. Lily's laughing and crying and saying yes and flying into his arms and the nanny and the pipe fitter's lips collide as the British army thunders past.

Had the troops of the Prince of Wales's 1st Battalion looked down from their Shorland armoured cars, they would have witnessed one of Northern Ireland's happiest moments.

Many Fridays later, Lily's ill. Saturday morning as well. Sunday, she barely chokes down her toast and doesn't even touch her tea and by Monday she's certain and tells him as much.

For once in his life, Nolan's speechless, rooted to the spot, grinning like a National Lottery winner and when he finally finds his tongue it's only to echo his wife.

"You're going to be a dad," he repeats, savouring the sentence like it's single malt and it tastes so good he tries it again. "You're going to be a dad." Then it sinks in and he sinks to the couch only to jump back up immediately and bound to the window, throwing it open and bellowing the news to all of Belfast. "I'm going to be a dad!"

He kisses her face, her belly, promises to take her away, far away from the rubble and ruckus of Belfast. Promises to give her a good life. And Nolan Doyle keeps his promises.

"Don't tell anyone yet. Not yet," she pleads, shiny-eyed. He nods, clenches his jaw, inhales through his nose because some wounds feel like they'll never heal.

Because Northern Ireland in 1969 is no place for a baby.

"AND WHERE EXACTLY IN THE Godforsaken Arctic is this Sault Ste. Marie?" inquires Lily's Ma as if doubting that the place exists at all.

"Canada, Ma. It's on the Great Lakes," says Lily.

"Settled by Jesuits and named after the Holy Mother. Ideal place for a tot," adds Nolan, shooting his wife a wink that flies in just below the maternal radar. Ma's still skeptical but her eyebrows return from her hairline to their rightful place on her forehead, and rightly so. Ontario is lovely by all accounts and Sault Ste. Marie sounds as good a place as any. Most importantly, there's work. Ma sighs in resignation as she clears away the teacups.

"I'm not sure what I'm going to tell your father," she says, which really means, *I wish I didn't have to.*

"We'll be gone until The Troubles end. No more than a year tops, thank the Lord," assures Nolan, hoping he sounds more convincing than he feels.

"Too true," adds Lily, a little too quickly. They're halfway home in the taxi before she lets herself cry.

It's a windy Wednesday when the Queen Mary leaves Belfast Harbour, heading for the open sea. Nolan and Lily stand on the aft deck hand-in-hand, watching as their bonnie green isle disappears, as the bombs and the bastards and the bad memories turn to froth, slide away and vanish in the ship's marbled green wake.

Eight months later, Nolan's trudging across a snowy car park through a cloud of his own icy breath. Try as he might, there's no describing this cold without cursing. Lily (bless her) had gone off-menu at the start of her third trimester and these frigid, late-night convenience store excursions had become something of a ritual. Antacid, crisps, chocolate sauce, minus-forty Celsius. That's what love looks like sometimes.

Things hadn't gone exactly to plan. They were barely six months in Sault Ste. Marie before the work dried up, leaving Nolan no choice but to chase his losses West. Lily (who was pregnant in earnest by now) had to follow him by bus, which was a harrowing ordeal, even for her. Often she wouldn't get off at the derelict, drifter-infested station stops, not even to stretch her swollen legs. And she never made eye contact with anyone, not even the driver. A cross-country coach is no place for a pretty, pregnant Irish girl.

It's not that the work hadn't been plentiful here in Alberta but after freezing his knackers off in an Edmonton paper mill for the last eight weeks, Nolan was absolutely done with this nonsense.

He's under no delusions about Ireland either. Things are getting worse back home, not better. Even Ma and Da Gowan and the twins are packing their bags and no one who leaves buys return tickets anymore.

Nolan's never short of a plan, though: Prince Peaks, British Columbia, a booming mill town with more work than they know what to do with or so he's been told. They could make it to the coast before the kid arrives and Ma and Da and the twin aunties could join them. It's a long shot, but Nolan Doyle's not afraid to take a gamble and he's not afraid to have a *craic* and he's not afraid, full stop. He'll present the plan to Lily tonight, providing he doesn't die of cold in the next few moments.

Prince Peaks in the 1970s is the perfect place for a family: postcard pretty and obscenely green even by Irish standards. Between the mill, the fish cannery and the container port, it's more or less the poster-child for booming, beautiful British Columbia. The town's comprised of an island connected to the mainland by a short bridge and on certain days in deep January the harbour shimmers jade green and the trees looked like the ones from model railways. Thanks to her Ma's unmitigated advice, Lily's apprehensive about grizzly bears, but her husband reminds her that they're neither Protestant nor Catholic, nor interested.

As promised, the Toby Island Pulp Mill is booming. Nolan and Lily find a modest home only eight miles away: a ten-minute trip on a good day and a five-minute trip the day Lily's water breaks.

Ashlyn is born on a Tuesday. She's a happy child with her mother's eyes and her father's confidence and she's the centre of their universe.

DAD'S STILL AT THE MILL but it's grinding him down. He's there more often than not and he's working for a song and now four mouths are singing for their supper. Clearly something's got to give and Mum tries to ask him about it but he just pushes the peas around his plate and musters one-word answers.

Dad doesn't talk about going home anymore. Not with the land mines and the shoot-to-kill politics and the gift-wrapped grenades from Libya and the *Ulster Vanguard* and the *No Surrender to the IRA*. Westminster's digging its heels in and the Provisional IRA's prepping for the long game. Sunday was bloody indeed but bloodier days are coming and The Troubles are only getting more troublesome by the day. But Dad's got troubles of his own.

"To hell with Bobby Sands," he snaps, when Granddad brings up the hunger-striker-turned-politician at the dinner table. "I have no sympathy for a man who willingly starves himself while I'm breaking my back to make sure my family doesn't."

But later that week there's a spring in his step when he arrives home and a glimmer in his eye when he slides into his seat at the dinner table. Animated, excited, he explains between mouthfuls of mashed potatoes: there's a grocery store up for grabs with an apartment above it that's big enough for the lot of us. He's not afraid to take a gamble, he says. And he's not afraid to have a *craic* and he's not afraid, full stop. So it's a tip of the hat to the *Toby Island Pulp Mill* and time to tie on a blue apron and that's that. Because he promised Mum he'd take her away, far away, from the rubble and ruckus of Belfast. Promised to give her a good life. And Nolan Doyle keeps his promises.

It's a good grocery store by small town standards: thirteen hundred square feet of new linoleum and nearly-new shelving and fridges, four aisles, two cash registers, a little office in the back and a butcher counter that brings Granddad (and his legendary Irish sausages) out of retirement without anyone even having to ask him. It's not backbreaking work but it is a special kind of exhausting.

"Full-time, like living with an invalid," says Dad. But it's our invalid so everyone chips in. The twin aunties fall in behind the twin cash registers, Mum does the ordering while Nan watches Henry, and Ash and I are on self-appointed taste-test duty with special focus on chips, pop and particularly juicy pieces of fruit; a family business in every sense of the word. Gradually the gamble begins to pay off. And despite the long hours, Dad finally feels like we're booming along with the rest of Prince Peaks.

Welcome to Doyle's Foods.

"Things were good on the home front, then."

"Things were better."

"How about on the school front?"

"School was tormenting. Words can't express the excruciating boredom I endured every minute trapped in that stuffy little classroom and one-size-fits-all desks don't accommodate boys who are big for their age."

IT'S THE SLIVERS OF FREEDOM in between that are worth their weight in gold; the sweet reprieve of recess and lunch and recess again. But sadly, you don't get graded for tearing into a sandwich or tearing around a playground. If you did, I'd be top of the class and Report Card Day wouldn't be so unpleasant an ordeal. But it is and the first one of Grade 5 is no better than the last one of

Grade 4. Slowly, I walk home as the wind begins to gust and the clouds darken the sky prematurely, even for October. It's like God's unimpressed with my academic performance as well.

"Get me off the hook. *Please*," I hear myself say to no one in particular as I trudge up the stairs to our apartment above the grocery store like a condemned man en route to the gallows.

Mum's biggest fear is that I'll flunk out of school and never amount to anything. She's tried everything—even promising me a Ferrari when I turned sixteen—if I would *just* get on the Honour Roll and stay there. I know I can never pull that off as much as Mum knows she can never afford to buy me a sports car and we both know I'll never be a straight-A student like Ash. But that doesn't stop her dogged, desperate efforts to get the best out of me. Purse-lipped, she looks up from the incriminating document.

"Your father's going to hear about this when he gets home," she informs me somberly like I hadn't figured that much out already. I glance at the clock: 3:30 and Dad's not off until 6:00. The next two-and-a-half hours are going to feel like two-and-a-half days and I'm pretty sure that's an intentional part of the punishment. Dad's not one to take his belt off in these situations. His father did that to him and that's all the explanation I've ever received (although the look on his face fills in the blanks). No, he's far more clever than that. First, he'll just stare at me like any good Catholic father, letting the guilt do all the heavy lifting. Then, in case there's any doubt he'll tell me just how disappointed he is in me and that I'm going to have to pull my socks up or there'll be grave consequences, boy. And then, just so I know he's not kidding he'll dole out a smaller version of the grave consequences he was referring to: usually something that will at the very least blow an irreparable hole in the hull of *HMS Next Weekend*. That's what I'm in for and quite frankly, I'd prefer a good strapping.

I'm staring through the TV, the cartoons getting about as much attention as the untouched cheese and Stoned Wheat Thins at my elbow. On days like today, my after-school snack feels more like a Death Row inmate's last meal. It's only 4:30, I realize mournfully as the wind screams bloody murder, rattling the living room windows like bones and I'm partway through pondering just how badly my report card is going to sink my Saturday when suddenly there's a massive rending sound followed by an almighty crash.

Dashing to the window, I gawk at the carnage. Shingles pepper the road like leaves and what looks like a large chunk of someone's roof lies right in front of our grocery store. I'm wondering whose roof it is but only until Mum's scream provides a shrill answer.

Her eyes are wide and wild as she stands over the stove, apron pulled up over the pot roast like an umbrella as the rain lashes the countertop and the howling wind turns the dangling pots and pans into a crazy carillon. It's our roof, apparently, and suddenly it looks like we're dining al fresco tonight.

"Get your father!" she shrieks. I can't help grinning as I bolt down the stairs. Dad's cursing, Granddad's charging outside with a broom (like it's going to do any good whatsoever) and the rest of the evening is a frantic whirlwind of mops, buckets, roofers and tarpaulins. When all's said and done, my report card is as far from their minds as the roof is from the kitchen.

Glancing out the window before bed, I look up as the angry autumn Prince Peaks storm slowly tires from its tantrum.

"Thanks," I hear myself say, to no one in particular.

"Divine intervention?"

"Maybe. Old buildings have old roofs, though. And Prince Peaks does get crazy storms. But the timing was interesting."

"Still, you prayed…"

"Sure. But I was desperate. I would have prayed to anyone at that point."

"Praying's something you do only when you're desperate?"

"Let's talk about something else."

"Fair enough. Tell me about your interest in girls. When did that begin?"

"Oh God, even earlier. Kindergarten. I was never one of those kids that thought girls were gross. They fascinated me from day one."

IT's MORNING RECESS AND WE'RE racing around the playground at breakneck speed because that's the only speed boys know. We're chasing the girls and they're screaming in faux-horror and bolting like sheep before eventually letting us catch them. God knows why we're chasing them and God knows why they're letting us and no one seems to know the endgame. But invariably, they cluster like an over-excited, bobby-socked Roman phalanx as we pant and circle, shiny with sweat and braying like young barbarians.

Alexis is the girl I chase the most because quite simply, I love her. She's a brunette with huge hazel eyes and I'm going to marry her, I'm absolutely positive. One day after school she shows me her *Strawberry Shortcake* panties and the next week her dad catches us playing doctor behind King Coin Laundromat. That's the end of the chase and the beginning of my crash-course in shame though I'm still too young for any kind of guilt to stick.

"It's filthy and wicked," admonishes Mum. "And not how a gentleman treats a lady." Dad nods quietly but I swear his eyes are smiling.

I wait three weeks before calling on Alexis again and when I do it's her dad who answers.

"Can Alexis come out and play?" I ask bravely.

"Don't you think you've played with her enough already?" he replies before slamming the door in my face. I'd have to wait until grade twelve before getting the chance to play with her again.

BUT IT'S NOT JUST THE girls that are grabbing my attention. I'm an active kid and sports are attracting me too, and I'm getting the swing of one in particular: golf.

Dad's amazing work ethic is tempered by a healthy dose of Celtic practicality.

"I'll take a day off for three things: Weddings, funerals and golf," he says each Sunday like today's some kind of exception rather than our weekly ritual. Eighteen holes is as good a relationship as any to have with your old man, even as a kid. We're betting a dollar a hole and thanks to a generous handicap I'm winning quite nicely going into the back nine.

"Son," says Dad, throwing an affectionate arm over my shoulder, "see that sand trap? Tell your Ma I'm teaching you to gamble and I'll bludgeon you with your own putter and bury you in it."

THERE'S A TOURNAMENT AT THE club this weekend so we're working on our swing at the driving range instead. I'm knocking through my second bucket of balls (with a 5-wood that Dad sawed in half to make it seven-year-old friendly) when this kid from school comes bounding up. His name's Keegan and he's a grade ahead of me but I'm taller but he's already getting man muscle.

Danny 1, Keegan 2.

"You going to hockey practice tomorrow?" he asks.

"I can't skate," I reply.

Danny 1, Keegan 3.

"That's okay. My dad's the coach," he assures me benevolently like that's somehow going to change anything. Keegan blinks at me, waiting for my answer while I process his fundamentally flawed logic.

"Okay," I hear myself say. "See you tomorrow."

Danny 2, Keegan 3.

"So that was the beginning of hockey. And you were how old? Six?"

"Seven. Young enough to squeak into the last year of Mighty Mites but the other kids had been skating since they were in diapers so I was still the latecomer by a long shot."

DAD HAD TAKEN ME TO Olympic Sports after we left the driving range. Olympic was a cluttered, dimly lit second-hand place that reeked of feet and creosote but you couldn't go wrong with the prices. I remember my mouth dropping in awe as my eyes adjusted to the darkness as silhouettes slowly became sale items: balls, bats, skis, fishing rods, weight benches... But it was the back half of the store that had my heart hammering. Walls of skates, bins filled with pads, gloves, sticks... I was a knight suiting up for his first battle and the guy hunched over the spark-spitting skate sharpener was forging my Excalibur. Shirt, shorts, helmet, skates (I already had a floor hockey stick at home). Ready.

I'm undaunted in the locker room the next morning despite my plastic yellow stick and ill-fitting gear and confident in spite of the laughter. But fearlessness only gets you so far. I'm the son of Irish immigrant and the closest I've been to ice is Granddad's whiskey. It only takes one overconfident stride onto the glassy surface before the compass spins and I'm suddenly on my back trying to bring the rink's rafters into focus. A whoosh next to my head and I'm yanked out of my reverie by an icy slap of snow. Wiping the crystals from my eyes, I blink up at the face looming over me: a stern, steely-eyed visage with a hint of a smile carefully hidden behind a large moustache.

"Get up, son," says Keegan's dad, Gerry. And that's all he says, carrying on with the rest of the practice while I spend the better part of an hour wobbling and splaying across the ice like a baby deer.

Coach G was the son of an angry Belgian immigrant. He'd moved from Flin Flon, Manitoba to coach our local men's hockey team, the Prince Peaks Aviators. They occupied the majority of his time and coaching the Mighty Mites had been an afterthought but it gave him the chance to spend more time with his son. Coach G wasn't a big man but he didn't need to be, while he had eyes that could bore through you when you were messing around, you knew there was a heart of gold hidden somewhere behind that twitching moustache. In the off-season he worked for Canada Post. Forget the dog, beware of the mailman.

We're in the locker room after practice and I'm doubled over, recovering from a good-natured punch in the groin, courtesy of Keegan. The place is ringing with laughter and I'm gasping for breath and trying to navigate my way through that sickening pain as it travels up into my guts and becomes the God-awful cramp behind the belly button that women will simply never understand. Keegan's genuinely sympathetic once he's unloaded his unabashed mirth and wiped the tears of glee from his eyes.

"Whaddya mean, you're not wearing one?" he asks incredulously.

On the way home, I make Dad stop at Olympic again.

"Forgot something?" asks the pimply-face kid who sold me the oversized gear the day before and suddenly I realize that I don't know what it's called and I'm racking my brain and drawing a complete blank.

"I need a doogly protector," I mumble, cringing even as I'm saying it. Pimples just stares at me blankly. I glance left then right to make sure no one's looking before pointing meaningfully at my crotch. A smile of understanding slowly wraps itself across his oily face.

"Hey, Vern!" he yells. "Do we carry doogly protectors?"

"Huh?" comes a muffled reply from the guy on the skate/sword sharpener.

"Protectors," he yells, clearly enjoying himself, "for your doogly."

By the time I leave cup in hand, I'm ready for the earth to swallow me up.

Danny 0, Pimples 3.

As LUCK WOULD HAVE IT, the rink is right across the road from the grocery store and having a bedroom bird's-eye view of the parking lot means knowing *what* teams practice *when* without ever having to leave my pajamas.

There are three other Mighty Mite teams besides mine, each with its own coach, each with its own practice slot. Every dark, misty morning I watch these yawning kids trundling in, dragging their oversized hockey bags behind them, banging through the big blue double doors. These kids are training and I'm not and judging by their 5 a.m. body language, most would rather be dragging their asses to a funeral. A couple of weeks of this torture and I'm convinced I deserve the ice-time more than any of them (which I do if drive and desire are anything to go on). So I join them one morning, yawning and trundling and totally unnoticed and soon I'm going to all the Mighty Mite practices. Of course, it's not long before I'm spotted and the coaches are having a good laugh over the Doyle kid who can't skate and apparently can't read calendars either until they realize I'm doing it on purpose.

I'm relentless: playing floor hockey at school too and the girls will just have to wait because I've got better things to chase right now. I'm even going to Saturday public skates because God knows I need to catch up because I'm still whiffing shots, sending passes wide, clattering into clumsy challenges, collecting penalty minutes like hockey cards. These kids are fitter than me, faster than me and more skilled than me and I'm not okay with that. Forget the girls. For now, anyway.

Always the devoted parents, Mum and Dad are immediately, blindly supportive as are Nan, Granddad and the aunties but I do get the sense that they're all a little thrown by the new passion I've found for a sport I hardly know.

"There's no denying you're the competitive one," observes Mum quietly, somewhere between pride and fascination.

"Maybe he's adopted," suggests Nan, something to which Granddad takes particular exception.

"Rubbish," he declares, lowering the newspaper and peering over his giant reading glasses. "He gets it from me."

"Which is why you became a butcher instead of a footballer?" asks Nan as she heads to the kitchen with the breakfast dishes.

"I'll have you know, woman, I made the best bloody sausages in Belfast," he thunders after her, getting only retreating apron strings for a reply.

WHEN THE COACHING STAFF DISCOVER I'm poaching ice-time from the other Mighty Mite teams, they tell me in no uncertain terms that I'm no longer welcome at any practices apart from my own. But I'm fast learning that whenever possible, finding the spaces between the rules is preferable to breaking them. There's no rule about loitering at the rink and from what I can tell the coaches' collective jurisdiction ends where the bleachers begin.

I'm sitting in the first row, hair still wet from the shower, wiggling my toes and enjoying that first half-hour out of skates when your sneakers feel like they're made of pillows. The Aviators are mid-practice and I'm watching and wishing and dreaming. They're *so* good. *So* fast and they make it all seem *so* effortless. A defenceman slams his teammate into the boards with a loud boom, rattling the Plexiglas in front of me before grinning and skating off. My stomach flutters. *Johnny Ronson just smiled at me! One day I'll be an Aviator*, I promise myself. *I'll be a defenceman, just like Johnny. And I'll drive a garbage truck in the off-season too. That would be the perfect life.*

"Whatcha still doing here?" asks Keegan, sidling up next to me. I shrug, not quite ready to share my hockey/sanitation department dreams. "Wanna help me do the chores?" he asks, which is actually a way more exciting proposition that it sounds. Keegan's the stick boy for the Aviators and despite the fact that the job mostly entails lugging around ripe hockey gear, it's also an all-access pass to our hometown heroes. I'm an eager assistant that day and the next day and the day after that and by my eighth birthday, I'm officially the Prince Peaks Aviators' *co*-stick boy.

Free admission to home games is an amazing perk but lurking in the locker room is the real privilege. I'm collecting gear after a game one night and it turns out I'm closer to the Gatorade than Ronson who by now I see as something of a hero.

"Danny Boy, throw me a bottle, would ya?" he says and when I leave the rink that night, I'm grinning like the Cheshire Cat. I'm Danny Boy and I'm unstoppable. I'll make the Rep team next season, I'll carve a path through Pee Wee, blaze through Bantam, get picked up by the Western Hockey League, then the National Hockey League then I'll win a Stanley Cup. That simple.

The Rocket, Mr. Hockey, Johnny Ronson, Number Four, Danny Boy… It all starts with a good nickname.

But a name does not the player make. I'm waiting at the Rep team cuts and I'm just oozing with confidence. This kid's come a long way and if drive and ambition are any measure, I'll be just fine.

We're taking a knee at centre ice. Shoe-ins, hopefuls, unlikelies, not-a-chancers—the whole lot of us—and Coach is calling names. Keegan's first. Then another and another and another and I'm waiting to hear mine and if I'm lucky, he'll call me *Danny Boy* and we can all get on the same page with that. But suddenly he's done and he's heading for the bench and the new Rep boys are congratulating each other and I'm not one of them. I've been measuring with the wrong yardstick and the prognosis reads eerily similar to my report card: 'needs improving'. Sure, this kid's come a long way but not far enough.

Danny 1, Reality 3.

"You were terribly disappointed, I imagine."

"I was gutted. And absolutely furious."

"You were angry? At whom?"

"Can't someone just be angry?"

THAT NIGHT IN THE BATHTUB, I bawl my heart out. And no matter how hard I cry it doesn't change anything, which only makes me cry harder. There's no consoling an eight-year-old kid who's this crushed and Mum and Dad know it so they leave me be while I wail and wallow and punch the water because nobody could possibly know how this feels. Eventually, I run out of tears and I'm just sitting there in the lukewarm water, eyes puffy like a boxer and just as exhausted. Henry wanders in, looking at me silent and solemn-eyed as he pees. Then he wanders out.

Shivering into a towel I wipe a hand across the fogged-out mirror, listening as the bath water gurgles away, taking with it the last of my hopes and dreams for this season. Eventually, I wrestle the sobs into hiccups and the hiccups into breaths and finally, I'm finding the thoughts that go with the feverish feelings: it's the House Team for me next season and there's nothing I can do about it. Nothing. But I'm Danny Boy Doyle. And just like Dad, I'm not afraid to take a gamble and just like Dad, I'm not afraid to have a *craic* and just like Dad, I'm not afraid, full stop. As long as there's a Rep team, I will *never* stop trying to get on it. Because quitting is for losers. And because losing really, really sucks.

I STILL HAVE MY JOB with the Aviators. I'm still training. Still hanging out full-time with Keegan and the Rep boys like I made the cut and had I not already been caught, I'd be sneaking into their practices as well.

Off the ice I'm still their equal and nothing provides a better proving ground than street hockey. Keegan's big brother Barry has organized a weekly game of shinny on the street behind mine and these Sunday spectacles are gradually developing something of a Game 7 seriousness, helped along by our custom of co-opting NHL team names. The day I captain the Leafs to a 6-1 victory over the Flyers is one of my proudest childhood moments.

Barry's as short as his Rottweiler dad, Coach G, but stockier with brown, wavy hair like a 1970's porn star and a neck that looks just a bit too big for his body. He recognizes my drive and he always gives me encouragement and tips and claps on the back and all without barking too loudly. Winning the House League Championship that year was a whole different report card: 'shows great promise.'

That summer, I'm in hockey school and the following fall I try out for the Rep team. I'm the last player to make the cut but I make the cut and that's all that matters.

Danny 1, Reality 1.

Barry's the coach that following year. He's still encouraging, still full of great tips but I find myself watching from the bench as the season slides by. Every time I buckle on my pads it feels a little more pointless and every time I spot Mum and Dad in the bleachers, their well-intentioned support seems a little more ridiculous.

"You just need to sharpen up, skill-wise. Need to understand the game better," suggests Barry with that trademark clap on the back that's beginning to feel more dismissive than supportive.

I'm near boiling point when we go to Thornhill for a tournament. Here we are, playing our Divisional rivals and I'm warming the bench again, thunderclouds forming on my brow as I realize that I get more ice-time picking up pucks after the Aviators' practices. Complete bullshit. Then Thornhill scores on a defensive error (one I *never* would have made had I been playing instead of babysitting the Gatorade) and that's the final straw. I can't stop myself and suddenly I'm leaning over the boards, banging my stick and cheering on the opposition thinking, *You can go to hell Barry, I'll cheer for whoever I feel like because that's what spectators do.*

Prince Peaks 2, Thornhill 5.

After the game, I'm in a different kind of trouble and the vein is bulging in Barry's thick neck as he comes at me like a wolverine and when he's done there's this ragged silence in the locker room and no one knows where to look but we're all certain of one thing: He is Coach G's son after all.

Later that night I'm in the kitchen, lamenting to Dad as I miserably choke down cold macaroni and cheese. He's a dad so all he sees is his upset son and all he hears is that his kid didn't play *again* and he's done with it so out comes the hero hat.

"We're going to sort this out," he tells me with a solemn, reassuring wink as he picks up the phone.

"Barry, Nolan Doyle here," he begins, all traces of congeniality gone from his voice. "Not so good actually, Barry…"

I'm only privy to half the conversation but it's the half that includes questions like *"What's the meaning of this?"* and, *"Shouldn't having fun be first and foremost?"* and statements like, *"It's only a game,"* and, *"They're just young lads,"* but all the indignation and parental rile in the world can't hold a candle to ice-cold coaching sensibility.

"What did he say?" I ask once the phone is back in its cradle. Dad looks at me evenly.

"Cheering for the other team?" he asks. I shrug, not with indifference but because that's what happens to a kid's shoulders when they have nothing else to say. Sighing, Dad pulls up a kitchen chair. Unlike my little stunt at the rink, Barry had assured him it was nothing personal. Apparently, Rep teams play to win (not for shits and giggles) and if I'm not contributing to that end, I won't see the ice and that's the bottom line. When I improve I'll get my chances.

"That's it?" I ask. Dad shrugs because I guess that's what happens to an adult's shoulders when they have nothing else to say too. The truth's harder to swallow than my macaroni and it feels more like a slap in the face than a clap on the back but it's reality: only a handful of players are naturals. The rest have to bust their asses. If I want to make it I'll have to work harder. Dad doesn't know hockey from handball but he does know a little bit about losing so it's something I take to heart.

The following season, I make the Rep Team again, but this time as a core player.

Danny 1, Bench 0.

THE HARD WORK'S FINALLY PAYING off. We're good (I mean on-fire good) and there are some pretty spectacular wins and yours truly is at the centre of most of them. Danny Boy: on top of the world and on the tip of every hockey-dad's tongue when conversations inevitably turned to promising Pup Rep defencemen.

There's a lot of travel when you're a Rep player and I'm getting billeted out like a foster kid every odd week with God-knows-who all over British Columbia. These trips are amazing, albeit a little nerve-wracking—not a Doyle in sight beyond my dirty reflection in the bus window—and I'm equally excited that we're throttling up after school on a Friday as I am gutted that I won't see Mum for forty-eight long hours but not like I'd *ever* admit that to *anyone*.

When we hit the highway, the hours race by like road-paint and the boisterous boy energy reaches critical mass and we're distracting ourselves by committing mild acts of torture on the kids who pass out first. Billy Coates is the first one to crash and conveniently, he sleeps with his mouth open so out comes the toothpaste. We're half a tube in when he wakes up, gagging and swearing and foaming at the mouth like a minty maniac and we're almost collapsing in the aisle with sadistic glee.

Pre-game bus trips, highway high-jinx and the games themselves provide ample distraction but I'm still pretty young and once the dust settles, homesickness still haunts me, lurking at each well-meaning billet's house, waiting to catch me alone. So far, the host families are amazing and there's no reason for these first few overnighters to be the knotted-stomach ordeals they are but I'm new at this. No matter how nice, these homes just aren't our cozy apartment above the grocery store. *There's nothing they can do about that*, I think as I lay on the bottom bunk of some kid I crosschecked two hours earlier and gnaw on a tasteless apple. *I wonder what Mum's making for dinner tonight?*

FINALLY, I'M THIRTEEN AND IN Pee Wee Rep and by now I'm harnessing homesickness, winning games and generally coming out on top, bunk bed-wise and ten-year-old Henry's coming up behind me like a little carbon copy. Despite my relentless teasing, he's doggedly following in my footsteps, right into my old pair of skates and he's had the luxury of hitting the ice early. And his stutter's all but g-g-g-gone.

But there's more to the Doyles than its brothers. Ash is also an athlete and ironically, no stranger to ice. The girl's an amazing figure skater and an even more amazing curler. The night her team wins the Junior Provincial Curling Championship is the first night I have the stones to get properly, illicitly drunk. There's a point in every boy's life when, for whatever reason, the adults collectively hit the bottle and drop the ball and tonight's that night. Granddad's passed out in the armchair, mouth hanging open while his giant glasses try to mount an escape off the end of his nose, Dad's working his way through a dirty joke and the women are starting to sound like the kindergarten girls at recess.

Not one to miss an opportunity, I'm slurping the last warm inch from a tall can, eyeballing the whiskey bottle like it's the Holy Grail and overall feeling pretty grown-up and glamourous. Henry watches intently from the bottom of the stairs but I shoot him a loaded look and make him promise not to t-t-t-t-tell.

"I don't do that anymore, jerk-face," he reminds me defiantly. Tousling his hair, I teeter down the hallway for a piss.

The great thing about winning? It's not like losing. Losing you do alone. Winning's something you get do with everybody.

chapter 2

"Encouraging news, I hope?"

"Not really."

"I'm sorry."

"The chest x-ray came back negative for a mediastinal mass, though."

"Well that's something."

"It's nothing. The bone marrow aspirate and biopsy confirmed their suspicions. White blood cell count 1.3, hemoglobin 86, platelet count 88, neutrophils 0.04."

"What's the reality of this?"

"What do you mean?"

"I mean clearly it's serious. How serious?"

"The cell blasts were positive on flow cytometry for CD10 and CD19 and expressed CD79A and TDT which was consistent with B-cell ALL. Cytogenetics on the initial bone marrow biopsy was positive for TEL/AML1 fusion."

"You've memorized all that?"

"It's hard not to."

"Clinical euphemism again?"

"'Fraid so."

"What's the layman's translation?"

"They call it 'Standard Risk'."

"Serious, then."

"As serious as cancer, as they say."

"Let's pick up where we left off last time. You said girls were a distraction..."

"Well there was this one girl but she was a distraction to everyone: blonde hair, blue eyes, huge smile and a chest like a woman, not a girl. Everyone wanted her or wanted to be her and that just sent her stock through the ceiling. I don't think I'd said three words to Jill until I asked 'when's your birthday' and two months later on the day in question I left two roses on her locker and that seemed to do it. We weren't really an item but the flowers seemed to symbolize some kind of retainer that was sporadically maintained throughout most of high school."

"But she wasn't your steady girlfriend?"

"Not as far as I was concerned."

IT'S STRICTLY HOCKEY AT THIS point. Junior high is a rugged stretch for most kids but hockey's my and Henry's easy ride. Ash plays a beautiful, non-begrudging second fiddle and she's one of my biggest fans because that's what amazing big sisters do, I guess.

The Doyle name is doing well off-ice too. The grocery store's become a thriving little operation since Dad took the place over and Granddad's legendary sausages are as big a hit in Prince Peaks as they were in Belfast although Dad swaggers about taking most of the credit.

"It's my sausages, not your charm that bring this shop its business," declares Granddad emphatically, whenever Dad's chest puffs out a little too far. "Truth be told," he adds, "We should have named the shop *Gowan's*," a suggestion that always garners a warning glance from Nan.

Granddad has a valid point, though. Bar none, his sausages are the best anyone's ever had and the recipe (passed on to him by *his* father) is a closely guarded secret that resides between his ears and nowhere else. Beyond the fresh ground pork, no one's quite sure what he stuffs into those sheep casings but customers keep coming back for more and that's what matters most.

Sausages aside, Dad's owning his success and it shows on his face.

He doesn't speak of Ireland anymore despite Granddad's relentless commentary. He says nothing when two PIRA volunteers and a British soldier are cut down in Dunloy. Eats his toast quietly when a pair of RUC officers are killed by a land mine near Camlough.

"They've blown up the Grand Hotel in Brighton. Blasted it to smithereens. Disgraceful," tolls Granddad mournfully from behind his paper. Dad stands up a bit taller, gulps the last of his tea and squeezes the narrow cardigan shoulder as he strides by.

"Never mind that now, Da. Come on, that side of beef's coming in this morning and it's not going to cut itself."

My dad's words hung in the air as he left the room; and we all hung our heads for the dead.

It's a Friday night road-game again and we're on the bus and Minty Coates (poor kid) is wired on strong coffee and shooting everyone dirty looks and hiding his toothpaste even though Thornhill is only two hours away.

It's an easy 4-1 victory plus I get into it at the end of the third period with this blonde kid who looks like a sad greyhound. Pleased as punch. Game over.

We're in the parking lot and I'm waiting for my regular billet, looking forward to a good sleep and a cartoons-and-Lucky-Charms type of Saturday morning. Minty Coates is grinding his teeth like a machine, still hopped up on his mum's French Roast. He won't sleep a wink tonight and he'll crash hard on the bus ride home tomorrow and that's when we'll get him. But the best laid plans of mice and men...

Suddenly, Barry's clapping my back, telling me about the flu-bug that swept through town like a tornado and levelled my regular billet like bowling pins, which is why I'm going to some other kid's house for the night and it turns out to be the sad greyhound looking only sadder with a lump above his eye courtesy of my earlier elbow. Naturally, he's as thrilled with the whole arrangement as I am.

We're piling into his mum's rust-bucket Rambler along with his kid brother and sister and I'm thinking, *they better have Lucky Charms, at least.* One frigid hour later, we're pulling into an abandoned lot in the middle of nowhere and I'm tripping in the darkness over hard clay tire tracks and his mum's tripping over excuses as a mobile home looms out of the gloom. *I'm going to blast Barry for this tomorrow.*

It's late and I'm starving and we're sitting on these cracked vinyl chairs at this greasy little table and I'm getting cereal alright—for dinner—the kind in the yellow box that just says *cereal* in stark black letters like it's defying you to imagine that it's anything better or more interesting. There's milk too but it's powdered and smells rancid and makes me gag with each swallow. No TV. No Lucky Charms. Not a marshmallow horseshoe in sight.

Sad Greyhound's done first and he's up and outside chopping wood in the dark (so we don't die of cold, although the powdered milk might get me first). Little brother and sister, they just seem to dissolve into the shadows like ghost-kids and I'm sitting there at the table with the mum who looks broken somehow as she plucks a cigarette butt from the ashtray with yellow-stained fingers that tremble slightly if you watch closely enough. She lights the crushed stub on her fourth attempt and I'm staring at her through the smoke and she's staring back at me with these empty eyes.

Sad Greyhound comes back inside, arms full of hacked up 2x4s with ugly, rusty nails gnarling from them like brown thorns. I want to tell him I'm sorry that I busted his eye but it sounds dumb, even when I say it in my head. Anyway, you can tell it's not his first whack in the face so I just leave it. When we turn in, his mum secures the door shut with a pair of forks and a rubber band, peering out the window twice before finally turning out the light.

It's me, not Minty Coates, who doesn't sleep that night. I'm tossing and turning and this couch smells like beer and angry sweat and engine grease. At some point the kid brother gets up because he's wet the bed and later, there's these dry, desperate sobs coming from the mum's room.

Morning: more cereal and powdered milk for breakfast and no packed lunch. On the way home, I fall asleep on the bus but no one's dumb enough to crack out the toothpaste.

That night, while I'm eating homemade pizza, in my cozy home, with my big fun family, I think about Sad Greyhound and his tough spot and suddenly I'm not so hungry.

"How's the pizza?" asks Mum. I give her a hug; a long, warm hug. "What was that for?" she asks.

"Nothing," I say.

Everything, I think.

AGE FOURTEEN, AND THINGS ARE really starting to happen. I make first round selection for a Junior A evaluation camp in Alberta along with two brothers from my Rep team named Marv and Alphonso. The Fort Saskatchewan Blades' Rookie Camp is part of the Capital Region Board or *Greater* Greater Edmonton if we're being completely honest.

Just one day in and the boyish excitement has evaporated leaving nothing but the noxious fumes of adrenaline and the disconcerting stench of boys finally sweating like men. This isn't Minor Hockey anymore. This is the Juniors and any of these guys would cut your throat for a place on a Western Hockey League team, you just know it. These are the real proving grounds and when they say *leave everything on the ice*, they mean it.

My first hockey fight is a proper gloves-off-let's-do-this affair and as terrifying as it would be for any kid. We've been playing the same team four games straight now and it's game five and this kid has had it with me because I've introduced him to the boards one too many times.

"We're going!" he yells, red with rage as his gloves go skittering across the ice. I can feel the blood drain from my face and everything seems to slow down, except for the pulse thumping in my neck, which gets exponentially faster. This kid's twice my size and a good two years older and *I've bitten off more than I can chew*, I think, as I pull off my helmet. It feels like we're circling forever before we finally lock up and as soon as we do, he's swinging for the fences. At first, I'm getting the wrong end of this and he's landing punch after punch to the back of my head before finally catching me in the mouth; but fear's a funny thing because sometimes it gets the job done faster than you realize. It's one desperate punch but as luck would have it, noses are made of soft cartilage and before I know what's happening, he's on the ice and I'm on him and officials are swarming like black and white bumblebees. I'm grinning all the way to the penalty box, covered in blood. But not mine.

Danny 3, Other Guy 0.

Apparently, a quicksilver uppercut's not all I bring to the table because I get selected for their Main Camp as well. Here's the catch, though: playing for a Major Junior Club means losing eligibility for an American four-year scholarship program and I'm all about creating opportunities for myself, not eliminating them. It's a tough decision but I cool my jets and head back to Prince Peaks for a final year of Bantam Rep, instead. Both roads lead to the NHL—potentially—one just comes with a college degree, which is a very appealing insurance policy in a career that can get cut off at the knees by one bad hit.

By now, Marv's my best friend but this Fort Saskatchewan business has put us on thin ice and Sunday afternoon when the calls come in, it's his phone that doesn't ring. It's weird the next day at school because suddenly we're out of things to say and it goes on like that all week. Boys this age are resilient and by lunch hour Friday we're finally finding our voices.

"Can't believe you turned it down," he mutters into his ham sandwich.

"Can't believe you got cut," I offer but my insincerity makes me feel worse so instead I re-gift the honesty bestowed on me by Barry via my father:

"Only a handful of players are naturals. The rest have to bust their asses. If you want to make it, you have to work harder."

"Go to hell, Doyle," he suggests. There's a moment of straight-faced silence before both of us burst out laughing and just like that we're back to normal. When hockey season rolls around again, we'll be playing together in Bantam Rep and he'll have completely forgotten that I'm there by choice, not necessity. Boys this age are resilient.

BUT BOYS BECOME MEN AND men grow old. And resilience like everything else slowly slips away. Nan stops in her tracks, surprised to see Granddad with the Tuesday edition spread out on the table before him like a war-room map instead of propped up like a newsprint fortress.

"Lily," she calls to the kitchen. "Did you know a little old man lives behind the newspaper?" Granddad doesn't chuckle. Doesn't even smile.

"A *grumpy* little old man," she observes curtly, turning on her heels. Granddad waits until she's left before knocking back an aspirin with his tea and gingerly rubbing his wrists and hands. The last few months, his lunches have gone from an hour to two hours to four and eventually it's anyone's guess if he's coming down after his tea and cheese sandwich at all.

Granddad's a proud man whose excuse for his absences is a head cold that mysteriously seems to come and go sans symptoms but it hasn't gone unnoticed that his fingers are getting stiffer, uglier, more gnarled. One Friday morning, he packs up his butcher knives once and for all and he doesn't want to talk about it, not with anybody. Bloody arthritis.

SIX WEEKS LATER, GRANDDAD HAS a stroke. It's awful seeing him like this. Silent. Stuck in a body that doesn't want him but won't let him go. Once, he was happy, carefree, conversational, whistling when he wasn't singing and smiling when he wasn't whistling. Now he can't move, can't speak, can't write, can't do anything. When a tear rolls down his craggy cheek, we leave so the nurses can change him.

Overnight, Mum's life changes as her and the twin aunties hold rolling vigil by Granddad's bedside. She's going to the hospital and she's coming from the hospital and she's going back again and that's life now because it's her dad in there, she reminds us like we were questioning it. But that's my mum in there too, and I'm pulling my weight as best I can because I know I can't make her happy right now. But I would settle for less sad.

The empty butcher counter is a common enough sight already but the empty seat at the kitchen table is what makes my throat ache and eyes sting. Nan seems the strongest, really: so organized, so busy reassuring everyone else. But the day she cancels the newspaper is the first time I see her cry.

GRANDDAD'S STROKE IS AN OMEN: a harbinger, heralding hard times ahead and no one in Prince Peaks is exempt. Grimly, Dad realizes Granddad's sausages had indeed attracted a sizable chunk of the shop's clientele. Without its butcher, the once bustling grocery store gradually becomes a local afterthought for milk, newspapers, batteries, and other items otherwise forgotten at Safeway.

As the high-flying economy chokes, sputters, and finally stalls, Doyle's isn't the only local business going into a tailspin. The rights dispute with Alaska kills the fishery, the softwood lumber fiasco kills the mill and a freak fire kills the cannery. Prince Peaks is so busy just surviving, there's no way it can carry a men's senior hockey team, as well.

Despite empty plants and abandoned machinery, the eight thousand people who still call Prince Peaks home have some fight left in them but the day the Aviators get grounded is the day the town loses its soul. Then the rains come—week after wet week—washing away the last of anyone's hope and lashing the crippled community into a wet, miserable container port shanty town.

"Your father didn't close the store?"

"Oh God, no. He still runs it to this day or should I say, it still runs him. He should have euthanized Doyle's when it was still his invalid. Hung a closed sign on the door like a giant toe-tag and left town and never looked back. But somewhere in the middle of him not being afraid of anything and promising to give Mum a better life, it stopped being his invalid and became his captor."

"What made him choose to stay initially?"

"Dad's a gambling man. But the best gamblers sometimes back the wrong horse."

"Let's go back to the hockey. How long was Prince Peaks without a Senior Men's team?"

"Five years, almost. It's a different place at this point. Smaller. Unhappier. Lots of folks are unemployed and most of the ones who

aren't work at the container port. Throw in a smattering of riffraff and alcoholics and you get the picture."

"Was it really that bad?"

"Bad enough for the Alaskan cruise ships to find a different port of call en route to the icebergs."

FIFTEEN'S A BIG YEAR FOR me and not just because my voice is starting to crack and not just because I'm growing body-hair like a Chia Pet. Barry calls and I can tell he's excited because I have to hold the phone an inch from my ear. He's been out of the coaching game for a few years now but apart from a few extra belt notches and a thin spot in his '70's porn star hair, he's the same old Barry. He ran into Johnny Ronson at the hardware store yesterday, he tells me. It got him feeling sentimental so he paid a visit to the barn and was looking at the old silverware in the trophy case, which got him thinking…

"Went down to the vault," he continues, "and that's when I found them!"

"Found what?" I ask.

"The jerseys, Danny Boy! The old Aviators' jerseys!" This town can't carry a men's Aviators team, he concedes, but maybe it doesn't need to. Maybe it just needs to be able to carry a Bantam team…

"I'm bringing back the Aviators, Danny Boy! And you're going to be my captain and wear number two and we're gonna win the Provincials! Whaddya say?"

Suddenly, my mouth's gone dry and my head's thumping pleasantly with the prequel to a happy headache from too much good news, too fast. *I'm going to be the captain of the Aviators! And I'm going to be wearing number two. Johnny Ronson's jersey!*

"You were finally an Aviator."

"Finally."

"How did that make you feel?"

"Invincible. Amazing. And you can't imagine what it did for the town."

Word of the Aviators' reincarnation spreads like wildfire. It's been years since anything happy has happened here. Prince Peaks is gagging for good news and our Bantam outfit is just that but we're more than that too. More than hockey. We're hope. On opening night, the whole town's jammed into the barn. And when we dust off those Aviators jerseys and take to the ice there's a roar like peeling thunder and it's for Prince Peaks the town as much as for its resurrected team.

There's a new crackle of anticipation in the chilly coastal air. Housewives are chatting excitedly in the grocery store line and husbands are bantering over beers at the bar and kids can't shut up about it at school and it's Aviators this and Aviators that and no one seems to care about anything else.

Something's crackling in me as well. It seems like only yesterday I was picking up pucks after Aviators' practices and now I'm putting pucks in the back of the net. Now I *am* an Aviator. Number 2. Danny Boy Doyle. Attacking defenceman. Captain, not stick boy. The sharp end of the spear. This is the first time I know what it's like to have fans and I mean *real* fans and nothing compares to that feeling: racing up to the boards while the horn's blaring and the goal's lighting up like a Christmas tree and they're hammering on the Plexiglas, roaring in jubilation at you and you're roaring right back and in that exquisite moment, you're all in it together. Don't let anyone ever tell you that home ice advantage doesn't matter.

Overnight, we're the new hot ticket in town and naturally it goes straight to our teenage heads and mine in particular. Six games into the season, we're on a streak and these score lines aren't even close. 17-3, 11-2, 14-3, and it's mostly Marv and I scoring or assisting.

I'm unstoppable on the ice but that goes for solid ground as well. Sure, the autumn weather's as wet and miserable as always but I love it. It gives me something to push against when I'm training; hood up, hammering through the downpour as cars whizz by with honks and thumbs-ups. This hometown hero hat fits nicely, even on my big head.

Maybe it's a little obnoxious the way I strut around school, navigating the hallways like I'm in slow motion and imagining some sort of victorious soundtrack filling my sails. But I've always been the one catching up, the one at the bottom of the hill, the one with something to prove. Not now. This time, I've caught the long end of the stick. This time is my time.

Our Friday night fixtures quickly become all-out spectacles that consistently attract a full house, which makes our Halloween game an irresistible opportunity for self-promotion. Marv and me and the guys, we're papering the town with flyers that we made ourselves and our self-belief is nothing short of scary: *Feel the Thunder when Tamittik goes Under* in bold, black, block letters. But the town's as ramped up as we are, and the buzz is bigger than usual if that's even possible.

But after all that buildup, the squibs are wet. Forget fireworks, there isn't even a spark. Despite a gallant performance, we don't run away with it. We don't even win. And when the final horn sounds, the score's 9-8 and we're stunned, swallowing our first loss of the season. It wouldn't feel like such a defeat if we hadn't grandly advertised how comprehensively we were going to dismember Tamittik. Fans are fickle, even in Prince Peaks, even the adoring ones. Having our Halloween lunch handed to us doesn't sit well with anyone and at our game the next day the stands are as quiet as a graveyard. Ironically, we win 12-3, but no one cares, not even me. The Halloween nightmare has been humbling. And the soundtrack in my head disappears after that.

Good thing too, because we have some business to take care of. Sorel, Quebec is coming to town, and after decimating Tamittik and Thornhill en route, they're making noises about shooting the Aviators out of the sky as well. We're training like young Spartans and everyone knows that this is a signature chance to put Halloween well and truly behind us but just in case there's any confusion, I corral the boys in the locker room for a Stanley Cup-calibre pre-game pep talk.

"Boys," I begin, impressed with how well my deepening voice booms through the locker room. "We embarrassed ourselves on Halloween and we learned a valuable lesson. But we are *not* going to get our asses handed to us by a bunch of poutine-eating pricks from back east. Now let's get out there and show them what Prince Peaks is made of!"

Judging by the enthusiastic response, I'm feeling confident that we're all on the same page but I'm feeling something else as well: heartburn. Nerves are a funny thing. I get them before big games sometimes and nothing calms the storm quite like *Kentucky Fried Chicken*. Mum came through with a big bucket earlier but now I'm wincing into my gum guard, fighting the searing smolder behind my jersey, feeling like I'm the one who ate poutine.

But adrenalin's a funny thing too. As soon as the puck drops, I'm as good as new and I contribute two goals and three assists. You could have fed me engine grease and we still would have won 7–2. The barn stays packed after the final horn because this is about regional pride and everyone wants to milk every last moment. Barry's dad Gerry is off-leash, clearly re-living the glory days as he clacks across the ice in his cowboy boots, grinning like a deranged hyena and bellowing like a cup winner as he gesticulates obscenely at the visitors' bench.

"Au revoir, assholes!"

IT'S NOT JUST THE GAMES that are memorable. Sometimes, it's the stuff that happens outside of the games that you remember. Like this one Monday evening affair. We know we can beat them in our sleep and tonight feels more like shooting practice. Barry's quiet on the bench, saving his voice for more important games and Gerry (who always finds a way to be involved somehow) is as vocal as usual while he mans the score clock. We're keeping the old guy pretty busy too—winning handily—when a frustrated check sends one of our wingers to the ice. There's five minutes left in the third and mentally, I'm already in the locker room, stifling a yawn as I watch the trainers crowd around the concussion-case. Keegan looks as bored as me, fooling around with the puck, not far from Gerry. There's a single pane of Plexiglas separating Keegan from his dad and in that Plexiglas is a hole: *just* large enough for the scorekeeper to push a new puck through, if need be.

Our injured guy is still clearing the cobwebs from his helmet and

Keegan's bored with hot-dogging and stick-handling. That's a dangerous combination because intentionally or otherwise that's when boys get up to no good. Snapping a wrist shot at the glass probably isn't his best idea anyway and the chance of that shot making it through the puck-sized hole in the Plexiglas, next to impossible. But apparently, not impossible.

Gerry's expression doesn't change as the puck ricochets off his head. But his hackles slowly rise and his moustache twitches and some swear they can hear a growl and for a second, time stands still. Then he's over the glass.

"Who was that?! Was that you?"

We all stare at Gerry and then at Keegan but no one says a word. As he looks us over, he starts to laugh, albeit somewhat maniacally.

"You fucking bone head!"

We're all still in shock over the improbability of what just happened and the fact that there's this old man laughing hysterically. Maybe the puck gave him some sort of brain injury, but he's still laughing.

"That's my boy! Did you losers see that? Right through the hole! Impossible, but not for my boy!"

Gerry's still laughing, flecks of spit lacing the corners of his mouth.

The next day, when Gerry comes into the rink, his sunglasses only accentuate the purple hematoma above his eye. And since we're not sure whether he still thinks it's funny, no one says anything at all.

No matter how many times we've tried, no one's ever managed to put a puck through that hole again. It's next to impossible. But not impossible.

FREAK ACCIDENTS IN OUR REARVIEW, we're the new Bantam Aviators and we're flying high all season and (apart from the *very* occasional hiccup) we're coming up aces. First the Region, then the Zone Championships, and we're heading to the Provincials with an almost unmanageable sense of boyish confidence when freak luck rears its ugly head once more. Warming up for our first BC Qualifier, I hit a slapshot from outside the blue-line and break our goalie's arm.

Barry's beside himself, naturally, but I don't care if he rips my face clean off because all I can think about is two games in Fort St. James with our Number Two in goal. His name's R.D. but we call him The Joker. The Joker is a great guy, ready for a laugh at any time, and my wingman when it comes to teenage shenanigans. But The Joker is the first to admit he's a better prankster than goalie.

"The funny man's always laughing between the pipes," is how Barry puts it.

You have to feel sorry for The Joker, though. *He* knows how this will go down and *we* know how this will go down and suddenly none of us are fancying a win because it's been a long, long season. But then there's Dad. Always the die-hard fan, he's along on this road trip and he's pulling out his Blarney Stone charm and vial of something clear he claims is *horse medicine* and he's rubbing it on our bruised shoulders and niggling knees and aching elbows and I'm the only one who knows it's just tap water. Nolan Doyle: not afraid to have a *craic*.

It's five minutes to faceoff and The Joker's positively ashen stepping out from behind the Gatorade but valiantly, the ball cap comes off and the mask goes on. No more jokes on the bench it's GO TIME and The Joker's laughing in the net all the while and kicking out saves like a young Martin Brodeur. We are all shocked! He's doing it and laughing all the way. We manage to hold on for the win with some great defence on the part of yours truly and some crazy saves made by the backup goalie.

The next morning while we're warming up, comfortably firing pucks when we get an unlikely visitor. Keegan—being a year older—had already left for his Junior Tier 2 team had played in Prince George the night prior. He and Gerry were heading home when they realized the Bantam Aviators were in nearby Fort St. James fighting for a Provincial spot.

"Kick their asses!" growls Gerry. Despite my dad's horse medicine, the numbers don't favour another three periods of dogged defence. But you've heard of puck-luck? We have plenty of that tonight and Fort St. James is hitting the piping so much it sounds like a xylophone solo. By the third period, we're in a goalless dead heat and the place is just crackling and suddenly the ref makes a call against us that's so lousy, even the home fans are looking down awkwardly.

Bang! If you've never heard a collective gasp, it sounds like all the oxygen leaving a room. The rink door behind our goal has been flung wide open and framed in it like a snarling, snapping little Zamboni stands Gerry.

"He's ba-a-ack," whispers someone in the bleachers. What pours from Gerry's mouth is an education in obscenity and what follows is an ejection from the Fort St. James barn. And what follows that is the narrowest victory of our season. We're going to the Provincials.

"How did you do at the Provincials?"

"We lost. Thin line-up, too many injuries, and suspect calls."

"Getting that far was still a great accomplishment."

"Losing's not an accomplishment. It's losing."

WHILE WE WERE BUSY *not* winning the Provincials, the Fort Saskatchewan Blades were busy trading away my rights to the Vandermeer Cougars: a Western Hockey League team on the South Coast in a city the size of fifty Prince Peaks. Junior scouts are already scribbling in their notepads and if I'm lucky, I'll end up in Vandermeer or maybe in the British Columbia Hockey League. Danny Boy's coming up now! But there's another dream I'm chasing too…

For most kids, the countdown to their sixteenth birthday finishes with a white-knuckled driving test followed by two years of intense negotiations over when they get to use their parents' car. Not for me. Three years, I've been waiting for my crack at *Team Pacific*, a squad showcasing the cream of the crop from the *BC Best Ever* program. You know those World Junior hotshots that pull you out of your cranberry-tryptophan coma every Boxing Day? This tournament is pretty much the precursor. Danny Boy Doyle has caught up and then some and confident as ever, I'm fancying my chances and ready to test my mettle against the best from the Czech Republic, the US, Germany, Sweden and Russia. The Cold War might be over but not in my video games, not in my comics and *definitely* not in my fantasies because playing the Ruskies at Christmas is up there on my to-do list with winning a Stanley Cup. Being a year older than me, Keegan had his chance twelve months earlier but got cut after the first round. As far as Prince Peaks is concerned, I'm their shot this year.

First day of tryouts in Quesnel, I'm still pinching myself. I believe I belong here and the town believes I belong here but I still can't believe I'm *actually* here. In a word, it's surreal.

I'm at the rink early, hands jammed deep into my hoodie pockets as I watch my friend, Sam Dawson's, scrimmage. Sam's a big, husky fella whose cheeks go as red as his hair after half a shift. Usually, I don't have a lot of time for gingers but he's a good guy through-and-through so I make an exception. Besides, like my dad always says, *"Better to know the (red) devil beside you…"*

He's carving it up out there, determined to make an impression on the coaches when out of nowhere this even larger kid just steam-rolls him—I mean really flattens him—and suddenly the only thing he's making an impression on is the ice. Sam, poor guy, he looks so ridiculous scrambling back up, teetering about with this surprised look on his face and I'm not sure if it's tryout tension or the sheer slapstick of the whole thing but I just lose it and I'm trying *so* hard to stop laughing it just makes it even worse and then I make eye contact with Captain Concussion and it's game over. The Germans have a word for pleasure derived from the misfortune of others: *schadenfreude*. Apparently that's what I'm in the throes of as I take one fateful step off the bleachers and break my ankle. The Indians have a word for when *schadenfreude* bites you on the ass: *karma*. And she's pretty surreal too.

Sam will be fine in a day or two, but a break's a break, says the doctor. By the time I'm crutching into the hotel that night, my new roommates are fast asleep. We're sleeping four to a room and each room has two beds so you do the math. Me and the goalie from Prince George make strange bedfellows; stranger still, since we've yet to actually meet but it's not happening tonight since he's out cold: mouth hanging open and leg flung out of the covers like he's making a save. Slowly, I lower my head onto the pillow, positioning the ice pack on my ankle and hoping to God this guy's not a snorer.

In the morning, I roll out of bed to find Prince George standing over me, a disgusted look on his face.

"I'm Danny," I say, extending a hand.

"What the fuck, man!" he replies. "Did you piss the bed?" A hot, throbbing pain shoots up my leg as I contemplate the huge wet stain at the foot of the mattress, and in one cruel instant it all comes flooding back. I'm eight years old again, in my parents' bathroom, watching my dreams gurgle down the bathtub drain.

"As long as there's a Rep team, I will *never* stop trying to get on it."

"Huh?" says Prince George.

"It's water. Get over it," I reply with a scowl as I prod the melted ice pack with my crutch.

Location's everything, asshole. Piss the bed? Really? I think as I thump into the bathroom. All the determination in the world can't change reality. I'm fifteen. And as far as Team Pacific goes, this is my only chance. *My one and only chance*: that's my grim mantra as I wrap the offending ankle like an Egyptian mummy and stuff it into my skate. Covered in a thin sheen of sweat, I'm almost biting through my lip with pain but nothing hurts more than losing, I remind myself. Somehow, I make it through the camp. Somehow, I make the cut.

It's a strange reception that awaits me in Prince Peaks. Keegan had kicked the door open for me the year prior and as I'm running through it, imaginations are starting to soar and people are beginning to talk and the local papers are touting their native son, this kid on crutches, as the A-player who might actually be able to show these AAA players a thing or two. But right now, I can't even navigate the apartment stairs without help. Four weeks. That's what I have to endure in this cast, and the second round of tryouts are six weeks away. Thumping about and cursing quietly, my furrowed brow probably says it all.

"You're face will stay like that," warns Nan. Silently I stalk by, wondering what she'd say if she knew I commandeered one of her knitting needles every time my cast got itchy. But bones heal. And despite Nan's warning, my face returns to normal too.

Phase Two of the *BC Best Ever* program is in Oliver: a pleasant little town in the Interior, smack dab in the middle of wine country. It's a round robin tournament pitting the best Junior players in BC against each other because you don't get to beat the Russians without working for it. My ankle's as good as new now and my form must be bang-on because forty of us go to Oliver and only twenty of us get a ticket to Calgary and thank God I'm one of them. By Phase Three, I'm cruising on confidence and holding my own against the top twenty hopefuls from Alberta and when I return to Prince Peaks, I'm nothing but optimistic.

It's Saturday night. We're at a teammate's house, a bunch of us and a bunch of beers, when Sam Dawson comes bounding in with the phone.

"Danny Boy, it's your brother!" which means the call came in from Calgary, which means the *Team Pacific* squad's been picked which means the excruciating wait is finally over. The boys, they're clambering for me to call Calgary back then-and-there but I need to do this solo, so I walk home and suddenly, it's the longest five blocks in Prince Peaks.

I'm in our kitchen, in our apartment above the shop staring at the ceiling, at the clean wooden beams of a roof that once blew off in a winter storm on the heavenward plea of a desperate little boy. Picking up the phone, I call Calgary back.

"Let me hear you say it. Come on," coaxes Dad gently.

"Only a handful of players are naturals." I slowly work through a mouthful of macaroni.

"And?"

"And the rest have to bust their asses. If I want to make it, I'll have to work harder."

"There's a good lad," he says, tousling my hair before leaving me alone in the kitchen with my thoughts and my leftovers.

The phone returns to its cradle. At Christmas, Mother Russia's mettle is going to get tested big time. But not by me.

Danny 0, Ugly Truth 2.

chapter 3

"The surgery was successful?"

"Relatively. VAD put in and two blood transfusions. But that's the easy part."

"Now chemo?"

"Now chemo. First stage. Consolidation Therapy."

"How long's that?"

"Twenty-eight days."

"Initial thoughts and feelings?"

"It's complicated. And awful. Worse with all the Christmas crap in the hospital. Like anyone in the oncology ward gives a shit about trees and bobbles and bows. Not the most festive place on the planet."

"I imagine. Walk me through the treatment."

"Let's see... Day 1, intravenous dose of Vincristine followed by Methotrexate. Daily oral dose of Mercaptopurine too. Methotrexate's administered on Day 8 and Day 15 as well."

"The Methotrexate's administered orally?"

"No."

"How then?"

"Spinal Tap. I don't want to talk about it."

"I can hardly blame you. Let's talk about hockey, then. Last visit, you'd just missed the cut for Team Pacific. Did quitting ever cross your mind?"

"God, no! It's never crossed my mind to quit anything. But it was tough regardless. Real tough. It was my first man-sized failure."

"Was it worse, having gone so far?"

"Absolutely. Missing the bus is bad enough when you're a block behind but when the door slams in your face it's hard not to take it harder. The local media attention didn't help either. Hero-to-zero. That's what it felt like."

"But you persevered."

"I didn't have a choice. Winners don't have back-up plans. It's like planning on losing."

"That sounds like a t-shirt."

"It should be."

THE WORST PART IS THE sympathy from my friends: their faces and forearms brown from beery lake-days and warm from beach bonfires. Even when they don't say anything you can see it in their eyes. *Poor rink-pale Danny Boy, fresh off his stationary bike summer, fit as a fiddle, ten percent less body fat and for nothing.* For absolutely nothing.

I REMEMBER ONE SUNDAY AS a kid, golfing with Dad.

"Nice putt," he says, coughing up the requisite wager. I'm a million miles away as I stuff the dollar in my pocket, lost in my little boy thoughts as I squint into the sky. High above, a passenger jet splits the blue in half like a little silver zipper. All those people going somewhere. Anywhere. Just leaving here.

"Coming?" asks Dad.

"Yeah," I reply. *But one day, I'll be going,* I think to myself.

That was nine years ago. If discontent was stirring then, you can imagine how I feel now. I don't hate Prince Peaks. Far from it. But Johnny Ronson's jersey isn't going to fit forever. Sometimes, you outgrow the things you love, and that's just what life looks like sometimes. The realization is heavy. Melancholy. Like the space between deciding you're going to break up with somebody and actually doing it. Bantam's over and there's still a gaping, penniless hole where the men's Aviators use to be. Hockey or home is what it's come down to. Prince Peaks makes the decision for me.

Two weeks after the Calgary call, I'm standing at Granddad's bedside saying goodbye.

"Most kids play two more years in Midget before leaving to playing Junior," I explain. "But I'm not most kids, I guess." Turns out that old eyes can twinkle, even if everything else is broken. Turns out they can also say, *I'm proud of you, Danny*.

That night, I call Jill. She's on her way out with her friends but drops everything when I tell her I'm leaving in the morning. Jill drops everything whenever I call and I only call when it suits me and that's why her friends hate me. She's in my room half an hour later and naked five minutes after that and it's clumsy and urgent and when we're done, she tells me she'll miss me. I tell her I'll miss her too because not saying anything would just make it awkward.

The next day at the bus depot, it's a flurry of crying and cuddles from Mum and Ash and the aunties. Then it's Henry, with a rough hug and a self-conscious, *See ya around, asshole*, because that's what brothers look like sometimes. Dad (by his own admission) is absolute rubbish at this goodbye business so he keeps it short and sweet and that's fine by me.

"Knock 'em dead, Danny." That's all he says.

I REST MY HEAD AGAINST the window as the bus pulls away, as the sleepy container port town disappears in the rearview mirror. It's all behind me now. Barry, Gerry, Keegan, Marv, Sam, the Rep team, the Bantam Aviators, *Team Pacific* tryouts...

Now, it's time to shine. Cold War aspirations might be off the table but my Major Junior Hockey dream is still alive and kicking. I'm Danny Boy Doyle. I'm sixteen. And I'm going to the Vandermeer Cougars Rookie Camp.

Vandermeer is a picturesque harbour city just a two-hour ferry ride from the Mainland. Big by small town standards and small for a city, it's blustery and beautiful and full of tourists and cherry blossoms but most importantly, it's not Prince Peaks.

Rookie Camp is a weekend on the outskirts of town, in the city's most western communities. We're talking sixteen to twenty year-olds here, so size isn't on my side any more than time. These guys mean business and from where I'm sitting, a lot of them are men. And they're fast. And they hit hard. And to make it worse, we've graduated from full facemasks to just visors. It's in the Juniors when hockey players start looking like hockey players.

As expected, I'm invited back for the Main Camp—an intense Sunday through Tuesday affair—followed by a few exhibition friendlies that are anything *but*. Adding insult to injury, I'm now up against guys from the new *Team Pacific*, which makes each hit as rueful as it is painful.

I hope to God you dish it out at least this hard to the Ruskies at Christmas, I think, as this kid goes through me and my newly exposed chin smacks the ice sending pain knifing up my jaw into my head.

It's all business now. No one's here to make friends and no one's here to clap your back and if you're not good enough, all you'll get is a white slip on your locker and a notice to be out by noon. It could happen to any of us at any time and I'm discovering that having your head about you is as important as having your skates on. It's all or nothing at this point and losing is terrifying when you're sixteen and hockey's all (you think) you have. Losing perspective is even worse, though. One kid who the Cougars cut twice in two years drove his car head-on into a tractor-trailer and you'd better believe it was a closed-casket funeral.

Getting the nod from the coaching staff is difficult enough but once you're on the team you still need to get the nod from your teammates and that's a whole other kettle of fish. Hazing is still a part of the game at this point, and it's not the cruel cocktail of bullying and psychological torture it's branded as by today's standards. I've got a pretty good idea of what I'm in for because I've heard the horror stories: kids with water bottles tied to their balls marching around the dressing room at the unbiased mercy of gravity; kids tied to wooden crosses and blindfolded, ball hair shaved, legs barber-poled with hockey tape and shaved too. That's how you get in. Get accepted. That's all it really comes down to.

But getting rooked is the least of my worries. I've seen more of the bench than the ice, even in the pre-season and a few days after

Main Camp I'm meeting with the Cougar's coaching staff in the closest thing that hockey has to a heart-to-heart.

"Truth is, Doyle," comes the frank prognosis, "You're good enough for a spot on the team but I'll tell you right now, you're not going to get a lot of ice time. At this point in your career, you might be better off with the Clippers."

The Regal Clippers are a farm team: a lower league outfit with affiliations to a higher league team and in this particular case, the Clippers serve the Cougars in this capacity. It seems like a step backwards but it's more of a tactical shuffle sideways because the minute I pull on that Clippers jersey I'll be eligible for a coveted U.S. scholarship (which despite the academic element, has always been a part of my long-game). Most importantly, it means I won't be on Gatorade duty and moreover, I've barely been in Vandermeer long enough for a cup of coffee let alone hazing and that's a bullet I'm fine with dodging for now.

"Sure," I say. "Send me to Regal."

REGAL'S A TWO-HOUR DRIVE NORTH of Vandermeer and smaller by a long shot. Two underwhelming strip malls unofficially delineate the city limits; one on the north end of town and one on the south and in between there isn't much to speak of beyond a small town centre, a casino and a couple of car dealerships. A few years back, they threw a bunch of money at a *re-gentrification project* but you know how awkward an unattractive girl looks in a prom dress? That's Regal. Either way, I'm going to ask her to dance.

By now, there's one thing of which I'm completely certain: uncertainty. Plans never go exactly to plan, and as I stand on the stoop of my new billet's house looking down at the giant pot leaf on the welcome mat, I'm reminded of this yet again. Ringing the doorbell one last time, I heave my hockey bag back onto my shoulder and turn to leave when the door finally opens.

This guy's got to be forty-something. He's wearing a *Frankie Says Relax* t-shirt and sporting dirty blonde hair that looked suspiciously like it might just be blonde after a good shower. Tugging on his half-hearted goatee, he stares at me blankly until a grin gradually spreads across his face like he's clawed through a fog and found what he's looking for.

"Hockey dude!"

"Hockey dude," I confirm flatly, which only stretches the grin around his dopey mug even further. His name's Tony, he tells me as I follow him into the dim house. And his wife is Skyler but she won't be home until the party. *Party?*

"And this… is your room," he announces grandly, flinging open the door to what must have been at one point a closet. "Throw your stuff in here and I'll introduce you to the kids."

I know what a house full of kids sounds like but I can't hear a thing (not even after-school cartoons) as I follow Tony down into the basement. And these walls look like they've been soundproofed or something. Gulping, I glance over my shoulder, making sure I have a clear escape route should things get as weird as they're beginning to look.

"How many kids do you have?" I inquire, my voice sounding strangely hollow in the small space that's suddenly starting to smell like beneath the bleachers in the school playing fields back home.

"About seventy," he replies, as we reach the bottom of the narrow concrete stairs. Before us, mounted on a large wooden frame sit row upon row of green PVC pipes. In each pipe is six perfect holes. In each hole is a young marijuana seedling and above the whole operation hangs a large hydroponic lighting array.

"These," he says, grinning proudly, "are my babies."

Tony and Skyler's party goes long into the night and well into the next day too. Come six a.m. I'm a complete write-off; something the Clippers coaches thankfully attribute to first-day nerves, and when that first day comes to a close no one's happier than me. But heading to the locker room after practice, the raucous laughter and knot in my stomach remind me that hockey has rituals…

One of the other new guys has been tied to a chair as a huge veteran defenceman goes at him with a pair of surgical scissors, a razor and a tub of Vaseline. The hair on his head's no luckier than the hair on his balls.

"How did they haze you in Vandermeer, Doyle?" one of my new

teammates asks, handing me a permanent marker.

"Oh, you don't want to know," I reply, autographing the poor Rookie's forehead. *Sorry, kid. Luck of the Irish.*

He got off easy, anyway. The last guy who came through the Clippers earned himself the 'Puck in a Bucket' treatment: a special reception reserved for rookies too big for their own skates that involving a penis, a noose, a bucket and an ever-increasing number of pucks…

Dodging genital trauma is the least of my worries.

Within a couple of weeks I'm discovering that Tony and Skyler's parties are the standard, not the exception. Weekdays, weekends, whenever. Night after night I fall into a fitful sleep, pillow wrapped tightly around my head and morning after morning I wake to brown and green forests of empty bottles and overflowing ashtrays. It's hard enough navigating a new high school and keeping my skates underneath me on a team I have no excuse being anything but the best on but after wading through a smoky seven week haze of Doritos bags, zip-lock baggies and rolling papers, I've pretty much had enough. Hockey's suffering, school's taking a serious hit and the rings under my eyes are starting to look like bruised apples. Snitches get stitches but screw it. This is career stuff and all bets are off. Time to talk to the coach.

But nothing. Six days later, I'm still living in the weed dealer's closet, the perpetual party shows no signs of abating and the Clippers' interest in my wellbeing seems to end where the ice does. Even Sad Greyhound's couch seems like a Simmons Beautyrest compared to what I'm getting. Sometimes I miss Pup and Pee Wee Rep. Hockey still felt like a game back then. Not a business.

"What did you do?"

"The only thing I could, really. I went over their heads. Took it up directly with the Vandermeer Cougars. I was moved to a new billet the next day."

"And taking things into your own hands, that didn't ruffle a few feathers in Regal?"

"Oh it sure did. They dropped me a week later, right after I scored

the game winner against their arch-rivals. 'No one decides how we run our show.' That's what they told me."

"Lesson learned?"

"Lesson learned. Snitches don't get stitches. However, they do get cut."

LUCKILY, I HAVEN'T BURNT ANY other bridges (at least not yet) and the dark cloud of my close call with the *BC Best Ever* program has a silver lining in the connections it's afforded me. A flurry of phone calls later I'm getting a tentative offer from the Purcell Rockies. All things considered, it's a long way to fall from *Team Pacific* tryouts to the Major Junior Cougars to the Junior A Clippers to this Junior B outfit in the Kootenays. And it's a long way to travel too. Purcell's so far east it might as well be in Alberta. But it's hockey. And it's not Prince Peaks.

"Your confidence must have taken a hit going to Junior B."

"Not really. It was bad luck that got me where I was, not bad hockey. There's one way to get to the Carnegie Hall, but several routes to the NHL. I wasn't off course. I just wasn't in the express lane anymore."

THE BILLET SITUATION IN PURCELL is an easy improvement on Regal. My teammate, Travis, and I are sharing the coach's basement with the washing machine and dryer. Travis likes to complain about the noise, especially when both machines are firing on all pistons but compared to Tony's party pad, the industrial din sounds like a Maytag lullaby and the place smells like lilacs, not beer and bong water. Coach and his wife have a son. A *real* kid. The kind that sleeps under a Winnie-the-Pooh mobile, not a hydroponic lamp. This is more like it, I'm thinking and Travis is easy going and quiet and the family seems nice enough too. But all good things must come to an end and in my case, usually sooner than later.

They're up in the kitchen and we can't hear what they're saying but it's louder than usual and cupboard doors are slamming and Mrs. Coach is doing most of the talking and by the time she clomps down the stairs, Travis has connected the dots and is already packing his gear.

Mrs. Coach is expecting another kid; any minute now apparently, judging by her sway-back, her swollen sweater and the way her belly button protrudes like some kind of weird emergency button. Having a pair of 16-year-old defencemen living in her basement is a little too much excitement for a woman in the family way, she explains apologetically, before puffing and waddling away.

Ruefully, I stuff my socks into the top of my bag, hoping karma gives her another boy so she'll eventually get stuck with two defencemen in her basement whether she likes it or not.

Travis ends up elsewhere and true to my recent bad beat, I get shuttled off to the home of Mr. Bruce, who is (by an exceptionally cruel twist of fate) my new algebra teacher as well. Mr. B is as much of a stick-in-the-mud as Tony was a loose cannon. Apparently he subsists on a diet of dour comments and CBC Radio because there's little else in his annoyingly immaculate home. At least at Tony's there were always Doritos…

The curfew's a bit tight and the guy gets a hard-on for homework, but this *no eating between meals* nonsense is the only house-rule I have significant issues with. Mr. B knows numbers, I'll give him that but clearly he has no interest in caloric intake nor how much food a regular growing boy needs let alone an aspiring hockey star. And since there's no arguing the point, I pick my battles carefully and resort to covert means of sustenance.

He's out and won't be back for a bit so I'm foraging through the fridge, almost ready to attack the hamburger relish with a spoon when I spot the mother lode: a lonely, lovely egg. Gazing at that oblong little beauty almost gets my pulse up and the thirty-second wait while it pirouettes in the microwave is the longest half-minute of my young life. But patience is a virtue. Stupidity, on the other hand, is not. Turns out I'm about as good at physics and chemistry as I am algebra because the minute I pop the thing in my mouth it explodes like a hot grenade, sending sizzling yellow lava shooting up my face. I'm still running my mouth under the cold tap when Mr. B arrives home.

Matt McCoy

"Thirsty," I explain thickly, hoping he doesn't spot the yolk splatter on the ceiling. *Man, I miss Mum's cooking. Man... I miss Mum.*

Amazingly, egg burns and hunger pains are the least of my problems. Between the endless list of chores and the staggering stacks of homework, Mr. B's working me harder than a kid in a Dickens novel.

"For a nominal fee, I'd be happy to give you extra tutoring," he offers, bemusedly watching as I get beat up by a polynomial equation. Lifting my forehead from the textbook, I give him a withering look.

"Don't they pay you enough for starving me?" I ask, gathering up my books and stalking off to my bedroom. That semester, Mr. B fails me. Asshole.

Danny 0, Living situation $0=x^2+2x+5$ (solve for x)

HOMEWORK ISN'T THE ONLY THING keeping me humble. These Kootenay kids are worryingly exuberant about their hazing rituals and I can just hear karma killing herself laughing because finally I'm bearing this long-overdue cross. No bullet dodging now.

One particularly ragged road trip, five of us are stripped naked and herded into the bus bathroom: a squalid little chemical closet barely big enough for one. We're crammed in there like pink, pissed-off sardines with nothing but a knotted rope that used to be our clothes and four hours of open road to figure it out. One kid's wide-eyed and hyperventilating even before the sliding door slams shut and when it does, it's dizzying how quickly the temperature skyrockets, as the salty, slippery heat becomes suffocating and raucous gay jokes give way to grim silence and desperate attempts at dressing. By the time the driver puts the brakes on the situation, three of us are halfway clothed and the wide-eyed kid has passed out, lying in the aisle naked and grey.

I'm getting it on the ice too, and suddenly this dream-chasing business feels more like hard work. Any preconceived notions I had as an A-Player gracing a B-squad have evaporated with the arrival of this new kid that Coach brought in from his hometown and suddenly the Purcell Rockies have turned into a showcase for the new golden boy. Being benched because you're bad is one thing but losing out to barefaced nepotism is a slap in the face. Again, I'm holding the line less and holding the Gatorade more and wondering what I have to do to get off this losing streak and win a hand or two.

It's dangerous when frustration gives way to discouragement. Frustration you can push against but discouragement? That just sucks the will out of you and it's in this disconcerting vacuum that certain things become crystal clear. There's more to life than just hockey. There are cars, for instance. And girls too. These are growing pains I guess, and growing pains aren't meant to be pretty.

It's eight on a Friday night and I'm already pretty wasted.

"Good job, Doyle," booms one of my tenured teammates, as I zip up my pants. "You kicked that guy's ass." Morbidly I watch my fellow rookie gag his way through the pickle I just pulled from between my butt-cheeks. Lose your pickle, eat the other guy's; those are the rules of *Pickle Race*, a Purcell Rockies' favourite. Honestly, I think I'd rather lose an eyebrow. But there's one way to avoid the eating part: volunteer first, when you're the least drunk. If any one game underlines my *losing sucks* philosophy, it's this.

A shrill whistle starts the second heat and two more rookies shuffle frantically across the room on their knees, hands tied behind their back, gherkins protruding from their backsides. *It's funny*, I think as the winner crosses the finish line to thunderous applause. *I've never seen anyone so happy and relieved to have a pickle in their ass.*

"That's appalling."

"I guess, yeah."

"Was this behaviour condoned by the league?"

"Not condoned so much as accepted. Once you hit Junior Hockey it was just a part of the game. Not now, though."

"No?"

"No way. Didn't you hear about that team last year, out of the Manitoba Junior League?"

"You'll have to forgive me."

"They were busted suspending water bottles from rookies'

scrotums. Even the assistant coach was in on it. The team was fined five-grand and suspended fifteen games too. But I bet it still didn't hurt as bad as stretched nuts. Anyway, enough of that."

KOOTENAY WINTERS ARE LIKE AN icy backhand from an unloving God but that doesn't deter time-strapped truckers from using the lake's frozen surface as a secondary highway. It doesn't deter drunk kids either even when spring's thumping at the door, thinning the ice to Russian Roulette thickness.

Pickle Races behind us, we've piled into a couple of cars near some of the big houses that line the lake and corralled some Kootenay cuties. We're rum-fueled, randy and revving our engines because that's what a few girls do to a few boys after a few Bacardis.

"Come on, Danny," says the brunette with the bright red lips whose name went in one ear and out the other an hour earlier. She flings the car door open but she might as well be flinging her legs open for all that it suggests. I've never been out here before and thin ice breaks and so do condoms and it's already a quarter past curfew but the alcohol's burning the couplings off my thoughts before that train has a chance to leave the station.

I'm no coward, I remind myself as I climb in. *And they need to know it.*

We're doing donuts on the frozen lake in the dark; tires hissing like *Starbucks* steam-wands, shoulders jarring into shoulders like backseat pinball, everyone crowing with glee whenever we see the other car's headlights because it means they haven't gone through the ice yet either.

Red Lips has her hand on my leg but I don't even care because there's a knot in my stomach not my pants and it's all coming together in one drunk, lucid moment. *I'm not in control. Not of anything. If I don't change something soon, whatever happens next will happen next, regardless of me. Because I'm not in control.* That's when we hear the crash.

No one in the other car remembers whose dumb idea it was to kill the headlights but they did it anyway and they hit the retaining wall near one of the lakefront houses pretty hard, judging by the sickening crunch. The girls are crying of course, and there are some cuts and bruises and a couple of missing teeth but no one dies. No one gets laid either.

That night, I make myself a promise: Thick ice or thin, from now on whatever I do I'll do from the driver's seat.

AND DRIVE I DO. HOCKEY'S a hall pass to adulthood and hanging out with 21-year-old teammates means little details like my age often fall through the floorboards. They're good guys, sliding me drinks down the bar so I can avoid the bartender and several doubles later I'm standing at the stainless steel trough having a man-sized piss, particularly pleased with myself and suitably buzzed.

Washing my hands, I study my reflection. Not sure if I'd call it stubble yet but it's something. And I'm pretty big for my age too. *Tonight*, I decide, *I'm doing it. I.D. or not.*

"Jack and Coke," I pronounce grandly, striding up to the bartender. *Shit!* I think. *He's looking at me strangely.*

"Uh… lineup's over there, man," comes the reply. I can feel my ears burning as I fall in behind the five people to my right and when my time finally comes, I opt for a different approach.

"Jack and Coke," I repeat with casual disinterest, like the whole idea of bourbon suddenly bores the hell out of me. The bartender looks suspicious but he's pouring one anyway and he's hitting it with the soda gun and suddenly there it is, no questions. Driver's seat.

The other aspect of this hockey hall pass is the women and I mean *women*, not girls. They're plentiful, puck-drunk and about as interested in my age as the bartender, and suddenly bourbon's not the only thing I'm confidently asking for.

But I'm not twenty-one. I'm sixteen. And school still comes calling every Monday, whether I'm hung-over or not. No surprise, my grades are slipping and no surprise, Mr. B's riding me about it like a Korean Tiger Mum.

"I wish you'd just apply yourself, Daniel," he says.

I wish a storm would blow the egg-stained roof right off your kitchen and take you with it.

SOMEHOW, THE HANGOVERS THAT ARE hobbling my academic career are having little effect on my game. Soldiering through is what

I do best and clearing the cobwebs from a boozy night is no worse than running through a torrential Prince Peaks downpour. You just have to get it done.

In hockey there's something called a *depth chart:* a tool used to communicate the placement of starting and secondary players, usually in relation to their position. Well, the Purcell depth chart is more populated than a Mormon family tree and despite my mid-way position, it's a case of too many players and not enough ice and again I'm finding myself contributing a couple of frustrating minutes per game. I'm miserable. Miles away from anyone I know and everyone I love and more than anything else, I just want something good to happen this year. Then I meet Nicola.

Nicola's not my first girl, not by a country mile. But she's the first girl I let in, and I'm not just talking about my bedroom. No more ghosting away in the dead of night, one leg in my jeans. I'm waking up next to this one. Watching her sleep. Nuzzling that nook in her neck that smells like almonds and whispering things into her shoulder I've never even thought, let alone said.

It's mid-afternoon and we're back in bed with our secrets and our sex and our inside jokes because to hell with fifth and sixth block English and Algebra. She's wearing my t-shirt and a pair of cotton panties and that's a deadly combination, even without those bouncing brown curls and emerald green eyes. Kneeling on the bed, she's singing into a hairbrush, doing a terrible impression of a terrible pop song but I just can't keep my hands off her. We're laughing as I tackle her to the mattress, as giggles turn to heavy, horny breaths.

"I love you," I mutter into her soft shoulder, fumbling for the clasp on her bra but that's what love looks like, sometimes.

"It's on the front, silly," she replies. I forget myself when I'm with Nicola. I forget everything because I'm someone else. Someone better. Someone happier, and God knows hockey isn't making me feel that way anymore.

When we lose the BC Championships Final, I'm not even disappointed because how can you be when your only contribution is the warm-up skate? Honestly, it's not even *we* anymore. It's *them.* I'm still pulling on the jersey, still lacing up the skates but I haven't felt like a part of the Purcell Rockies for weeks.

"I've got nothing to hold on to here." I tell Nicola, and she's hurt because she says, *You've got me*, but it's hockey I'm talking about and she should know that without me having to explain. After a long long-distance call with Mum, it's decided: Prince Peaks for the rest of Grade 11 and the summer too. Home doesn't have to be where the heart is for it to still be home and the minute I make the decision, the loathing for Purcell sets in like Kootenay cold and there's no shaking it. I hate this town now. And everything it represents and every way it's let me down and if my exit isn't going to be proud it'll at least be loud, that's for sure.

Mr. B's the first on the end of my spear.

"I hate you and your Algebra," I tell him, "and your CBC radio and your stupid curfews, and the wartime rations that pass for dinners around here." And when I'm done with him, I unload on the rest of the teaching staff, then the coaching staff, then anyone else who has the misfortune of making eye contact with me. A lot of good people get hurt the day that Hurricane Danny roars through town.

Nicola's near hysterical when I leave and it's my first hard goodbye because I've never missed anyone like this except Mum. But she's coming out in summer to visit, I remind her, wiping her wet cheek with the back of my hand and funny enough it's not the kiss I remember, it's the long, desperate hug. Sometimes words just don't cut it when you're sixteen.

And so I head west, back to Prince Peaks, while the Purcell Rockies head east for an inevitable Western Hockey Championships spanking at the hands of a shit-hot Manitoba outfit. But that's their problem, not mine.

As far as anticlimactic homecomings go, this takes the cake. Henry's hockey has taken him elsewhere and Ash is off collecting A's at university so Mum's a little more thrilled than everyone else to have me home. Granddad's happy to see me too, they inform me when I visit the hospital, but I don't know when they started putting words in his mouth. He looks exactly the same as the day I said goodbye except his eyes look more desperate, more pleading.

Jill's happy to see me too but devastated when I tell her about Nicola.

"We're over?" she asks tearfully, and I don't know how to tell her that you can't end something that wasn't really something to begin with.

"Well, we can't do *this* anymore," I concede. But she's so pretty when she's sad and I'm not going to see Nicola for another six weeks so we do it one more time, just to bookend the situation. Jill makes me take her from behind but I think it's just so I don't see her cry.

Coasting through the last quarter of the school year is empty and lacklustre because all I can think about is Nicola and when she finally arrives, it's the best three weeks of the summer and when she leaves it hurts like a sunburn.

Danny 0, Cupid 1.

"You know the worst part about being cheated on?"

"Enlighten me."

"Finding out accidentally. Because no matter what they say afterwards, you know no one would have ever told you. Nicola's friend Kelly spilled the beans accidentally when I was making a crack about it. 'Oh my God, you know?' that's how I found out. The worst part isn't the betrayal. It's being played like a fool."

"She was the one who broke your heart?"

"She's the one who broke everything. It was my teammate, Travis, my old roommate. Happened when she went back to Purcell. After I'd brought her to my home. Introduced her to my family. She wore him down, I guess; always showing up at his house playing the 'I miss Danny' card. One day she waltzed in and announced she wasn't wearing panties and you can guess the rest. It happened twice. Twice I know of, anyway."

"It sounds like you blame her primarily."

"Absolutely."

"Doesn't it take two to tango?"

"She wasn't wearing panties. What did you expect him to do?"

chapter 4

"Happy New Year."

"Sure."

"How did the Consolidation Therapy go?"

"Okay. Had to deal with Streptococcus pneumonia but that's normal, apparently. Cleared up after a cycle of antibiotics."

"Good. And the Interim Maintenance begins today?"

"Yeah. Fifty-six days of it."

"What's the run down?"

"More of the same, really. Intravenous Vincristine again, Day 1 and Day 29 this time. Oral doses of Dexamethasone on Days 1 through 5 and 29 through 33, Mercaptopurine Days 1 through 50, Methotrexate Days 1, 8, 15, 22, 29, 36, 43 and 50."

"Spinal tap?"

"Yeah. Day 29."

"How are you doing?"

"I've been better."

"I imagine. Let's get back to Nicola, which I believe is where we left things. Is it fair to say that her betrayal made you more angry than upset?"

"Here's the thing I know about myself now that I didn't know then: I put things in boxes. It's how I manage my life. Manage myself."

"Compartmentalization."

"Sure. I was horribly upset by the Nicola thing. Shattered, even.

Matt McCoy

NICOLA'S PUT MY ENTIRE LIFE through a tumble dryer, leaving everything ill fitting and uncomfortable and I hate her for it and I hate myself for letting her do this to me, which only makes me hate her more. And the worst part? I'm the one hurting, not the girl with the curly brown hair and the emerald green eyes. She's probably panty-less somewhere, bunkered up with another hockey player. God, I hate her. God, I love her.

When I leave Prince Peaks in the autumn for a new team in Salmon Arm, my departure's as anticlimactic as my arrival.

I'm stomping off the ice, down the corridor, frustrated and furious and those aren't the only f-words coming to mind as I hurl a water bottle against the locker room wall.

"Can't win 'em all, Doyle," comes the inane chirp from the assistant coach, but it's more than that. It's Nicola, goddammit. All I can think about is her and Travis and *I'm not wearing any panties* and she might as well be screwing him over and over and over in real life because she is in my head. No one can play good hockey when they're this angry.

I need a fresh start, a reboot, and the notion that I can somehow leave my baggage here in Salmon Arm makes perfect sense when I approach the coaching staff later that week.

"Two options, Doyle. Saskatoon or Purcell," says the coach matter-of-factly as he rifles through a sheaf of paper. Suddenly, my heart's hammering in my throat and all sorts of thoughts are elbowing for space in my head and all I can see is panty-less Nicola standing on the far side of a charred, smoking bridge and me on the other side holding a match.

"Purcell," I hear myself saying.

"Why would you go back, after everything that happened?"

"It's like a backdraft."

"I don't follow…"

"We were an inferno, Nicola and I. Crackling, roaring, all consuming and when she cheated on me the oxygen left the room. But the fire didn't die. It smoldered. It got hotter. All it needed was someone to open the door."

"What are you trying to say?"

"The only way to stop loving her was to hate her in equal measure. Kick the door open and feed the flames because honestly, at this point I was ready to set her on fire."

"You know how destructive that is, right?"

"I do now."

FIRST THINGS FIRST: THE LAWS of nature dictate that Travis can't get off scot-free and as soon as I get back to Eastern British Columbia I'm giving him a Western British Columbian smack-down and believe me, fists are balled for this one. A few hefty clouts in and he's all hands in front of the face, babbling the truth, the whole truth, and nothing but the truth like a D.A. just offered him a plea deal. Travis rattles into the locker as I stalk off and that's the end of our beef as far as I'm concerned because that's how guys deal with things.

Travis taken care of, my next priority is that charred, smoking bridge still standing between me and Purcell. If I'm going to make a second run at this town in any sense of the word, I'm going to have to slice myself off an enormous piece of humble pie because between teachers, coaches and billets it's a piece that's going to take several weeks to swallow.

"Not a chance in hell," says Mr. Duff, the history teacher with the pronounced limp who I'd terrorized mercilessly the year prior. Shadowing him down the hall had seemed like a hilarious idea at the time, catching his temple with carefully aimed blasts from the squirt gun while he defended himself with a thick copy of Sir Kenneth Clark's *Civilisation*. But it wasn't and in retrospect I realize that I should have listened to that quiet little voice in my head that all

Matt McCoy

along was chiming, *You're being an asshole, you're being an asshole, you're being an asshole...* Now, that voice was louder: *You're an idiot, you're an idiot, you're an idiot...*

To their credit, some teachers let me back into their classrooms despite the notoriously bad reputation I'd managed to build over the last two terms. Not all the faculty are singing the same tune but enough of them recognize the balls it takes to come back and face the music at all.

Getting Nicola back is no easy task either. It takes several months in fact, and she's doing her best to put her whole panty-less past behind her. Me, Travis, everything. But guilt's a funny thing because she's taken something away from me and she knows it and I know it and now I want it back because she owes me that much. When Nicola finally agrees to help pick up the pieces, it momentarily crosses my mind that this might actually work, that maybe we can put this behind us together. Rewind. Go back to singing into hairbrushes and romping the afternoon away on her narrow pink bed. Even as I'm thinking it though, the door's swinging open and the oxygen's rushing back in, sucking at the flames, urging them back to life. News travels fast in a small town like Purcell. The newspaper boy, the mum at the grocery store, the coaches, my teammates, everywhere I turn I see the looks, almost hear the murmured conversations. *Look at that dumb-ass Doyle, back with the panty-less slut who screwed his friend. What an idiot...*

I've already choked down a lot of humble pie, but this piece is catching in my craw and staying there. The worst part about being cheated on isn't the betrayal. It's being played like a fool.

Once we're back together, I do everything in my power to punish Nicola, my first order of business being the seduction of Kelly (her friend who broke the bad news in the first place) because if you can't shoot the messenger, at least you can screw her. But that doesn't make me feel any better, any more vindicated nor do my daily attempts to make her cry. She's taking it all on the chin, accepting her fate and doing her time, mostly in the bedroom, which earns me a couple more checked boxes on fucket-list, anyway (and don't let any boy tell you he doesn't keep one half-intentionally, at least). Nothing

I conceive is killing this fire though, and kicking someone when they're down is only gratifying the first couple of toe-to-temples. But that doesn't stop me trying.

Ironically, as I'm wading through hate on the home front everything else is going swimmingly. School couldn't be better. Hockey too, and finally I've clawed my way to the top of the Rockies' depth chart, playing the best hockey of my life. But let's face it, no one can play bad hockey when they're this angry. Compartmentalization.

Danny 2, Purcell 1.

"Did you realize at the time how horrible you were being?"

"On some level. But I remember rationalizing it. Would God have let everything else in my life go so well if I was really behaving that badly?"

"You believe that with God, the crime always fits the punishment?"

"I'm not sure I even believe in God."

"Well if your philosophy holds true, the situation you're in now seems to suggest a divine debt unpaid."

"You think I'm to blame for what's happening now?"

"Do you?"

ROUND TWO IN PURCELL FINDS me camping out in coach's basement again but this time it's a new basement and this time there's the new baby (a boy) so one day, Mrs. Coach might just get stuck with two defencemen after all.

I'm still sharing the space with that loudmouth washing machine/dryer combo but it still beats the hell out of bunkering down with Mr. B and his wartime rations and his CBC Radio and his endless algebra. Incidentally, Mr. B was one of the teachers who *didn't* welcome me back into their class and believe me, no love lost.

Hockey's finally happening since I've started aiming my animosity at Nicola and on-ice Danny is a picture of positive focus, regularly winning games for a team that (although weaker than the year prior) has one determined West Coast kid leading the charge. Sometimes, it's not about pound-for-pound skill; it's about gelling as a team and we're cohesive come playoff time. Confident, greater than the sum of our parts, and that year we win the BC Championship and then the Western Canadian Championship. Fifty-seven wins, three ties, six losses and three of those L's were before I returned anyway. That was how the year in Purcell ends and that's how I want to keep it but there's one piece of unfinished business: Nicola.

After a year of punishing her, tormenting her, cheating on her, trying and failing miserably to forgive her, the fire has finally burnt itself out leaving a blackened, sooty skeleton of a room where our dysfunctional free-for-all of a relationship used to be. We're in coach's basement when I tell her as much.

"You can't just go," she chokes, a captive mourning her captor even as he unties the ropes.

"Watch me," I reply coldly, feeling a small pang of something… curious, disarticulated and strangely detached, like a sociopathic kid pulling legs off a bug. She's desperate, pleading, asking forgiveness for the hundredth time and all I can think is I'm done hurting this girl, I'm done even looking at her. She stomps out of the basement, two sobs a stair.

"Keep your chin up, Nicola," Coach says from the kitchen.

"Fuck you, you fucking cocksucker!" she screams at him, adding exclamation marks with the slam of the front door. Nicola finally got angry, just at the wrong guy. I wait five minutes just to make sure she's gone and I mean really gone before I venture upstairs for a sandwich.

"*That*, was the best move you made all year," observes Coach as I yank the fridge open and mine for sandwich stuff. He's not wrong. But if I could just roll back time and freeze it, I'd find that afternoon in that narrow pink bed—Nicola in my t-shirt and a pair of cotton panties, Nicola with those bouncing brown curls and those emerald green eyes, Nicola kneeling on the bed singing into a hairbrush— and I'd stay there forever.

Danny 0, Cupid 0.

RETURNING TO PRINCE PEAKS IS different this time. Henry's back and Ash is soon and I'm going to graduate high school with all my old friends and summer's just around the corner. The hard part is visiting Granddad because it's like talking to yourself; a weird, one-sided conversation comprised of inane updates and useless anecdotes while all along he just gazes into space, the whites of his eyes a sticky, distant yellow.

"He's living in the past now, in a happier time," intones Nan quietly, like that means anything at all. *Define 'living'*, I think, squeezing his clammy, skeletal hand. At least Mum still comes up twice a day.

IT'S A WARM SUMMER EVENING in Prince Peaks and probably even warmer in the Bahamas where Sam Dawson's parents are enjoying their cruise, oblivious to the party slowly building steam under their roof back home. The town's entire under-twenty population is packed into the house—Henry and I and everyone I've ever known—and the second keg's just getting tapped. Jill's there too, but she's finally started listening to her girlfriends and no-one's going to use her like Danny Doyle ever again, which would be more believable if Keegan wasn't making such obvious headway. More power to him. I've had enough drama the last couple of years and not enough beer tonight, although this piss is surprisingly large. Shaking, zipping, I'm on my way out of the bathroom when I hear a familiar voice in the hallway behind me.

"Didn't you promise to marry me one day?" Her thick brown hair is pulled back in a ponytail, her eyes are still that gorgeous hazel and her little blue summer dress leaves no doubt that somebody's definitely grown up.

"Alexis!" I stammer, suddenly aware of my beery breath, wishing I'd snaked a dab of Sam's toothpaste from the medicine cabinet a moment earlier. I'm barely listening as she tells me about her parents' return to town, about her imminent departure to university, about the summer she's anticipating here in Prince Peaks first. *God, her legs are golden against that little blue summer dress...*

"You still wear Strawberry Shortcake panties?" I venture, realizing too late that it sounded better in my head.

"I don't wear panties," she replies. *Jeez Travis*, I think abruptly, as my jeans grow uncomfortably tight. *I totally get it, man.*

Matt McCoy

A few hours and countless plastic cups of beer later, we're in the dark on Sam's parents' bed and I'm on top and her little blue summer dress is hiked up and bunched around her waist.

"I love you," I grunt, coming inside her.

"No, you don't," she giggles, biting my shoulder.

"You're right," I admit. "But I've always wanted to tell you that."

The next morning, Sam interrupts my hangover sleep-in with an irate phone-call.

"Doyle, what the fuck did you do to my parents' bed? Everyone saw you go in there with Alexis…"

"Why? What's up?" I reply, sitting up with a wince, my head hammering like hell's bells.

"There's blood all over the middle of the mattress!" he yells. *Oh God, Alexis*, I think, as I foggily connect the dots. *Timing's everything.*

"Uh, I must have cut my foot…"

"In the centre of the bed?" thunders Sam, hanging up. Dully, I listen to the dial tone. *Location's everything, asshole*, I remind myself as I totter to the bathroom. *Cut your foot? Really?*

MUM'S STILL ANGLING FOR MY academic future.

"You'll be useless to anyone if you blow out your knee," she warns for the hundredth time and she's not wrong. When I get the transfer call from Castlegar, she's as relieved as I am excited. The Castlegar Kings from British Columbia's south interior are a Tier 2 outfit, which means a much-coveted U.S. College Scholarship could be glimmering on the horizon providing I stay on form or don't 'blow out my knee'. Originally the plan feels like a coup d'état, with my coach from Purcell in line to take the helm bringing with him myself and a handful of other bright hopefuls from last season's illustrious Rockies. But when the opportunity arises for him to take on the Presidency of the British Columbia Amateur Hockey League, he takes it and who can blame him? On his advice, me and the boys still head to Castlegar, but it isn't with the same sense of entitled confidence as before and suddenly we have everything to prove and everything to lose all over again and there's that goddamned word: the great equalizer, the toss of the coin, the show-me-what-you've-got: tryouts.

As luck (and skill) would have it, all us ex-Rockies make the team but 'team' is a generous term to use at this point. The Kings are a storied franchise and for all the wrong reasons. Their previous season had been a fall-on-the-face disaster due to the fact that their best efforts were put in at the bar, not on the ice and in a desperate attempt to salvage the organization the entire boozy lot of them had been let go. When we arrive, the sum total of the Castlegar Kings is an empty rink, an awful reputation and basement level expectations.

Day One and the owner's giving us a pep-talk with the new coach (a hard-nose from the Prairies) standing next to him with a scowl, arms crossed high on his chest like he's daring any of us to even think about having a drink.

"I'm a good guy," begins the owner, and to be fair he looks like he's telling the truth. "My expectations are reasonable. But I have one and only one stipulation: No Night Moves. Ever. You put one foot in that place and you're off the team. Understood?" He looks around the room, smiling benevolently at the puzzled players. "Good. Welcome to Castlegar."

Night Moves, as it turns out, is a nightclub across town that was allegedly the downfall of the last Kings squad and the minute I learn about it, I know we have to go. But first things first: billets. Have to unpack my bag before I start tilting at the rulebook.

Prior to the move to Castlegar, I'd specifically asked to be placed alone. Nothing against my teammates but when you're already dawn-til-dusking it with a bunch of guys the last thing you feel like doing is making small talk with them while you're brushing your teeth. I'm not sure if it's accidental or if it's someone sending me a message for being cocky enough to try to special order my living situation but I end up in a house with five other guys. Five. The logistics are a nightmare, sleep patterns appalling, privacy nonexistent and the only effective way I find to vent my ire at being press-ganged into the Dirty Half-Dozen is via a series of semi-sadistic pranks. Marcel (a winger originally from Pictou and a fellow import from Purcell) is the object of most of my attacks, mostly because he's good-natured and a bit because he's just asking for it with that silly Nova Scotian accent. He has these beady, protruding eyes too, and they don't close entirely when he sleeps but apart from that, he's a stand-up guy.

Marcel works on the side for a siding company whose sole goal is turning every home in Castlegar into a generic Hardiplank box and such a grand endeavour involves a 7am start and a therefore a 6am ride to work. As soon as he's asleep, I'm re-setting his alarm two hours earlier than the prescribed time and by 4:30am there's the inevitable racket of Marcel coming back to bed, stomping and cursing as anyone would after spending an ice-cold half hour in the middle of the night sitting on the curb.

"Doyle, you fucking arsehole!" he hisses, as I grin into my blanket. God, that Nova Scotian accent's even more hilarious when he's mad.

"Stay outside, man. Your ride should be here any minute," I urge mirthfully. A hardhat whizzes through the dark, clattering against my shoulder. *Totally worth getting woken up for*, I decide. The poor guy ends up sleeping in and missing work, but I don't care. Castlegar can survive another day without yet another Hardiplanked home. Sometimes harassing Marcel just isn't enough, though. One night, I shut off the breaker and it's my billet's husband who's late for work that day. A hardhat would have been a welcome projectile instead of the abuse he hurls at me over the dinner table that night.

Sometimes though, Marcel's my partner in crime. One night, we're sneaking two girls into the house and that's mission enough but more importantly this small town Casanova bullshit is never going to take if we don't start using aliases because girls talk, we're learning. In a drunken bar bathroom conference earlier, we'd decided that Marcel would be *Peter* and I'd be *Rick*—which sounds easy enough—but throw in a few more double highballs and some beer chasers and we're having a hard enough time remembering our *real* names.

Anyway, we get them back to the house and it's raining bras before you know it and jeans are unzipping and the whole thing's turning into a hot, inebriated shit-show when Marcel's girl (who's straddling him by now) begins getting vocal.

"Oh, Peter, oh, Peter!" she's moaning and Marcel (peeking over her shoulder at me while I'm getting a midsection spit-polish from her friend) mouths, "Who da fuck is Peder?"

"You are, asshole," I mouth back, laughing so hard I almost lose my wood.

BY NOW, I'M NOT THE only one on the team fascinated by the off-limits Night Moves and having hit every other watering hole in town, that beautiful banned establishment has been imbued with something of a virginal appeal. Untouched. Alluring. And almost irresistible had it not been for the heavy-handed consequences attached to violating the Kings' one and only rule. But then I have an epiphany…

It happens while I'm disinterestedly watching the evening news with our billet's husband—a segment about labour union strikes in Poland—and with all the black-and-white common sense of an eighteen year-old, I decide to weigh in:

"I don't know why they don't just fire all those assholes."

"They can't," says the husband, swigging his beer. "Who'd run the factories? There's power in numbers, kid." Thoughtfully, I watch the workers with their sandwich boards and their placards and their broad, determined brows. *Can't fire all of us. Solidarity. We could go to Night Moves after all. We just had to go together…*

"What was so fascinating about Night Moves?"

"What's so fascinating about the hour after your curfew? The off-limits food in the fridge? Your teammate's girlfriend? It's the things you don't have that you want the most."

"Is that what drove your desire to become a pro hockey player?"

"No. That was something different. That was passion."

WE'RE AT *Darcy O'Brien's* ONE night, a local bar that's a favourite with the boys. There are at least eleven of us and we're hot off a win, guns still smoking, and the only thing going down faster than the Jameson is the Guinness and that's when I propose my idea. There's a collective balking at first but with each new round of drinks, I campaign a little harder and slowly they're starting to come around

Matt McCoy

because I'm a natural salesman and because blood-alcohol content's an even better salesman than me. Baby steps, though. First, we go to *Slack Alice's*, the strip bar right next to the forbidden fruit and after an hour of bad beer and balloon boobs even the most reluctant of us is ready to roar next door.

"Keep a low profile," I warn, because even with the Polish strike strategy, the ideal scenario is not getting caught, period. But low profile doesn't pair very well with a dozen half-cut, horny hockey players, especially not on ninety-nine cent Tequila Night. Night Moves itself is nothing special: dark and dingy and smelling like vomit and Armani, but it's Night Moves and we're in and that's my last clear thought as the lime pinches my jaw and the Cuervo fumes race up my nose…

That's not how my alarm clock should sound, I think, trying to open my gummy eyes. CLANG, CLANG, CLANG, CLANG… And it's not. It's our billet, a look like thunder on her brow as she trundles through the room beating the living daylights out of two saucepans. Everything spins as I stagger up, pulling the black puke-stained beach towel off my face, wincing at the white-hot pain behind my eyes. Reeling into the kitchen I find Marcel at the table, facedown in a sandwich. Somehow, the other guys have made it to 6am practice but the bastards hadn't woken us, probably because the whole thing was my idea and probably because Marcel was from Nova Scotia.

Fragments of the night come back to me as we race to the rink. I'm wearing a huge sombrero, dancing on a stage. Giving a shout-out to the Castlegar Kings. "Drinks are on us!" I'm bellowing. I'm leaving with the hot barmaid, a handful of ass as the sky begins to turn purple…

Keep a low profile. Fuck.

Marcel looks like he's going to soil himself as we're marched into the owner's office.

"I can't go back to Pictou! Not like this!" he moans to me almost tearfully.

"Shut up and let me do the talking," I hiss. *Everyone has a Prince Peaks I guess.*

I'm still loaded as we stand in the little office and it's already thirty-eight degrees in the shade so you can imagine what it feels like in here. The owner's in the middle of an unpleasant déjà-vu from last season and I'm sure he's picturing his investment going up in smoke as he lays into us like there's no tomorrow and by the look of Marcel, that might just be the case as he sways grey and waxy, sweating like a criminal. When the owner finally runs out of words, I (painfully) clear my throat, determined to take the rap like a man.

"Sir, it was all my idea. I take full responsibility for what happened last night and... excuse me..." *Well that went well*, I think, as I retch bile and blackness into the downstairs urinal. Undaunted, I drag myself back into his office where the owner's still waiting and poor Marcel's perspiring more than ever.

"Team morale," I continue with conviction. "I took the boys out to build team morale and it got out of hand and it won't happen again," I conclude hurriedly, realizing that Marcel's in real danger of his liver falling out his asshole. Gruffly, we're dismissed and miracle of all miracles, we're still on the team the next day.

Somehow we dodge the bullet, but I can't swallow for a week and Marcel never drinks tequila again. There's a silver lining because bad apples get pulled from buckets and almost immediately I'm moved to a new billet. The Dirty Half-Dozen's finally been disbanded and blisteringly hung over or otherwise, I'm ecstatic.

FINALLY, AFTER ALL THE SUBSTANDARD billets (Sad Greyhound, Tony, Mr. B, The Dirty Half Dozen) Karma's throwing me a bone and I'm landing very firmly on my feet.

The Pickfords are the poster-family as far as billets are concerned and Noreen's the mum-away-from-home that any boy my age would be lucky to land. With so many host families only in it for the money, it's amazing encountering a family in it for sheer love of the sport. They'd even take in kids who couldn't afford to pay elsewhere. If Junior Hockey sanctioned sainthoods, Noreen would get one.

The Pickfords have two little boys and it's a clever move putting me under this particular roof because just the way they gaze up at me with those star-struck eyes makes me want to do well by them. This is role model stuff, I guess and I'm good for it but there's still a bit of blowback left to deal with from the last few weeks: a steady stream of young ladies calling, asking for Rick. Noreen's no slouch I discover, as she sits me down for a frank and friendly chat.

"We love having Danny here," she begins, patting my knee. "But Rick's going to have to stay at a motel when he's entertaining his lady friends. Sounds fair?"

"Sounds fair," I grin.

Noreen's something else. Whenever I'm absent for Coach's curfew calls, she says I'll call him right back then she calls Rick wherever he is, asking him to get Danny to call in ASAP and the little system works like a charm.

One Sunday morning, I'm rolling in from a lusty weekend on a stiff bed with God-knows-who at the Castlegar Stay-n-Save, when Noreen greets me with a surprise in the living room.

"Hi, Danny," shrugs Jill self-consciously, waiting for me to react, probably imagining the stunned look on my face is due to the hot froth of emotions bubbling to the surface at the sight of her, when all I'm really thinking is, *Shit, I just used my last condom on what's-her-name at the motel.*

"Jill couldn't find accommodation so I'm putting her in the spare room," informs Noreen with a look that says, 'but don't try anything, buddy. I know your game.'

Against her better judgment (and all her friends' advice) Jill had been calling again recently because 'absence makes the heart grow fonder.' And although I was more a proponent of 'out of sight, out of mind,' I'd been encouraging the dialogue and had (three phone calls ago) half-heartedly suggested she visit me one of these days and now here she was. But not one to ignore when opportunity comes knocking (especially by Greyhound coach), I don't waste any time the minute we finally get the house to ourselves.

"You have condoms, right?" she asks breathlessly as I fight a losing battle with a bra strap that feels like it was designed by her dad.

"Right, yeah. Hold on," I say, jumping up and running downstairs stark naked, a three-legged man taking two stairs at a time. It's amazing how the male mind works under sexual duress because two minutes later I'm back upstairs, my ingenuity proudly protruding from my midsection.

"What the hell, Danny…" Jill trails off, staring in dismay at the Saran Wrap stretched over my erection and secured with elastic. "You're not putting that in me." Tearing it off, I vow to pull out as I tackle her to the mattress. That's the first and last time that I go in unsheathed with *anybody* and luckily I don't knock her up. But the episode haunts me for ages and it takes several years before I start answering the phone on Fathers' Day. I always wondered why Noreen had 'gone out shopping' five minutes after Jill arrived…

The long leash isn't the only thing I like about Noreen. Her fondness for a good prank is where we really bond. Kindred spirits in that respect, I'm joyously pulling out the classics from my repertoire: flipped breaker boxes, prank calls, late-night living room furniture re-arranging, that type of thing. One night, Noreen's baking a pie for one of her kids to take to school the next day and she's easy with the fridge privileges just as long as we keep a dialogue going about what's up for grabs and what's not.

"*Please*, don't touch the pie," she emphasizes *again*, clocking my hungry eyes as she pulls it from the oven. And I'm not about to, but this is an opportunity too good to miss on a totally different level. Late that night I grab the precious pastry and shove it onto a shelf too high for her to spot (and at five-foot-nothing, that's not even the top shelf). Taking some crumbs from a leftover wedge of quiche, I sprinkle them on an empty identical plate, leaving it on the counter in lieu if the pie. The next morning, I shuffle into the kitchen, staring dolefully at the empty plate.

"I'm sorry. I just couldn't stop myself," I admit remorsefully. Noreen's good nature evaporates instantly and it's hilarious watching decency and rage wrestling for pole-position on her face until finally, she manages a reply.

"I don't know how you could do this," she quavers. "I'm *so* disappointed in you." *Bless her heart, she's actually keeping her head on.*

"You could just grab a three-dollar pie from Safeway on your way in…" I suggest. By now, Noreen's actually vibrating.

"How dare you!" she gasps, all five feet of her storming out of the kitchen. By the time she's recomposed herself and returned, I've

Matt McCoy

put her beautiful homemade pie back on the countertop. The little lady just stands there, a completely blank look on her face.

"Gotcha!" I sing, giving her a big kiss on the cheek as I leave the kitchen. "Still love me?" She does, surprisingly. The next morning, I get a nasty surprise when I unwittingly sit on the Saran-wrapped toilet in my en suite bathroom.

"Shit!" I yell, figuratively as well as literally, realizing in dismay that in leaving the Saran Wrap in my bedroom after the Jill debacle, I'd more or less gift-wrapped this one for her.

"Still love me?" calls the feisty little lady from the hallway. That's the kind of person Noreen is. And I absolutely adore her.

"The Pickfords and I are still friends today."

"It sounds like you desperately needed a real mother figure in your life at that point."

"Probably more than I realized. They were the closest thing I'd had to a family since home. I would have been happy to stay there indefinitely."

"How long was your stay with them?"

"Not long enough. The Kings were a last-gasp outfit when I arrived. Sadly, the team folded three months later."

LUCKILY, I'M PICKED UP ALMOST immediately by Saskatchewan's Rayburn Redwings, but that still leaves me a two-week window to visit home.

This time, I only see Granddad once and only for about a quarter hour and I'm not even sure if he realizes I'm there. His room is dim and smells awful and heavy and dank and when the hospital doors swish behind me I gulp in the crisp, clean Prince Peaks air with a new emotion—something that comes with growing up, I guess—gratitude.

I see Jill again too. I owe her that much after her coming all that way to see me and besides, Alexis has left for university by now.

"I don't want to do this with you anymore. For real this time," I tell her as we pant and pound, our skin making obscene slapping noises.

"I hate you," she says, grinding underneath me.

"Yeah, looks like it," I reply, thrusting just a little harder to make my point. That's the last time I screw Jill. For real this time.

chapter 5

"Delayed Intensification?"

"That's what they call it. Nine different types of chemo. Starts tomorrow. It's supposed to be pretty intense."

"Hence the name, I guess."

"Yeah, it's like they threw the 'delayed' in front just to remind you that they've put it off as long as they possibly can, but now it's going to get bad."

"Yet another clinical euphemism?"

"Bingo."

"What's the rundown?"

"Vincristine, Dexamethasone, Doxorubicin, Cyclophosphamide, Cytarabine, Thioguanine, Methotrexate, Leucovorin and the worst, PEG Asparaginase."

"The worst?"

"Intramuscular injection. Large muscles. Two huge needles in the thighs."

"This must be terribly hard for you."

"It's breaking me."

"Let's talk about Saskatchewan. Tell me about Rayburn."

"What's to tell? It's like everywhere else in Saskatchewan. Unbearably cold in the winter, unbearably hot in the summer and flat as an ice rink. Its only saving grace are the warmhearted folk who call it home."

"What about the hockey?"

"The hockey was great. The Rayburn Redwings were a good little outfit. A reasonably sized depth chart, lots of seasoned players... It was definitely a more aggressive league than British Columbia too, which suited my playing style to a tee. A couple of teammates had followed me out from Castlegar but neither of them got the ice-time I did. I was the ex-King of the castle."

SASKATCHEWAN IN 1989 IS NO place for anybody, even under good billet circumstances but this is what welcomes me on the fridge door:

House Rules:
No eating between meals.
No drinking any of the home's soda.
No going to the fridge without permission.
No friends over.
No girls, period.

THIS ISN'T WORKING FOR ME, and by now I'm an ace at spotting the bastards who are just in it for the money. Bad enough leaving the balmy climes of beautiful British Columbia for the purgatory-on-earth that is Rayburn but these people make living at Mr. B's seem like a trip to Club Med. By now, I'm also ace at getting my own way and forty-eight hours later I'm lugging my bags into Home Number Two, hoping for an open-fridge policy and maybe just a glimmer of the warmth and familial love I experienced at the Pickfords'.

Make no doubt, there's love here, but not of the familial variety. There are two other teammates in the mix and one (our goon, who actually turns out to be a gigantic pussy) is way in there, and I mean *in* there, since he's regularly planking the house mum which is not cool on any level because a) she's a donkey and b) she's the house mum. House Number Two lasts three weeks and as Donkey's driving me to House Three she pulls the beat-up brown family minivan into an abandoned schoolyard, yanks open her beige blouse and flashes me her beat-up brown nipples.

"Want a quick ride?" she asks, leaning in and fingering the emergency brake obscenely. Seeing as she's technically already giving me a ride and seeing as the question is punctuated by those underwhelming boobs, I'm pretty sure I know what she's actually driving at. Sometimes, an answer isn't necessary. Sometimes just getting out of the car is answer enough.

By the time I arrive at House Number Three, my fingers are bluish at the tips and my face is too frozen to smile but I'm not much in the mood for smiling anyway.

"I'm Holly," announces the buttoned-down, bun-wearing woman in the ankle-length dress and suddenly I feel like I've walked onto the set of *Little House on the Prairie*. "And this is Wadie," she says, introducing the mild-mannered man at her side. You know that painting, *American Gothic*? You get the idea.

OPENING MY EYES, I let go of Holly and Wadie's hands. Irish Catholic and all, I'm no stranger to saying grace before a meal but this is a first at a billet's, as is the pre-dinner Bible-reading. But Holy Holly knows how to cook a spread and I'm pretty much ready to do back flips if that's what it takes to dig in. I'm three mouthfuls deep before I realize that no one else is eating.

"Uh, amen?" I offer again, thinking maybe they didn't hear me the first time but that can't be it because Holly's just staring at the knife in my left hand like it's sprouted horns and a tail.

"You're left-handed," she observes quietly.

"Yep," I confirm, happily shoveling a forkful of peas into my mouth.

"Homosexuality is an abomination," she says and it's only by the grace of God that I don't spit my mouthful across the table like little green bb's.

"Huh?" I manage after swallowing. Turns out that Holy Holly's beliefs are as archaic as her wardrobe because this woman actually thinks that all southpaws putt from the rough. That's when I spot the opportunity...

"Oh no, ma'am I'm not one of them. But I should probably sleep with a few girls soon, just to be sure," I offer, flashing a devilish smile at Mary, the couple's 17-year-old daughter, who's sitting opposite me, certifiably cute despite her lack of makeup. Now it's Holly's turn to almost spit out her peas and I'm informed in no uncertain terms that female company is *not* on the agenda, not under this roof. Holly tells me she'd much prefer it if I held my knife in my right hand, at least when I'm eating with the family. I explain to her that it's not a choice: it's the way God made me and I should be free to eat how I choose, because I'm not hurting anybody. But I do assure her that I will abstain from gay sex, at home or anywhere else.

Mary's a sweet girl and a little heartbroken since her boyfriend (if holding hands makes you that) was ironically traded to Yorkton to make space at Rayburn for me. I get to meet the male half of this virginal arrangement just two weeks later when Yorkton comes to town on a road trip and poor kid, I'm taunting him all game about what a firecracker his little hand-holder Mary is in the sack, before finally putting him through the wall just before the horn.

"I'll pray for you, Doyle," he says limping off the ice.

"That'll make two of you on your knees, I guess," I call after him with a shit-eating grin. Relentlessly teasing Mary about her boyfriend never gets old and she tolerates my needling with saintly patience. Mary's really a sweet girl.

I can handle Holy Holly and her clan and their Bible and their quiet, pious shtick but there's one thing I don't abide: cats. And since I don't have any love for redheads either, you can guess how I feel about the family's ginger tom. Chester takes an immediate, annoying liking to me (evident when he chooses me as the one to let him out in the mornings for his piss) and suddenly my alarm clock is playing second fiddle to the incessant scratching at my bedroom door. One morning, it's both: the scratching, and the beeping and I'm in the middle of a really good dream when the phone starts ringing too and in the half-stupor of someone desperate for an extra half-hour of shut-eye, I spring up, desperate for it all to just stop. Desperate for just a few more moments of peace. I'm halfway across the living room before I remember that I'm stark naked and by the time I hear a stereo gasp, it's too late. Holly and Mary sit on the couch, open-mouthed.

There's a horrible moment between realization and reaction when time stands still. The slack-jawed shock on mother and daughter's faces. The surprise on mine. And most memorably my proud, steamy morning glory craning toward them. Holly looks like she's never seen an erection before and Mary clearly hasn't, staring at my crotch with that combination of fear and excitement that kids get when they meet Mickey Mouse at Disneyland for the first time. It's only a moment in time and I'm back in the bedroom cursing and covering up almost faster than it happened but what's been seen cannot be unseen and that night at the dinner table, the Bible reading's a little longer than usual.

Amazingly, my penis isn't the body part causing the most disruption at Holy Holly's. It's my mouth. And this devout house mum is doing everything in her power to get me to clean up my language.

"Say fire truck instead," she implores gently prior to a family dinner that includes several aunts, some uncles and a few cousins but feels more like an Amish high holiday. I hold my own throughout the meal, minding my Ps and Qs and even managing to keep my knife in my right hand throughout.

"How was dinner?" asks Wadie amiably to no one in particular once Mary and her mother have dutifully cleared the plates from the table.

"Fire trucking delicious," I reply with a satisfied smile. The look Holly shoots me is decidedly non-Christian.

On and off the ice, the first year is good and (much to Holly's relief) the closet-case left-handed thing is getting easier and easier. Much to my relief the sanctity of this solo billet scenario is not being disrupted. But then comes the dreaded question:

"How would you like another player to share your room with?" asks Wadie with the condescending excitement of someone saying, 'How would you like a popsicle?'

"Not a fire trucking chance in H-E-double hockey sticks," I reply evenly. But apparently, the question is more of a courtesy than an actual question because Mary's off to university soon and Wadie and Holly's pockets just aren't that deep and 'God only helps those who help themselves.' Three hours later I'm sourly meeting my new roommate.

BUT EVEN NEW ROOMMATES ARE easier to tolerate than this bone-numbing cold. The Redwings' first road trip north is an eye-opener to just how frigid this Godforsaken province gets. I show up to the bus in my Prince Peaks-quality ski jacket to find Coach White kitted up like Sir Edmund Hillary in a water buffalo coat and a fur hat big enough to snap a lesser man's neck.

"Where are we going, the North Pole?" I ask.

"Yes, son. More or less," he replies grimly. I'm comfortable when we leave Rayburn at a balmy seven degrees Celsius but by the time we reach Flin Flon, Manitoba, the temperature's plummeted to a not-so-comfortable minus forty-seven. I get off the bus and gaze into the greyness, teeth chattering like maracas. Dogsleds sit in the parking lot like cars (no shit!), and giant above-ground sewage pipes give the landscape the feel of an icy, post-apocalyptic Mario World. I remember this was where Gerry hailed from. *No wonder he was such a crazy bastard*, I think.

After playing Flin Flon, we head southwest to Nipawan, but not south enough because this ski jacket is still a joke in these conditions. En route, the bus breaks down (probably frostbitten pistons) and the mercury drops out the bottom of the thermometer so violently, Coach White's actually worried we'll freeze to death. *We can always cram six of us at a time naked in the bus bathroom. That's how you go from unbearably cold to unbearably hot;* but there's no way I'm suggesting that until our first casualty. Luckily, things never go that far because a rig comes along inside the hour and a new bus inside two. Could have been worse. They could have sent the dog sleds…

EVENTUALLY, I THAW OUT AND the team's just getting hotter all season and here we are, the first game of the playoffs and here I am on the bench.

"Are you kidding me?" I groan to Coach White in his office later. "Carry the mail. That's what you told me I was here to do. If you're not going to play me, I might as well go home!" It's not like my outbursts have had a history of doing me any favours but luckily, this is one coach who recognizes the difference between hungry and entitled and next game, against our bitter rivals Estevan, I'm on the ice. And I'm on fire. It's a double-overtime nail-biter and they put up one helluva fight but we walk away with the win. And Danny Boy scores the game-winner!

'Doyle scores in Double OT,' says the Leader Post the next day and that's a headline I can't stop staring at and I swear, my pulse hasn't slowed down, even the next day and I haven't felt this tall since Game 1 with the Bantam Aviators. That series behind us, we head back to Nipawan and that's a seven-game series even more grueling than the weather.

We take the first two games at home and it's Game 3 at their barn and we're going hammer and tong for three periods. Pound-for-pound skill's marginally on our side but they have some serious bulk on their bench which they're using with maddening effect. We're losing 2-0 with about a minute left on the clock when I get speared in the back by this overgrown bag of meat named Rackie Woods who's widely considered the toughest sonofabitch in the league, which is saying something. I'm not overly thrilled at the prospect of getting into it with this goon but he's been banging me around all series and this one's inevitable, I guess. An hour later, I'm sitting in this sorry excuse for a hospital getting a badly broken nose set but so is he, which is saying something too, and it's amazing how much space I'm given on the ice next game. That's what hockey looks like sometimes.

Losing at home in Game 7 is a devastating blow and as I head back to Prince Peaks for another summer, it's with a new level of gravitas, one that's been steadily growing since I started shaving daily. I'm getting bigger. Stronger. But I'm getting older, too, and every birthday's a stark reminder that the window of opportunity that is my hockey career is slowly, steadily closing.

"Did you ever doubt yourself? Question your dream?"

"I hadn't. But fear's one helluva motivator. There weren't any keggers for me that summer. No Alexis or Jill or any other girls either. Nothing. There was only training. Only hockey."

"What were you afraid of?"

"Failure. What else?"

BACK IN RAYBURN THE NEXT season, I couldn't have been more focused, more driven, more optimistic. God knows I'm locked and loaded with a full season ahead of me and a U.S. College Scholarship in my sights and things get off to a great start with scouts sniffing around from Colorado College and Ferris State. But sometimes you're only as good as the guys you play with.

Most of our veterans had left the season prior, leaving a non-cohesive squad with second rate goalie and two pretenders for enforcers.

"There's no 'I' in 'Team'," Coach White reminds me as yet another underwhelmed scout closes his notepad and goes home. *No, but there is in 'scholarship'*, I think darkly.

In an attempt to give us a little more muscle to flex, Coach White has collared a couple of goons from the top Winnipeg Junior League. This one kid, Hank Lois ends up being my defence partner and I couldn't be more thrilled having this 245 pound monster to my left because he's a card-carrying brawler in every sense of the word. Hank's reputation precedes him. Rumour has it he trains in the off-season by fighting 250 pound toothless Native women.

The problem with Hank is that he sees the Rayburn Redwings as his opportunity to turn over a new leaf; a chance to put his violent ways behind him and finally become the finesse player he never was (still isn't and never will be).

One-third of the way through another disappointingly mild-mannered performance from the big man, Coach White storms into the locker room staring at Lois like he's appraising a broken refrigerator.

"I didn't bring you onto this team to put the puck in the net, I brought you here to punish people. Do your fucking job!" he barks, storming out. Hank looks like a hurt kid, but only for a moment. When he steps back on the ice for the second period he has a different look on his face altogether and by the end of the third, several Notre Dame players have (involuntary) different looks on their faces too. That night, a bunch of us order pizza and Hank's so fired

Matt McCoy

up he beats the crap out of the delivery boy as well. Begrudgingly, Coach White trades him away the next day. I feel sorry for Hank because I really think he almost had it licked. I feel even sorrier for his anger-management counsellor. All that time wasted…

SHORTLY AFTER HANK'S UNTIMELY EXIT, I get a letter in the mail from Mum, which isn't a strange thing in itself. It's the letter *inside* the letter that sends my eyebrows north. Clearly Mum has read it since a) it didn't come in its own envelope and b) she refers to it in *her* letter. Mum has Stasi-like sensibilities when it comes to her kids and their personal lives. Once, she opened a letter addressed to Henry who was eighteen and away at the time playing for an out-of-province team. Inside were lewd photos of the 26-year-old woman he was seeing and you can imagine that Mum had something to say about that; as did Henry, railing (in no uncertain terms) against the blatant violation of his privacy.

I scan to the bottom of Mum's letter. 'I hope you don't go back to that girl,' she finishes in lieu of 'hope you're eating enough,' which is the usual salutation that precedes 'Love, Mum' in these correspondences.

The second letter is on lilac-coloured paper that smells like a chemical astringent version of the same flower. The cursive is bubbly and ridiculous: pretty to view but surprisingly hard to read because it looks like squished balloons. This is Nicola's little purple version of a Hail Mary play: She misses me. She's sorry. Still so, so sorry. And she wants a fresh start… Indifferently, I toss the little lilac ball of paper into the trash. *Sorry, sweetheart. That box is closed already.*

BUT OTHER BOXES ARE OPEN, like the 'Take-it-or leave-it-because-it's-just-sex' box. That one's got loads of room left in it. I'm half-heartedly dating this girl in Regina, or 'Vagina' as my teammates call it whenever I embark on one of my single-purpose visits and finally it's becoming worth the drive. The first couple of visits, she thought we were 'moving too fast', but right when I was about to hit the ejection button, she changed her tune so here I am, on the road again to Vagina. But this time someone else has a problem with how fast I'm moving. Ruefully, I take the speeding ticket from the cop, looking at it like he just handed me a dog turd.

"Are you serious?" I ask with disgust.

"Are you?" responds the officer. "I could have dinged you with excessive as well. Now get outta here and if you know what's good for you, you'll pay that fine the minute you get into town."

DOING COMMUNITY SERVICE IN LIEU of paying the speeding ticket seems like a good idea at the time. Not so much because it *is* a good idea but more because it *isn't* what the cop told me to do, and that in itself comes with a certain level of satisfaction. But now, halfway through my stint at a home for the mentally challenged (is that the correct term?) I'm realizing how painless coughing up the money would have been. Now, I am hauling trash, sweeping floors and wiping down urinals while back home my ever-expanding fan base is cheering me on with every new T.V. highlight reel. If they could see me now, five bucks an hour, three days a week wiping up piss that would be in the hallway if it was any further from the porcelain... I'm getting screwed here.

But apparently I'm not the only one getting screwed.

This new kid (a rookie from Manitoba) has been giving it to Coach White's boss' daughter since he stepped off the bus and ask anyone, that's one degree of separation too close. Piss drunk, the idiot's planking Daddy's little girl in her dad's basement, the pair of them unabashedly going at it like they're doing a porn-shoot for the sight-impaired and judging by the dad's reaction they may as well have sent him snapshots.

"One of your little filthy little fuckers is screwing my daughter!" the dad thunders at an unsuspecting Coach White the next morning and the rest is just gravity because shit rolls downhill.

Our next practice is a puck-less, sadistic ninety-minute bag-skate and when we're done Coach White lets us have it both barrels.

"You fucking cock-sucking faggots with your earrings and tattoos!" he spits and sputters, the Tums he's furiously chewing turning the corners of his mouth into an angry yellow froth. "You pansy-ass motherfuckers! I'm sick of this!" he screams, and no one's quite sure what he's talking about but it's a safe bet that it has something to do with his boss' daughter. And since we're a team and he's a good coach, the shit-kicking's distributed between us evenly. It's the first time I've reaped the whirlwind for *not* screwing someone but there's no 'I' in team, I guess.

There is in 'horny idiot', though.

SOMETIMES, THINGS HAPPEN FAST. BUT not bad things. Bad things happen in slow motion because you're not in control. You're not driving. You're in the back seat just watching as the car skids across the ice, as the sidewall looms out of the darkness…

That's how the season feels as it winds down. Expectations are low going into the Playoffs and we don't disappoint, in that we do: an early First Round fizzle and somehow it's a weird relief because I'm on the outside looking in like the spectator in someone else's sad saga. As the last of the college scouts close their notebooks, shaking their heads as they leave the barn, as the final horn sounds for the final time, I walk down the hallway toward the dressing room and no one's cheering for me. No one's grabbing my elbow and talking up their campus programs. Nobody's there but the janitor, who looks at me and shrugs as if to say, 'Whaddya want me to tell ya, kid? I'm a janitor.' Somehow I'm expecting something more awful, more monumental. But as my hockey aspirations fade then vanish, the window of opportunity doesn't close with a bang. As these things do, it has been slowly closing for years and when pane finally meets frame, it shuts with the quietest of clicks.

Then life just carries on.

"This must have been devastating. You can't expect me to believe it was that simple. That it was just over and that was that…"

"Why not?"

"Because hockey had defined you since the age of seven and your professional aspirations were the only things that had ever given you purpose."

"You're forgetting, I have boxes for that."

BACK IN PRINCE PEAKS, I don't even have time to lick my wounds because if there isn't a scholarship in my immediate future I'm going to have to scrape and scramble a Plan B together (and quick) and it's as simple as that, says Mum. She's striking while the iron is hot and she has no intention of letting me lose my inertia and no problem telling me as much.

"What do you want to study?" she asks with the same matter-of-fact tone usually reserved for, 'What do you want for lunch?'

"WHAT'S ON THE MENU TODAY?" asks Keegan, with the hungry anticipation of a typical teenager.

"Lasagna," I announce grandly, brandishing a second Tupperware container that matches the first one I'm already making short work of. Keegan cracks the plastic lid, grinning in anticipation as a little bit of Italy wafts up to his waiting nostrils.

"Two bucks," I remind him. Keegan can't put the money in my hand fast enough and by the time I've stuffed eight quarters into my pocket and turned back to my own container, he's all but caught up.

Mum didn't want me to develop a misplaced sense of entitlement, but that wasn't going to stop her spoiling her son.

"These warm lunches are a favour to me more than to you," she would fib. "No mother in their right mind wants to get up extra early in the morning just to pack brown bags." Of course that wasn't true, but I was as happy with the arrangement as she was so the flawed logic remained unchallenged and every weekday at 11:45, she'd walk the three blocks to my school and drop off a container of something warm.

It had taken just one week of jealous stares from classmates for me to realize that I had a viable commodity on my hands and the wheeler-dealer wheels in my adolescent head had started turning almost immediately.

"I'm still hungry after lunch," I had informed her dolefully one morning, watching as her maternal concern completely eclipsed any suspicions that I was working an angle.

"How much more hungry, honey?" she had asked.

"Honestly, I could eat twice as much," I'd replied tentatively, citing several unsubstantiated claims about the nutritional needs of young athletes, for good measure. Ever since, Mum had been delivering two containers daily and like clockwork I'd unload one container on the highest bidder on the playground by noon.

Suddenly, the answer to Mum's question is crystal clear.

"Business," I reply. "I want to go to Business School."

I KNOW HOCKEY (I KNOW that much) and I'm pretty prolific with the ladies too. But school's another kettle of fish. I'm no Rhodes Scholar...hell, I'm not even an Ashlyn. But I do hate losing, so that's something worth working with anyway.

Mum and Dad, they're just like most parents who want better for their kids than they had. Mum had called it quits in Grade 8 and moved to Boston shortly thereafter, nannying for a rich Jewish family to help support her poor Irish one back home and Dad went straight to trade school to get his pipefitting certificate then moved to Chicago for a spell because that's where the work was. So while neither was a stranger to hard work and huge moves, the concept of higher education had been to them more abstract than anything else.

Whatever the case, it's better for their kids than they had so my new tack is greeted with enthusiastic support and no small amount of relief. Mum and Dad were fleeing the bullshit in Belfast when most kids were enjoying the luxury of a tertiary education and I'm pretty sure they (especially Mum) would be happy if I'd gone anywhere to study anything at this point.

But first, the fallout from a high school education that to date, has been fragmented at best and scattered between three provinces: Part of Grade 11 in Vandermeer, three months more in Regal, five months in Purcell, Prince Peaks for the rest of it, two months of Grade 12 in Salmon Arm, five more back in Purcell and now, the last gasps of my secondary school career back in Prince Peaks.

"Your transcripts look more like a passport and you're missing credits all over the map," my high school counsellor tells me flatly when I go in for a 'How-the-hell-am-I-going-to-make-this-happen' meeting. "You're going to need to put in a solid month of day and night studying. Honestly, I'm not sure you'll be able to pull it off." But that sounds more like a dare than anything else and *it can't be worse than hitting the ice hung over*, I think.

But it is worse. Far worse, and it makes my head hurt in an entirely different way. But losing hurts worse and come graduation time I'm up front in a ridiculous blue gown with everyone else, smiling smugly and shaking hands and taking photos and grasping that rolled up piece of paper like it's a trophy and boy-o you better believe we're getting hammered tonight!

But my celebration's short-lived. It's just gone June and I'm still six months' short of the prerequisites needed for business school. Unless I'm prepared to wait a year-and-a-bit (which I'm not because quite frankly, I'm never prepared to wait for anything) I'm going to have to get this done in half the time. There's no way that's happening on my own steam and God knows no one around here's going to tutor someone up that steep a hill. But then I remember A. Tunbridge…

A.T. is a Rayburn school teacher who lives next door to Wadie and Holly and he's as smart and bearded as his name suggests. The year prior, I'd taken a wild stab at a university-level English course and A.T. had been my saving grace, although Holly had given all credit to Jesus and her fervent prayers to Him on my behalf.

A.T. sounds genuinely pleased to hear from me, is pleased to board me for the summer and thrilled at my academic aspirations regardless of the rigor they imply. I think secretly, A.T. has always envied hockey coaches and the devotion their players give them and the dogged determination they foster in these kids and tutoring me is the closest he's going to get to a playoff rush. Team Doyle has a coach and a game-plan and God willing, this summer nerding out in Rayburn will produce the desired results by the fall.

"You're like a Ferrari," explains A.T. trying to regain my interest as I make obscene blowjob gestures out the window at Mary who's hanging laundry on the line next door. If I can just catch her eye, this is going to be priceless…

"Enough!" thunders my new tutor, slamming his hand down on the table and satisfied that (at least for now) he's in sole possession of my attention, continues quietly. "You're like a Ferrari. When you find your gear, you'll be unstoppable. But as long as you're just sitting in the pits, you're nothing but a shiny piece of metal. Did I mention that the race started ages ago?" A.T. strides from the kitchen, taking with him his massive 19th century beard and his not-so-massive dog Chino. "Catch up, Doyle!" he calls over his shoulder. "I know exactly what you're made of."

Wow, I think. *Way to go, coach*. Forgetting Mary and her clothespins, I buckle down and bury my head in the book before me, enjoying the pleasant, familiar warmth of the fire that's just been re-lit under my ass.

VANCOUVER'S NOT LIKE ANYWHERE ELSE I've ever lived, not even a city like Vandermeer (which is just a huge town by comparison). Vancouver's a proper city, sprawling at the foot of the Coast Mountains like a shiny pile of glass and scrap metal; a big beautiful bipolar mess of rain and sun and yoga and coffee that just keeps going and going and going, right across the floodplain, right to the American border, more or less, if you count the suburbs.

Just like A.T. and his beard had predicted, I've found my gear, only it's a new gear, one I didn't even know existed in my gearbox: one that whirs away eight hours a day, eight courses a semester. Two Year Plan: Get this damned diploma, get good and drunk and the next day, go into business for myself. But Coach A.T. isn't over my shoulder anymore and if this Ferrari's going to finish this race, it's going to need a willing pit crew…

The library seems like the smartest place to meet smart women. There's table after long, brown tables of them to choose from, the field only narrowing by necessity as I look for stacks of text books that match my own. *Fyodor Dosteovsky – Crime and Punishment…* no. *An Introduction to Conversational Analysis…* no. *Franz Kafka – The Metamorphosis…* no. *An Introduction to Quantum Physics…* not a chance. *Vis-à-vis: French for Beginners…* fuck no. *Operational Management, Human Resource Management, Corporate Finance…* Bingo. Suddenly nothing's hotter than reading glasses, hair held up with ballpoint pens and track pants with large white letters on the asses.

"I'm Danny," I say with affected shyness, sliding into one of three empty seats. "This stuff's tough, huh?" And suddenly, the struggling ex-hockey player with the dimples is getting unsolicited help from every ponytail at the table.

Danny's GPA 2, Worry 0

One girl named Mona is especially helpful and soon, we're meeting up all over campus: the cafeteria, the quad, the Student Union Building, her dorm room and not surprisingly, it's only a matter of time before we're *really* getting down to business.

"Here's the thing, Danny," she explains as she rides me on her single mattress. "I don't mind helping you with your homework and fucking you even, but I'm not looking for a boyfriend. I'm just here to have fun. Is that cool?" Appreciatively, I palm Mona's tits.

"Absolutely," I assure her emphatically. *Thank-you, Jesus!*

"Good," she replies, placing her hands on my chest and bucking a little faster. "Now shut up." *Who says guys and girls can't just be friends*, I think as she tumbles forward all gasps and groans and cascading black hair.

Mona's right. College is as much about having fun as anything else and if you can't kick back and enjoy yourself amid the masses of papers and essays and exams then what's the point? Her dating philosophy's given me a permission I probably would have taken anyway and between parties, pranks and getting my leg over the next freshman filly, this Ferrari's dropping a few positions. That being said, Mona is hands-down awesome. From her long-legged, coltish beauty and that gorgeous body and shiny dark hair to her general attitude about pretty much everything. I respected this one.

"Of course failing your Math midterm gets you kicked out of class," grates the instructor in question who has by now had it up to *here* with me. "Even if you aced the rest of the year you'd still fail my course and seeing as you can't do the simple arithmetic to even figure *that* much out on your own, I think it's safe to say that to continue with this charade would equate to nothing more than a massive waste of time for both of us."

"Fine," I respond, closing the office door with an unceremonious bang. *You don't have to be an asshole about it.* The ejection's an unprecedented pit stop and suddenly, Saturdays morning's are for Make-up Math, which isn't just cutting my weekend in half; it's murdering my Friday nights as well. And that's not even the sum total of my academic woes. Economics is no better because the asshole in charge of *that* class fails twenty people this year and you better believe I'm one of them.

To make matters worse, several local hockey teams come knocking, all past pretending their propositions are anything more than dead end job offers. No dream-spinning. No scholarship promises. Just, 'Hey, you're a veteran D-man. Want to come help us out?' *Not enough to pull me out of school, not after what it took to get here, thanks.* Their efforts might as well be written in bubble letters on lilac-scented paper for all the good it does them.

By the end of my first year at Business School, I've failed economics and nailed my second run at math and as summer school looms on the horizon like a month of bad weather, the fleeting Vancouver summer looks like it's going to be a failure too.

Then I get the phone call from Mum. All she has to say is, 'Hi honey,' and I know she's been crying…

It's a small funeral. They bury Granddad on a Friday, right next to my baby sister, Kelly, in a plot in Seaview Cemetery at the base of Mount Jayne. When he died, his sausage recipe died with him. Mum and Nan and Ash and the aunties, they're all crying, but not me. I'm relieved because anything's better than being trapped in that broken body in that sunless hospital. Sometimes, death is the fair end. Rest in peace, Paddy Gowan. I miss you. And the world misses your sausages.

It's a grey and listless summer but that's what summer in Vancouver looks like sometimes. Just as well, though. Summer school leaves me zero time to work which means zero cash, which means

I'm broke and bored and dark and cloudy anyway. But it does pay off. And come September, I'm in good shape for year two and this time I mean business.

Inside the first week I get friendly with some interesting characters; a good move because it gave me access to some archived exams. I still have to put in the footwork to some degree but these exams are the difference between me passing and me passing with flying colours. It's not what you know…

I've made friends with the Head of Marketing too. Cheri McG is like Noreen Pickford if Noreen was a bit younger, a bit taller, and a Head of Marketing. We get along famously and become great friends almost instantly because finally I'm at that weird age when it's understood that (roles aside) we're all more or less adults, even if one of us has been at it a bit longer than the other. It's this sense of novelty that initially builds our bond, I think, but it's definitely our shared sense of humour that sustains it.

Monday mornings are usually pretty arduous: all bags and binders and hangover coffees in beige paper cups, but not today. On the weekend, local magazine show *Sports Page* had featured me in a lighthearted student segment where I was aping about, doing what I considered to be a pretty accurate impression of one of my teachers. It's not even nine o'clock when my classmate, Kevin, comes bustling into Marketing 202 waving a video cassette above his head like a TV evangelist.

"Funniest shit I've ever seen! Seriously, Doyle, you should do comedy, man," he brays, rolling the monitor to the front of the room. By the time Cheri McG shows up, we're chortling through the *Sports Page* segment, enjoying my fifteen seconds of fame for the fourth time and no one even sees her there at the back of the room until we hear her laugh, which sounds somewhere between a shriek and a hiccup. Cracking up the class is one thing but getting a rise out of Cheri McG is a whole different kind of gratifying.

"Wow," she says, wiping her eyes. "Mimicry: The sincerest form of flattery." Which gets me thinking because I'd love to find a way of flattering *her*—or maybe just make her shriek-hiccup some more…

No one suspects a thing next class when a police officer interrupts the lecture on analytics and conversation rate tracking. No one suspects a thing, least of all Cheri McG. She's too busy being concerned and maybe a bit embarrassed because she swears she doesn't recall seeing an accident let alone leaving the scene of one and, 'what do you mean you have to book me?' when said cop pulls out a tape recorder because it's either a recorded statement or a ride downtown and this guy's not fooling around. If the look on Cheri McG's face as she sits down is hard to describe, the expression that follows is harder because there's a fundamental disconnect that happens when you think you're getting arrested and suddenly you're not. When suddenly you're being assaulted with obnoxious techno music and accosted by an oiled up, gyrating pretender in a policeman's hat and not much else. The shriek-hiccup. There it was. Mission accomplished. Marketing 202 is more or less a write-off that day, which is why the entire class is in the campus bar by 10am, Cheri McG included. I got an 'A' in that class and on my final exam, scrawled in green gel-tip was this:

Marketing is more than theory.
It's about working a room and getting things done too.
PS: Thanks for the stripper.
~ Cheri

"Let's go back to the cheating."

"Nicola?"

"No. Your cheating. School. Answer keys, exams…"

"I'd hardly call that cheating. More 'working the system'. I mean no one got hurt. I even flogged a few term papers so technically I paid it forward."

"It could be argued that cheating oneself and one's peers out of a proper education isn't exactly a victimless crime but that's another conversation. What intrigues me is your rationale: Are you suggesting that the moral fabric of any action is dependent upon if and how it's perceived by others?"

"You lost me."

"Do you believe it's not a crime until you get caught?"

"If a tree falls in the forest, right?"

"Then why are you here?"

"Because maybe I'm wrong."

EITHER WAY, I'M STILL SUBSISTING on a few hours sleep a night and come January, I'm on coffee and not for the love of it. I hate the charred black sludge, in fact, and the foul sour reek it leaves in the back of your throat, and all the cream or sugar in the world is not going to change that. I can't sacrifice school and I won't sacrifice my social life and sometimes there just aren't enough hours in a day, I lament to myself as I push through my dorm room door, arms heavy with textbooks and eyes heavy from reading them. Flopping onto the couch, I'm just about to slide into a blissful twenty-minutes of well-needed shut-eye when the phone begins to ring.

"Danny, it's Henry." My little brother's voice is hollow, desperate. "You have to get me out of here."

chapter 6

"How's the Delayed Intensification going?"

"It's going."

"About a week left now?"

"Eight days."

"I imagine it's taking its toll…"

"Yeah, it is. But the PEG Asparaginase is done for good and the Methotrexate spinal tap's done for now, so that's something."

"Good. And the response?"

"Promising. It's a long road with Acute Lymphoblastic Leukemia, though. Not like getting a mole lanced, you know?"

"No. No, I imagine it's not. Let's get back to Henry. He calls you. He's upset. This must have been troubling."

"Yeah, sort of."

"Did you speak to your brother often?"

"Not on the phone. That wasn't our thing. He was in Winnipeg playing hockey and with me being in British Columbia, we usually only caught up at home on the holidays. We were tight though."

"So it was strange for him to call?"

"Oh yeah. Would have been strange enough if he was calling just to say hi."

DESPITE THE EARLY STUTTER AND the teasing and tormenting it won him, Henry and I were always close. Three years difference is nothing between brothers, especially when you're old enough to play sports together which beats beating the shit out of each other. Baseball, basketball, soccer—you name it—and of course, hockey. Pushing him to do better was a job I took seriously and as he got older and got better, he pushed me to be better. Henry was a natural. Not like me and my blood-sweat-and-tears approach. He had genuine talent. Gifted even, making every sport he attempted look effortless. I might have hated losing but Henry simply didn't know how to. Mum always said that if he combined his skill with my heart, he could have played any sport he chose professionally.

When I embarked on my Junior Hockey career, Henry had just turned fourteen and fourteen's a hard enough age for a boy but even harder for a kid like him—all skill—twisting in the breeze in a town that had nothing to offer. Henry was miserable. And after a worrying two weeks of watching their dark-browed youngest bang slapshots against the garage door, Mum and Dad knew they had to do something.

But what? By now, *Doyle's* was the invalid which made it next to impossible to leave and it's not like anyone was buying even if they had tried to sell anyway. Sadly for Mum, sending Henry away to greener pastures was the intelligent option and Riegers the obvious choice. An exclusive boys' school in Alberta, Riegers specialized in wunderkinds of the sporting variety; a veritable prep-school for young jocks with honest-to-goodness scholarship shots. But the scholarships came later, not now, so moving heaven and earth, Mum and Dad sent him there on their own dime. God knows how, but they did, and going into Grade Nine, Henry found himself surrounded by elite kids like himself with every chance of a scholarship and a good chance at a crack at the National Hockey League as well.

For two years, Henry was at Riegers and it was worth every penny as far as the folks were concerned because suddenly he was turning heads at the Winnipeg Warriors. Not many kids headed straight for the Juniors after junior high but Henry wasn't just any kid. The Warriors knew it and Mum and Dad knew it and by sixteen, he was being seriously courted by the organization via a Western League Championship player.

"Sign with the team, kid. You can have what I have. Do well and you'll be NHL bound," the champ had told him and all Henry could think as he munched his burger was 'Holy shit, this guy has his own hockey card!' Not surprisingly, little brother signed.

That was two years ago and if he thought Year One was tough, Year Two was even worse and with high school almost in his rearview, he was desperate to get out and that's when he called me.

"What was the problem?"

"Not what. Who."

"Who was the problem?"

"J.G. His coach. The guy had been coming up with this core squad of players through Pee Wee to Junior and that's when Henry arrived. No one had a clue he was a pedophile. Sick fuck had been grooming his victims for years, escalating the abuse as they grew older."

"That's horrific. No one knew?"

"Allegedly some of the billets did but no one came forward."

"Did any of the boys refuse?"

"That's what happened to Henry. If you didn't do what J.G. wanted off the ice, he'd make your life hell on it. Pushing you harder than anyone else, limiting your ice-time, verbal abuse, even sabotaging your career with awful references when other teams came calling... He'd try to break you mentally if he couldn't physically. When I finally saw my brother, he'd lost weight. Lost his smile. Had these dark half-moons under his eyes. I got him on a new team fast enough but he didn't last long there and spent the rest of his Junior career being traded from one team to the next to the next. Henry wasn't the same player after being on J.G.'s team. Wasn't even the same person."

"Do you think Henry might have been abused as well?"

"That's a helluva question to ask. And one I wish I could answer."

I'M PRETTY MUCH RETCHING ON my toothbrush as I brush my tongue, furiously trying to get rid of the fuzzy taste of French Roast, when my roommate Jarv sticks his head in the bathroom.

"Here," he says, lobbing me a pill bottle like it's a white, rattling grenade.

"I don't do that shit," I say, tossing it back without so much as a glance at the label. If it came from Jarv, safe bet was that I indeed *didn't do that shit.*

"You sure?" he says with a grin, tossing it back. Skeptically, I read the label. *Maximum Strength NoNapz – Fast Acting Alertness Aid – 200mg CAFFEINE – Easy to swallow coated caplets – Safer than coffee.* "No more nasty java for you, bro!" he says, flashing me a blinding white smile.

The best part about caffeine pills is caffeine pills. Suddenly, the world's a bigger place filled with details you never notice when you're wasting time with things like blinking and sleeping. There are more hours in the day too: like 4am and 5am, when the sky's a different kind of purple and the quiet's so quiet you can feel it as much as hear it. And there I am, grinding my teeth and pouring with sweat and plowing through textbooks like my life depends on it. I'm confident; four out of five exams behind me, strolling into the hall to write my *final* final, chawing away on a wad of tasteless gum, drumming on the edge of the desk in counterpoint to my heart palpitations. That's the last thing I remember.

The worst part about caffeine pills is coming off caffeine pills. I've misjudged my mileage by about four hours and as my engine sputters and dies, I succumb to the gravity of four hours sleep in five days and begin a rather short, rather violent freefall. The force of my face hitting the desk wakes me up just long enough to put in a gallant (albeit stunned) effort that earns me a solid C+ in Global Economics. And with that, I limp across the finish line and Business School is over.

A DIPLOMA IN MARKETING MANAGEMENT isn't the only thing I take away from Business School. Two years of beer and pizza and vending machines have added an undue 55 pounds to the post-college situation leaving me at a soft 250 and no surprise, no local teams are coming knocking anymore.

Undaunted, I'm determined to keep my sport in my periphery somehow so I'm as thrilled when Slapshot, an East Vancouver hockey store, offers me an apprenticeship when I agree to write them a business plan. General idea: spend the next twelve months learning the ropes and gaining valuable insights that I can take with me when the time comes to set up my own shop front. Plan B. Same name as my grade point average. At least I'm consistent.

THIRTEEN MONTHS LATER. I'M HUNCHED over the skate sharpener re-setting the grinding wheel radius from the goalie-friendly one-and-a half inches back to the regular skate half-inch. I swear, I could do this in my sleep: Adjust the wheel just enough so the bonding compound doesn't overheat. Insert skate blade into the holder (heel to the left) so the blade rests against the anvil plate and is centred on the high point of the grinding wheel. Turn the cam lever. Turn the cam-adjusting screw snug then releasing one-quarter turn. Lock cam lever at the twelve o'clock position. Cross grind. Put witness marks on the front and back of the blade to make sure it's centred. Adjust blade as necessary. Grind test line to ensure it's centered for the entire length of the blade. Sharpen in three to four passes, left to right, heel to toe, letting the wheel pull the skate through (don't force it and don't round the heel or the toe). Finish with a layer of *Gusto-Glide*, run the blade across the grinding wheel once more and hand-hone. And repeat.

I'm on my sixth pair and it's not even noon. *I'm pretty sure it takes more than getting a good edge to run a hockey store*, I think ruefully as a bouquet of clean yellow sparks blossom just beyond my left elbow. Finishing up, I slide the little skates across the counter. The dad pays as the seven-year-old kid looks up at me, eyes dancing with excitement and hopes and dreams and suddenly, it's me and I'm back in Olympic Sports in Prince Peaks and all I can think is: *what the fuck happened?*

"Two goals, one assist," booms Mario, as he bangs into the store, almost dismembering the little bell from the front door in the process. Mario owns Slapshot. His son Anton plays for the Vancouver Voodoo, an 'Original Twelve' team from the professional Roller Hockey International League. Anton works at the store occasionally; a quiet, humble sort of kid who definitely didn't get his personality from his old man.

"Two goals, one assist," repeats Mario, his moustache looking like it's going to jump off his lip.

"That's great, Mario," I murmur unenthusiastically. *Let the kid do his own bragging, goddammit.* "Maybe I'll try out next year, I hear myself say. Mario stops dead, looking me up and down scornfully.

"Yeah, okay, Danny. You do that. Don't be late back from lunch." It's only later when I catch my reflection in the mirror at Wendy's that I realize how ridiculous a comment that must have sounded coming from a guy who looked like this. That's when something happens, like a switch being flipped.

"What can I get you?" asks the kid behind the counter with the black lipstick and the band-aid unsuccessfully hiding her nose ring.

"Just a salad," I reply, a strange, familiar warmth creeping up from my gut into my face. "No dressing."

"You want a strength and conditioning program…" echoes the fit Ray Romano look-alike in front of me. Carlo Sferra is a UBC Exercise Science grad who runs *Hockey Dynamics*, an outfit just down the road from my apartment that specializes in player development and as far as I was concerned, he was the man for the job. "What for?" he asks, without a hint of Mario's scorn.

"My comeback," I reply. There's this pause—a long one—and I'm guessing this guy's trying to figure out whether or not to take me seriously, but that's the long and short of it. "When can we start?"

"Let's go for a walk," he suggests. Carlo and I stroll past rows of stationary cyclists racing toward the finish line in their heads. Past guys heaving medicine balls back and forth. Past the clinks and grunts of the weight area. "I've been doing this for a long time. I've seen every kind of person walk through these doors. Some people come in here and they succeed and I mean *really* succeed but I've seen more fail, and usually due to unrealistic expectations."

"Like mounting a professional comeback?" I suggest. Carlo shrugs. "Becoming an elite class of athlete is no small feat. It takes determination and mental strength. Commitment. Confidence. Even then, you need the right genetics…"

"What are you saying?" I ask. Carlo stops in the spacious lobby, palms upward.

"I can't guarantee you anything. This is more about what you bring to the table than what I do." I look back at Carlo, think about my efforts and failings, from Pee Wee to Bantam to Junior hockey. I think about Dad too. Taking a deep breath, I reply.

"I'm not afraid to take a gamble. I'm not afraid to have a *craic*. I'm not afraid, full stop."

"What's your name again?" asks Carlo, a curious expression on his face.

"I'm Danny Boy Doyle," I reply. "And I'm the real McCoy."

EIGHT MONTHS LATER, THE ATMOSPHERE'S a little different at Slapshot.

"What's this?" asks Mario as I slide a piece of paper across his cluttered little desk in his cluttered little back room.

"My resignation," I reply.

"You got another job?" he asks.

"You could say that," I nod. "Meet the latest Vancouver Voodoo defenceman." I watch with satisfaction as Mario's moustache drops. His pride and joy Anton got cut this year and while I do feel sorry for the kid, it serves his loudmouth dad right. In a way, I wish I wasn't leaving Slapshot, if only to see what a season of Mario shutting the hell up looks like, but the look on his face in this pristine little moment will have to do. "Oh, mind if I sharpen my skates on the way out?" I ask. Because given the circumstances, that's so much better than saying *fuck you*.

Danny 3, Fat Danny 0.

"You did it."

"I did it. Worked like a maniac and lost 50lbs in 32 weeks. I must have put a few thousand miles on the stationary bike, hit the weights like a beast and dieted like Suzanne Somers."

"No girls?"

"None."

"The Voodoo represented your comeback?"

"More the beginning of my comeback. But all credit goes to Carlo Sferra. Everything that came after, none of it would have happened without him. He was the missing puzzle piece."

ROLLER HOCKEY IS THE DE facto bridge between the end of real hockey and the beginning of real hockey so sadly I only have the chance to play half a dozen games before I'm released, long enough for the scouts to come sniffing again and this time, no one's shaking their heads and flipping their notepads closed. One from back east catches my ear the minute he catches me by the elbow in the tunnel.

"Ever thought about a professional ice hockey career in Europe?" he asks.

"Keep talking," I say coolly, listening to his spiel as I roll toward the locker room: Net money. No tax. Fully furnished apartment. Two paid trips back home every year.

"Where?" I ask.

"There's a team in Rungsted, Denmark with a defensive hole on their back end…" I'm grinning the rest of the way to the locker room. *Goodbye student loans. Hello Danish girls!*

"This was your first time abroad?"

"This was my first time anywhere outside of Western Canada."

"And what an eye-opener it must have been."

"I mean, sure. I guess. I was just happy to be playing hockey again."

"Tell me about Rungsted."

"Rungsted is in southern Denmark about an hour and a quarter south of the airport in Bilund if you take the E45 and Bøgvadvej. It's not much bigger than Prince Peaks really but it couldn't be more different with its quaint diorama of red brick two story buildings and Playmobil trees."

"Hockey's big there?"

"Not as big as motorcycle racing. They'd hosted the World Final just a few years prior and were the yearly venue for the Speedway Grand Prix of Denmark. But hockey was big enough and no players bigger

than the five imports they'd signed to bolster their Superisligaen
campaign: Sven from Sweden, a Czech named Libor, and Italian kid
named Gio, our player-coach Richard Head... and of course me."

THE PLAYER-COACH CONCEPT IS A big deal in Scandinavia mostly
because it's one less salary to pay; but fiscal smarts aside, Richard
Head (let's call him Dick) is more trouble than he's worth. He's only
been out here for five days but swaggers about like he's been here
for five generations.

"Welcome to the Rungsted Tigers," he says with a grand sweep
of his arm as I descend the airstairs and arrive on the runway tarmac
with the Swede, the Czech and the Italian right behind me. Half of
Rungsted and most of the team have come up to Bilund to welcome
us apparently, which would have been a nice touch if any of them
had the foresight to bring some food because that's all I can think
about at the moment. Screw the fanfare. Say it with a sandwich.

Thankfully, they whisk us away like diplomats more or less immediately and ninety minutes later, Gio and I are standing in our new
home—a pretty nice little furnished two-bedroom apartment, albeit
with a communal shower down the hall—in a pretty nice part of
town. I'm feeling good about the whole situation and that's pretty
much all I remember because jet lag's setting in like a bad hangover.
As soon as my head hits the starchy pillowcase, I'm in the blank,
black abyss of a dreamless sleep.

One of the downsides to passing out versus falling asleep is the
lack of any tangible passage of time, even on a subconscious level.
Sometimes it feels like you've just closed your eyes and opened them
again and since your body's failed to cross-reference the situation
with your mind, you may as well be just as tired as you were when
the lights went out because you sure as hell feel that way. That's how
I feel the next morning, waking up with a crick in my neck and a
parchment dry mouth, in a room that looks like a large, beige box.
I'm unimpressed enough that it's the phone not the alarm clock
that jolts me out of my coma but even more unimpressed when I
answer it.

"We're picking you guys up in ten minutes," crackles player-coach

Dick Head through the receiver. *It's Thursday and first practice isn't until the following Monday.*

"Why?" I ask, puzzled.

"Last ten Tigers are arriving in Bilund today. We're rolling out the welcome wagon like we did for you yesterday."

"No thanks," I reply, placing the receiver back on the cradle. I haven't taken two steps before the phone starts ringing again but this time more angrily.

"What?"

"Doyle, you damn well be outside in ten minutes! This is how things are done in Denmark. Got it?"

Screw you, Dick, I think. *Who do you think you are, Hamlet? You're from Ontario. And you're only two years older than me.*

"Is it in my contract?" I ask. *Hesitation on the other end. Ha!*

"No, but…"

"Have a nice drive, Dick. And bring those poor buggers some sandwiches for Chrissakes." This time the phone doesn't argue when I hang up.

"Who that was?" calls Gio from his bed.

"No one, I reply," slamming my bedroom door closed.

The next day is the team parade and that's a different story because find me a guy who doesn't want to ride a float through a small European town while its citizens cheer from their shop fronts, lining the streets and welcoming their new Tigers like we just liberated them from the Germans. Slowly we roll down Margrethegev, around the roundabout and past the *Q8* service station, then right on Vestergade past the shops: *Boger Papir, Brille Centret, Sun You* (must be a tanning salon), *Sydbank, Rungsted Radio,* and that's when I see her. Hair doesn't get blonder than that. Eyes don't get bluer and that body: that ridiculously lithe little frame in those tight jeans and obscenely tall leather boots… *Look at me, look at me, look at me,* I'm willing her in my head like a mantra and I'll be damned, she turns! Don't let anyone ever tell you that electricity between two people is figurative because I can *actually* feel it in my gut when those azure eyes drill into mine and something courses through me like a hot current and I swear sparks are going to fly out my dick in a second.

You know that girl from ABBA? The hot one? She's like that. Wrong country I know, but you know the look.

"WHAT YOU ARE LOOKING FOR?" asks Gio, as I stand on my toes and crane my neck over the beer garden crowd, combing the milling masses of hockey-mad locals who are happily mingling with their hometown heroes under the soft glow of countless patio lanterns.

"Who," I correct him.

"What you are looking who?" he replies. Gio's English is a bit suspect at the best of times but after a few icy glasses of heady, hoppy beer, it has the tendency of going into the occasional, unexpected tailspin.

She has to be here, I think. *Somewhere. I mean, it just stands to reason. This is a Prince Peaks sized town that more or less turned itself inside out at the parade earlier and she was at that and there wasn't even beer on offer. She must be here.* Suddenly, I spot a head in the crowd: a white-blonde head and my heart's in my throat and I'm leaving Gio with his beer and bastardized English and plowing through the sea of fans like King Canute crossing the North Sea. *Must be her.* But she's walking away and I don't even know how to say, 'Wait!' in Danish so grabbing her shoulder is about the best I can do and I can barely do that in this maddening crowd.

That shoulder doesn't feel right. The young man turns around, tucking his long, blond Bjorn Borg-like hair behind his ear, smiling amiably. The only thing that trumps my embarrassment is my disappointment.

"Sorry, man," I mutter, quickly turning away and that's when I run into her. Literally. I'm toe-to-toe with the gorgeous creature, our faces just inches apart. Same boots, same jeans and even more breathtakingly beautiful this close, if that's even possible. I'm tongue-tied, lost, free-falling through those sky-blue eyes when someone jostles past, knocking her forward. For a moment her hand's on my chest and her body's crushed against mine and all I can smell is hops and vanilla.

"Sorry," I say again but this time I couldn't mean it less. She looks up at me and those full pink lips move and as far as I'm concerned, it's game over.

"I'm Astrid," she says, offering me the prettiest little hand I've ever seen.

"I'm Danny," I reply, with absolutely no clue what to say next.

"I know," she replies, and with a look that means one thing and one thing alone, she turns and disappears through the crowd like a soft, golden vision.

"No, Danny! This is what they say to me and I know it is true words. She is the bad choice!" Gio's well and truly drunk by now. He's been hanging out with a group of Danish teammates for the better part of the evening while I've been busy gazing across the crowd exchanging loaded looks and wordless promises with Astrid. And every time, sparks: hard, fast, skate sharpener sparks and I haven't even noticed the glowering or the glaring and if I had, I wouldn't have cared because the way this girl has got me going is verging on obscene.

Gio's intel is hard to decipher but I eventually get the picture. Apparently, Astrid broke up with her long-time boyfriend earlier that day (timing's everything) but there's a catch. The ex is friends with most of the guys on my team (hence the collective shitty attitude). Also, he's allegedly seven feet tall and built like a Lego brick shithouse. And purportedly psychotic. *The Great Dane* is a doorman at a club in Haslo (a nearby town) and the whole situation makes personal safety as much an issue as political correctness as far as my designs on Astrid go and Gio's imploring Ligurian eyes are only lending another level of gravitas to the whole situation. Laboriously, I pull my common sense from my pants and put it back in my head. If I screw Astrid, I run the risk of falling out of grace with my new teammates and incur the wrath of a giant, unstable Viking. On the other hand, if I don't screw Astrid, I don't screw Astrid. Taking a deep breath, I carefully remove my common sense from between my ears and tuck it safely below my belt.

"Fuck it," I reply. "I'm going in." I can feel the eyes of my teammates follow me as I bee-line toward the blond goddess: the gorgeous forbidden fruit with her leather boots and her tight jeans and her absolutely irresistible everything.

"Number 3, 9442 Fuglesoveg. Meet me there in one hour. Now look disappointed," I say quietly, hoping her English is as good as I think it is as I turn on my heels and stride away. Passing my skeptical fellow Tigers, I give them a friendly grin and a shrug that they can translate however they like. Suckers.

"I'm going home. Totally exhausted," I inform Gio, giving him a clap on the back that sends him teetering back towards the bar, clearly the last place he needs to be heading at this point in his evening but exactly where I need him to be.

My porch light's burnt out but I can see Astrid's silhouette waiting for me outside my apartment door.

"Hi," I say.

"Hi," she whispers back. English and Danish are both abandoned as I push her against the wall, burying my face in that vanilla neck, feeling the heat radiate from that tight little body as she gasps and arches and moans into me. Fumbling behind her like I'm looking for a bra strap, I find the lock, slide the key in and turn, sending us staggering into the living room like a drunk horse.

"I'm not going to sleep with you," she informs me.

"I know," I reply because what else am I going to say? *Really? That sucks. I was really hoping we could knock boots. Can I make you a grilled cheese?*

Male persistence isn't a character trait. It's a malfunction: the brain neglecting to send a memo to the midsection. It's the little soldier jumping over the trench all by himself and charging across no man's land towards the enemy lines, completely oblivious to the ceasefire. Male persistence isn't admirable. It's stupid. But sometimes stupid wins wars.

"What are you doing?" she asks as I strip down to my Tommy Hilfiger boxers, grabbing the TV remote and casually flopping down onto the couch.

"Getting comfortable. You know," I reply, looking at her like her question was the strange thing, not my behaviour.

"This is what you do in Canada?" she asks skeptically.

"Of course," I reply. Satisfied, she sits down on the futon beside me, but not before a surreptitious look at my barely clad body. *The con is on...*

"That feels nice," she breathes as I begin squeezing her neck and shoulders, casually pumping the brakes on my advances by asking her to translate the Danish infomercial on the TV. The product's called SuperRag (which oddly translates directly from English to Danish) but beyond that, I'm lost.

"It's a wiping cloth. For the kitchen," she explains. "He's saying it picks up twenty percent more liquid than a normal towel..."

"If you take your shirt off, I can massage you better..." I suggest. *Thank-you*, I mouth skyward as Astrid shrugs out of her top without turning around. Half an hour later, no one's talking about infomercials anymore.

"Do you have a condom?" she whispers, as I kiss the nape of her neck, coaxing the soft blond angel hairs to stand up as the goose bumps spread across her back and down her arms, the internationally recognized reaction to a change of heart.

"I didn't come prepared. I didn't want to treat you like that," I reply. *God, I'm good...*

"I'm on birth control," she assures me, standing up and wiggling out of her jeans and suddenly I'm the one who's overdressed. Speechless, I lean back and soak in the vision. She's beautiful. Perfect, honey skin glowing against the white lace of her tiny bra and panties (must tan at *Sun You*). She has the body of an off-season Olympian: soft but firm. Taut, with small, brown-sugar nipples and tiny dimples just above a tiny, small-hipped, perfect ass; a Nordic sculpture that would have given Hans Christian Andersen a woody.

"God, you are smoking!" I manage to utter and it's the most honest thing out of my mouth all evening. A shadow crosses Astrid's face and her brow furrows in puzzlement.

"No, Danny. I do not smoke." *God, she's adorable too.* I pull her forward.

"What do you do for work, anyway?" I ask, kicking my underwear past my ankles.

"I'm a lingerie model," she replies, straddling my lap and slowly lowering herself, gasping as the couch begins to move with deep, rhythmic creaks. *God, I love Denmark. Where's a SuperRag when you need one?*

"Pax huic dómui et ómnibus habitántibus in ea. Asspérges me, Dómine, hyssópo, et mundábor; lavábis me, et super nivem dealbábor, Miserére mei, Deus: secúndum..."

"What in the hell are you doing?" I ask groggily, opening my eyes to find a very drunk Gio looming over the couch. The poor Italian sways unsteadily, grief written all over his face.

"The Last Rites," he intones sadly, pointing at the sleeping Astrid, whose gorgeous golden head lies in the crook of my shoulder. "You are going to death, Danny. I will miss you."

"No one's going to die," I assure him as I sit up.

"What time is it?" asks Astrid, waking with a yawn. The alcohol and testosterone have receded, leaving me with an uncomfortably large amount of space for stark reality. *Oh man, I'm going to have to do some damage control on this one if I want to keep it up.*

"Time for me to give you a ride home," I reply gently, standing up. That's when I notice the leggy brunette in the armchair.

"Who's she? Isn't your wife visiting next week?" I ask.

Gio shrugs. "I will say some Ave Marias tomorrow."

If I was driving a regular car through Rungsted in the wee hours of the morning, it wouldn't have been such a big deal. But I wasn't. Like Gio and Dick Head, my contract included a vehicle. It was a flashy, new Alfa Romeo, which would have attracted enough attention on its own even without the huge sponsorship decals, the largest being a massive *Rungsted Tigers* logo splashed right across the hood. Heading down Norregade, I feel like it might as well say, *Just Banged the Great Dane's Ex-Girlfriend.*

After Astrid thanks me for the ride, I zip up my fly and begin the quiet drive home. There's no way I'm going to stop seeing this girl. No way in hell. Sooner or later, I'm going to have to face the music. I just hope the Great Dane doesn't want to dance.

I'M GETTING SOME SERIOUS COLD shoulder from the Danish boys Monday morning in the locker room and by the time we're on the ice, six of them have button-holed me for a solemn conversation on the blue line. Astrid's off-limits, they've collectively decided, because the Great Dane's their friend and the relationship might be dead in the water but the body's still warm and me swooping in like this is so many kinds of offside. *I wonder how you say, 'Fuck off and mind your own business' in Danish...*

These guys, they're thrilled I've given them reason to hate me. Resentment's never far below the surface with the domestic players. Only us imports have the luxury of calling hockey a full-time job whereas the rest of these pork-lovers are getting a pittance for their on-ice efforts and have to subsidize with thankless day jobs like bricklayer and baker and video store clerk. Of course, the flip side of this is that we (the imports) get stuck with the responsibility and expectation and that's as thankless a role as slathering mortar on clay, I'm soon to find out. When you're winning, the papers curtly acknowledge that you're doing your job and when you're losing, they absolutely crucify you.

But that's the least of my worries at the moment. I've got a psychotic giant one town over who is probably leafing through an enormous recipe book looking for tasty ways to prepare Canadian ass-meat after kicking it. There's no way I'm giving up Astrid though, so I've got to get proactive about this: send the message that I don't tolerate getting pushed around and if that means taking what's coming to me then so be it because I'll do what I want but I won't go skulking about doing it. I'm still Danny Boy Doyle. Still not afraid to take a gamble. Still not afraid to have a *craic*. Still not afraid, full stop. But I do have a peculiar knot in my gut as I step off the little commuter bus and look up at the town sign: Welcome to Haslo.

"But no hard feelings..." I gulp, staring across the café table, waiting for a response. Silently, I shift my weight to the leg tucked under my chair in case I need to execute a hasty exit. Worse case scenario: I can spring up, flip the table in his face and have a clear run at the door. At that point it would come down to a foot race but I fancy my chances.

He's not seven feet tall. Closer to six and a half but that's of little comfort. His forehead is as broad as a windshield, his jaw the size of a fender, his shoulders almost as wide as my Alpha Romeo itself. BANG! I flinch as two huge fists slam down onto the table, creating tempests in each of our untouched teacups. His arms resemble young samplings. Paint them black and they'd look like medieval maces (and probably capable of inflicting as much damage).

"You come here," he says in a quiet, grave-deep voice. "You come here and you tell me you're with Astrid now..."

"Yes," I nod, wishing I can remember Gio's panicked Latin send-off from a few nights prior. *Pax hoot domino omnibus something...* "Because it's the respectful thing to do."

"Is she happy?" asks the Great Dane.

"Huh?"

"Is she happy?" he thunders. I think back to the couch: Astrid moaning and bucking and bouncing on my lap like it's her last night on earth.

"She appears to be," I reply. And suddenly that huge, meaty head drops and those Alpha Romeo shoulders sag and when he looks back up, his eyes are shining. *Oh my God, he's crying!*

"You treat her well," he says huskily. "And you don't hurt her because if you do, I will take your face off of your head and feed it to your mouth." Some things get lost in translation, but I get the gist of what he's trying to say and when we shake hands at the bus stop, his envelops mine up to the wrist like when Dad use to hold my hand as a kid.

"Look after her. And good luck," he says.

On the bus on the way back to Rungsted, I'm not feeling as smug as I should be. No one likes to see a big man broken, but more than that, there's something about the way he said goodbye. 'Look after her. And good luck...'

chapter 7

"*How's the treatment going?*"

"*Maintenance Therapy.*"

"*I'm sorry, Maintenance Therapy. Well?*"

"*Can we not talk about it today?*"

"*Of course. I trust everything's okay?*"

"*It's fine. Well, not fine. Same shit, but less of it. Down to four: Vincristine, Dexamethasone, Methotrexate and Mercaptopurine. And apart from the Mercaptopurine, everything else is once a week or less. It's just nice to have days… whole days…*"

"*Where you don't have to think about it at all?*"

"*Thanks for understanding. It's just… I'm tired.*"

"*You're human. Let's get back to Astrid. Were your teammates accepting of your relationship with her?*"

"*No. But like I said, there was a collective chip on the Danish players' shoulders with us imports so if it wasn't that it would have been something else. My rocky start with Player-Coach Dick Head didn't help the situation either. Pretty sure the guy was fanning the flames just out of spite.*"

"*But it was worth it?*"

"*Every minute. Astrid was amazing. She spoke five languages and was dynamite in the sack.*"

"*What about the Great Dane's strange goodbye. Look after her and good luck…*"

"*Well as it turns out, nobody's perfect…*"

Matt McCoy

"YOU'RE WHAT?" I REPLY, TYING a knot in the rubber and three-pointing it across the room into the trashcan. *Nothing but net.*

"Severely diabetic," replies Astrid casually, like she'd said, 'Gemini with Scorpio rising.'

"You're not dying are you?" I ask.

"No!" she laughs, aiming her shapely golden legs skyward as she squirms into tight denim. "Not as long as I'm eating."

"How often?" I inquire.

"All the time," she replies.

"You must be constantly cooking."

"Oh, I don't cook, she replies nonchalantly. *Look after her. And good luck. Oh boy…*

I'm not much into cooking for myself let alone for anyone else but I'd rather be feeding a lingerie model than burying one so dutifully my take-out orders double in size while my expendable income halves. But hey—lingerie model. Between the screwing and the eating it's a pretty two-dimensional relationship but I love doing both and she loves doing one and has no choice with the other so it's actually a pretty good fit. Besides, the sex makes up for the lack of insulin.

One afternoon, we're marathoning away in the bedroom, her with palms flat against the wall and me behind, holding on to her hips when suddenly, there's an almighty SNAP! Furnished places can sometimes come with a few cut corners and the bed I've been allocated is an old futon (first generation by the look of it) with straps across the frame holding the mattress up. Theoretically, anyway. The short abrupt twelve-inch plummet surprises both of us so much we freeze, like a bizarre diagram from a Scandinavian edition of the Kama Sutra.

"You okay?" she asks with a breathless laugh.

"I think so," I reply, gingerly making sure I haven't snapped off inside her. Satisfied I'm still attached to the rest of me, we get back to business at a slightly lower altitude. "I thought you guys had good strong Ikea shit," I grunt, mid-thrust.

"That's Sweden, stupid," she half moans.

It's not the last time we break this particular piece of substandard

Danish engineering. After the third episode, the usually good-natured maintenance guy closes his toolbox, looks at me in desperation and pulls out the little English he knows for one pleading request:

"Danny, stop fucking! Please!" Naturally, I can't oblige him, but after he leaves, I lug the futon frame outside and heave it into the rubbish tip behind the building, resigning myself to a mattress on the floor.

LONG STORY SHORT, DENMARK'S WORKING out. The Tigers are pulling their socks up, making a good run at the league and the storm of controversy around Astrid and I seems to have blown over. But Denmark's not working out for everyone. Sven the Swede never makes it past the training camp in Prague and the hole he leaves in our otherwise impressive depth chart gets me thinking.

"Oh yeah sure, Doyle," responds Dick Head when I tell him about my brother. "We'll call him up right now and fly him out tomorrow. Because the one thing this team needs is two of you." Undaunted, I take it up with the Board because going over heads is how I get things done and going over this Head is particularly satisfying. The Board's collective English is better than my Danish but regardless, I come to the meeting armed with a pocket-sized copy of *Conversational Danish*, thumping it for emphasis like a travelling preacher. Apparently, I make my case because the next day they call Henry's agent and the next week they fly him out. *Ya like fruit, Dick? How ya like them apples?*

When Henry arrives, it's one trip to the Bilund airport that I'm happy to make.

"This is actually our car?" asks my little brother for the tenth time as we drive south toward Rungsted.

"My car, but you can use it," I reply, modifying his contract on the fly because that's a big brother's prerogative. Apartment-wise, Gio's out and Henry's in but the Italian's fine with that. He still stares at Astrid like she's an evil omen and he's clearly not convinced that the Great Dane won't have a change of heart and come murder us both in our sleep one night. As far as he's concerned, the change in living arrangements is likely his lifesaver.

Henry unfolds from the Alpha Romeo, stretching and yawning as he looks up at the apartment.

"Not bad," he nods with approval.

"Yeah man," I agree. "Good place, solid team and the people are actually pretty nice…" SLAP!

"Asshole!" screams the tiny Danish woman. Henry reels back, eyes saucering in surprise as she comes at him, all openhanded anger, whacking him repeatedly around the head. The tirade of Danish that follows is peppered with dashes of recognizable English words like *wife*, *Italian*, and *cheating bastard* and although poor Henry hasn't got a clue what's happening, I'm connecting the dots pretty fast.

"What the hell, man?" he asks desperately, backing up, his hands raised in front of his face. By now, I'm weeping with laughter.

"She thinks you're Gio!" I gasp, wiping the tears from my eyes and making zero effort to intervene.

"Well, tell her I'm not!" sputters my brother. Shrugging, I grab his bag from the trunk and walk toward the apartment as the little Danish woman continues to slap him around.

"Sorry," I call over my shoulder. "I don't speak Danish."

Turns out that the furious little lady is the aunt of the leggy brunette Gio had over the first night I brought Astrid home. The leggy brunette who didn't know he was married. The leggy brunette who he snubbed the minute his wife came to town for a visit. The girl had purportedly been a heartbroken mess and Aunt Frida wasn't having it and all the Ave Marias in the world weren't going to save Gio from her wrath; or as it turns out, Henry, whose Hail Marys wouldn't have made a stitch of difference either.

APART FROM THE ISOLATED INCIDENT of mistaken identity, Henry's received with welcome arms by the team and the town (with the exception of Dick Head, who's by now learned to loathe anything with Doyle for a last name). Henry's more diplomatic than I am, though. Half as much a handful and (let's face it) twice the hockey player, so you can imagine that he's a bit miffed to be running public relations on my amorous impulses and heavy-handed honesty. But we're finally playing for the same team and we're finally rooming together and we're winning more than we're losing. Denmark's working out.

Henry and Astrid get along like siblings too, which is convenient since she's over more nights than not. We'd tried doing it a couple of times at her parents' place (she still lives at home) but that was just weird. Danish parents have a slightly different attitude toward sex than their Canadian counterparts. When kids back home start screwing, parents don't want to know about it or talk about it and that's why there are condom wrappers under high school bleachers and cars parked in far corners of dark parking lots and two pairs of shoes under washroom stalls. Not in Denmark. Astrid's parents (like all Danish parents) are ballsy and pragmatic and want that sort of thing happening under their roof because no one wants their little girl taking it over a park bench or on the seat of an Alpha Romeo. That's just slutty. You want to have sex? You do it in your bedroom like a civilized human being and your boyfriend stays the night and he eats his waffles in the morning at the table like a respectable, horny young man. *No thanks.* I've spent too long fornicating in a suppressed, puritanical, shame-based society. That's my comfort zone. Besides, Astrid's as vocal as an opera diva in the sack. Daddy down the hall watching TV, completely within earshot just isn't how I spell sexy.

Even without the weird openness I'd still opt for my apartment over her house because just getting in the door is more trouble than it's worth. Two rings for Astrid or her sister and one ring for the folks. That's the deal with the doorbell but no one informed me and it's not like there's a little plaque on the mailbox explaining the rules so the first time I visit, I'm ringing away and I can see her Dad through the cut glass window completely ignoring me because that's how it works. Two rings for the girls and one ring for the folks. Ridiculous.

Henry's a good roommate. Astrid and I can bugger off to the bedroom or the shower whenever the mood hits day or night and all he does is look up from the TV with a mouthful of chips and says *hey*. No stupid comments, no shit-eating grins, no nothing. Just *hey*. Even on the afternoon I come barreling out of the bedroom white as a sheet, buck naked except for my socks.

"Hey," says Henry, stuffing another handful of chips into his mouth.

"Holy shit man, I think I killed her!" I croak. You've never seen someone drop a bag of Crispos faster.

Henry and I stand over the still, waxy form of Astrid.

"Don't look at her tits," I tell him.

"I'm not," he replies, pressing her throat for a pulse. "She's not dead, but I think she's having one of those diabetic things."

"What do we do?" I ask.

"I dunno," replies Henry. "Feed her I guess?"

Racing to the kitchen I skid across the linoleum, crashing into the fridge and hauling it open. Nothing but a half loaf of bread and some apple juice. It'll have to do. Cradling her head, I trickle the juice past her lips. It takes a few moments but as soon as she's sputtering and coughing and her eyelids are fluttering open, I'm stuffing bread in her mouth like she's in an eating contest. From that day onwards, I spend as much time feeding Astrid as I do screwing her.

"What about hockey?"

"What about it?"

"It seems like you've told me an awful lot about everything else since you got to Denmark. What about the hockey?"

"Do I really have to spell it out? I'd been out of the game for four years, made the mother of all comebacks and got snapped up by a professional European team as one of their top imports. I'd arrived, hockey-wise. That's all there was to it."

"Okay, okay. So hockey still mattered the most?"

"Of course."

"*Agurk?*" ASKS HENRY.

"No idiot, that's *cucumber*," I correct. My brother and I stare blankly at each other while the butcher waits patiently, albeit a bit bemusedly. Turning to the large mustachioed man, I make another attempt at making myself understood.

"Chiiiiii-cken," I repeat, slowing the word down to a crawl like my pace is magically going to make the word recognizable to the Danish speaker.

"Chiiiiii-cken," echoes Henry, enunciating loudly like the butcher's lack of English has left him hard of hearing. Still, the large man remains clueless, turning his mitt-sized hands ceiling-ward with a benevolent, apologetic smile.

"Try this," suggests Henry, tucking his hands into his armpits, thrusting his neck forward and wagging his elbows furiously as he stomps in a small circle.

"Unbelievable," I mutter, following my brother in his small, ridiculous orbit. Feeding Astrid is a full-time endeavour and worth the investment but ordering in every night has stopped being financially feasible. That's how we find ourselves playing charades in front of the meat counter.

"*Kyllinger*," says the middle-aged woman behind us, a look of pity on her face as Henry and I begin the third lap of our chicken dance.

"Aaah," says the butcher, but I swear there's a twinkle in his eye when he passes the paper-wrapped poultry over the counter. *I wonder what the Danish term is for cheeky bastard...*

My brother and I are doing a bang-on impersonation of Angus Young and Bryan Johnson while Astrid hangs over the back of the couch, watching from the living room and laughing uproariously and I'm pretty sure any good time a Danish guy could show her would look a little less awesome than this. Henry and I have two great loves: playing hockey and eating, and nothing gets us more ramped up for both than good, loud music and nothing sounds better loud than AC/DC. *No wonder the downstairs neighbours hate us.* Henry pulls the now golden bird from the oven.

"Fuckin' kyllinger!" he announces grandly.

"Smells amazing," calls Astrid.

"Don't die on me, woman! It'll be ready in ten," I call back, causing Henry to almost choke on the piece of carrot he's just swiped from the chopping board. Astrid's a great girl, even if keeping her above ground takes a little more effort than the average girl. High-maintenance just doesn't seem like such a pain in the ass when they can't help it. And there's something gratifying about being indispensable.

I'm feeling pretty indispensable on the ice too, and the local boys are finally getting it through their blond heads that I'm with Astrid now. I'm not saying they like it necessarily (there's this funny territorial thing with guys, wherever in the world you are) but the success of my suicide mission to Haslo seems to have sent some kind of message. I'm not sure if it's that they respect me for doing the right thing or that they're just impressed that I didn't come back in a casket but either way, I'm with Astrid now.

"Brownies?" offers Michael, a die-hard Rungsted Tigers fan who hasn't missed a game since he was out of diapers. He's about our age and looks like a hockey player (mullet and all) despite the fact that he can't even skate. At this point on this particular evening, he's having a helluva time walking, as well. Michael and his girlfriend (fans that they are) have invited the whole team over for dinner. The Carlsberg and Tuborg seem limitless and the spread's amazing, tables bending with mountains of mouth-watering food: meat balls, roast pork with crackling, poached cod in mustard sauce, smoked salmon, pickled herring in sweet pepper vinegar on rye bread topped with fresh onion rings and curried salad and hard boiled eggs and sliced tomatoes... a Viking feast if I ever saw one. By the time they pull out dessert, I'm stuffed to the gills with zero room for negotiation.

There's another entire table laden with cakes and tarts and strudel-ish looking things and I'm not sure why Michael's taken it upon himself to do the rounds with the brownie plate but nonetheless, I decline. No love lost, though. My sweet tooth is all but nonexistent and given the choice between cheesecake and chicken wings I'll almost always go for the latter. Henry on the other hand? It's a miracle the kid hasn't got a mouthful of cavities. Happily, he helps himself to one of Michael's brownies.

"It's one of my girlfriend's specialties," says our host with a wink. Henry shoots me a withering look.

"Probably sweetened with apple juice," he laments. Despite the fantastic feast she's produced, Michael's girlfriend is a vegan; a lifestyle choice she enthusiastically shares with anyone who's willing to listen (and a conversation that's undoubtedly annoying in any language). Regardless, Henry takes a bite. "Hmm," he nods approvingly. "Not bad, actually…"

"WHAT THE HELL, MAN!" I exclaim, skating up to my brother. We're away at our regional rivals' and this warm-up skate's an uphill battle for Henry for some reason.

He was strangely quiet on the pain-in-the-ass road trip that morning (a bus ride, a ferry ride to another island in the Danish archipelago then another bus ride) and now he was seriously falling apart, skating like it was his first time, clutching the boards and scissoring his feet beneath him like a three-year-old. "I told you to go easy last night!" I hiss. Henry's on pain meds for a niggling shoulder injury and really, he should know better than hitting the beer like that, free or not. But this? The guy's acting completely pissed and I'm sure he wasn't like this last night. "Hey, I'm serious, man! What's the matter with you?" I snap.

"I saw Bob Marley last night, Danny," responds a pale-faced Henry, a strange, distant look on his face.

"You heard him alright," I reply, "and you sang along to *Buffalo Soldier* and you sounded like complete shit."

"No, man. I saw him," he replies with quiet sincerity. "He was there. He was singing with me." Visor-to-visor, I stare into Henry's eyes. The whites are a soft pink and that's what I can see of them because his eyelids hang heavily like melting candle wax. *Oh no, the brownies…*

"Those weren't vegan brownies!" I whisper urgently. If Henry was pale before, he's even more pale now and as Dick Head approaches, my brother's complexion more or less matches the ice. Usually I glean a small amount of glee from Henry's misfortunes (schadenfreude is big brother's prerogative) but this one's no laughing matter. Every game, the Danish Hockey Federation's regulating body makes one player from each team piss in a bottle and if they find dope in the lemonade it means one thing and one thing only: Termination. Immediate, unforgiving, irreversible. Usually, it's us import players they liked to pick on because let's face it, why would they want to shame one of their own? For an average Joe like a plumber or a shopkeeper this would be a laughable hiccup and a day's work missed but for a guy like Henry, a professional hockey player, this is potentially career ending shit.

"Follow my lead," I mouth, as Dick Head skates over.

"Jesus and Mary!" he growls at my brother. "What is the matter with you?"

"It's his shoulder, coach," I offer unconvincingly. "The thing's really giving him some trouble. I don't think he should play today."

I might hate Dick Head like a saint hates a sinner, but I'll give him this: Nothing gets by him. Nothing. The asshole's eyes narrow.

"Michael's hash brownies?" he asks quietly. Henry blinks at him in dismay.

"I didn't know!"

"Of course you didn't. Even you're not *that* stupid." He glowers, grabbing Henry's elbow and pulling him to the bench. "Doyle's out!" he barks, loud enough for everyone to hear. "Shoulder's fucked." I might hate Dick Head, but he doesn't throw his own guys under the bus. Not when it would make him look bad, anyway. It's an anxious three periods for little brother, but when the final horn sounds, it's our stocky Danish winger who gets the post-game plastic cup instead of a urinal. Not the stoned Canadian kid. *He was a Buffalo soldier, dreadlock Rasta, fighting on arrival, fighting for survival...*

"Did you and Henry ever play on the same team again?"

"Unfortunately, no. Just the one season. That backstabbing asshole Dick Head made it his duty to convince the board not to renew our contracts for the next season even though we took the Tigers to the playoffs for the first time in their history and finished the season third out of nine teams."

"That hardly sounds fair..."

"Well, life's not fair, is it. Dick Head got canned the next year anyway. He'd brought his girlfriend with him from Ontario and the two of them were responsible for something like fifteen percent of the gross annual liquor sales at the local Kvickly convenience store. When the

Tigers finished a lackluster fifth place that season, the Board sent him packing back to Canada with nothing but his memories and a blistering schnapps hangover."

"Where did you and Henry end up?"

"England, eventually. Two different teams, though. But that's jumping ahead."

"It sounds like you and your brother are very close."

"We are."

ASTRID'S PRETTY UPSET WHEN SHE drops us off at the airport but she's just had a sandwich so at least I know it's only her heart that's in danger of breaking today. I'm trying my hardest to feel sad too, but I think I've already put most of Denmark in my *Danish box* and the lid's all but closed by the time we're staring down Gate 410. No doubt I'll miss her but realistically, this relationship has run its course and ended on as good a note as could be so I'd rather leave it like that. Compartmentalization doesn't mean you can't put a bow on the box if you want to.

"Come visit me," I suggest as the beautiful blonde sniffs, furiously wiping away her tears with the back of her hand. Henry shoots me a withering look. He's been ringside in my life long enough to know how often I've used that phrase. *Well fuck, what am I supposed to say? She's crying…*

At least she's had something to eat.

"So you went back to Prince Peaks?"

"Not right away. We found a bit of home in England."

IT'S 1969 IN BELFAST. THERE'S a play opening at the Lyric tonight, and Lily and Nolan are going with his brother Dominic and Dom's wife Annie. Dom and Annie have a son called Brennan, with hair as red as a freshly smacked bum. He's barely two, but all piss and vinegar already.

"Comes by it honestly," says Annie, glancing sidelong at her husband. Lily likes Annie and her conspiratorial winks and the way she makes being married to a Doyle brother feel like an exclusive club for tolerant women.

Brennan is off with Mrs. Finney, the landlady at the Moyola Arms where the two couples drink more nights than not. She's got seven grown-up ones of her own and loves to mind the feisty little fella, crushing him against her ample bosom while she chain smokes Pall Malls and sings song after song.

"It's good for the little 'uns," she says. "Like porridge for their wee souls."

No lover of the stage, Nolan would almost rather spend the evening crushed up against Mrs. Finney himself if it meant avoiding the play. When the curtains finally fall, Nolan is in such a hurry to leave he accidentally incites a standing ovation that to his dismay, takes the better part of ten minutes to escape.

"There must be a more effective ways to trim a theatre's electric bill without subjecting honest people to that rubbish," he declares, as they exit not a minute too soon. Lily thinks the play's reverse lighting scheme was quite clever but not being one to rock the boat, ignores her husband's grand indictment, instead suggesting that they walk back to the Moyola since it's dry out and not too chilly. It's barely gone ten. They'll have time for a quick pint with Mrs. Finney; and Brennan will be fast asleep by now. No point disturbing him until they have to.

The wives chat easily en route while the brothers smoke, a habit that for Dom is entirely dependent on his proximity to Nolan.

"The tie that binds," he quips. "I'd have no need for you if I quit the fags altogether." Nolan smiles, but secretly wonders if his brother is right.

Little Brennan is finally tired, having run himself into the ground chasing the good-nature out of the pub's dog and entertaining punters with his ruddy-cheeked curiosity. Eventually, he climbs into Mrs. Finney's lap on his own accord and as the embers in the fireplace crackle and glower, the old woman begins to sing an old Irish lullaby. The little man's tiny eyelids flutter closed, an exhausted smile on his cherub face. Mrs. Finney butts out her cigarette.

Control Zone. No vehicle may be left unattended Monday to Saturday 8am to 6pm, says the sign. But you can't control everything. The bastards leave a milk van loaded with Semtex. They park it right out front of the Moyola Arms.

There's an instant before an explosion. A horrible, shuddering inhale right before the blast when you know what's coming. Some think it's divine; a sort of tiny window to make your peace with God. But anyone who's survived will tell you that it's actually a cruel joke. A moment for Him to whisper in your ear, "This is happening and there's absolutely nothing you can do about it." In that pristinely silent second, as the shockwave ripples down the street to meet them, Lily sees only Nolan. And then nothing.

He's looming over her: fuzzy, distant, shouting for her to wake up and suddenly she's retching, hacking, head spinning, ears ringing. Ambulances shriek past like harpies and she's clutching him and they're stumbling up the pavement and Dom's bleeding from his head and Annie's croaking Brennan's name over and over and over and over. Closer, and the air is thick and it's awful the way Annie's eyes change as the hope drains from her body, as she pushes past the firemen, then falters, buckles, falls, claws the concrete (oh please God, oh please God no) as the shattered, blackened carcass of the Moyola Arms ghosts from the smoke.

There is no sound more terrible than a mother's grief.

Dominic and Annie bury Brennan on a Friday.

A year later, Dom and Annie moved to England. They'd never been back to Ireland because it's much easier to leave pain where it belongs than to take it with you. I guess putting things in boxes is a Doyle family tradition.

HENRY AND I HAD NEVER met our aunt and uncle, our relationship with them being relegated to birthday and Christmas cards containing crisp new ten-pound notes. Mum used to give us hell for shaking the money out of the cards before reading them but I always read mine afterwards and after years of seeing that familiar scrawl I felt like I knew them already.

Anyway, it was important to Mum and Dad that we saw them and even more important to Dom and Annie, so Henry and I arranged a month-long layover before heading back to Canada.

"Hear that?" I ask Henry as a soothing, spoonful-of-sugar female voice staccatos over the speakers and echoes through the massive cathedral-like concourse of Heathrow Airport.

"What'd she say?" asks my brother. I shrug, which makes my hockey bag travel an inch up and down my waist.

"Dunno. It's English, anyway. Nice change."

"Not if I still can't understand it," grumbles my brother. Henry took to Danish about as well as I took to Dick Head and it was with no small relief that he had put the little northern European country behind him and looked out the plane's window to see the green patchwork quilt that was the birthplace of his mother-tongue. "Fucking finally."

Exhausted, feet on the ground, we're both ready for heads to hit pillows but that's going to have to wait because London's not quite done reminding us that we're commuters. First, it's a crowded quarter hour on the Heathrow Express into Paddington Station, down the stairs to Paddington underground followed by a suffocating ride on the Circle Line toward High Street Kensington, getting off at Victoria Station followed by a forty-five minute over-ground train ride out of the city and into North Kent. *Now approaching Rochester, Chatham, Gillingham, Rainham...* and we're here. Railway Street is barely on a grade but luggage-laden and lead-footed, it feels like we've just left Everest's base camp and by the time we reach the door of Aunt Annie and Uncle Dom's terraced house, we're footsore, fucking beat and feel like planting a flag on their front lawn.

"Boys!" says Aunt Annie with an accent that's an odd mixture of Irish lilt and East London soot. She's a small woman with no-nonsense hair, sad eyes and a brittle bow to her shoulders like she's had to be strong for far too long.

Wiping her happy tears from my cheek, I follow Henry through the narrow front door into an even narrower hallway. "You get here alright?" she asks. I'm not sure if *alright* is the word to describe our arduous journey and I find it hard to believe there's not a faster way of getting around, but I nod nonetheless. "Never mind then," she responds, like she's read my mind. "I'll put on the kettle. We'll have a nice cuppa tea." *Nice cup of tea. I'd heard about this default. It's the English solution to everything, from hangovers to labour strikes to Luftwaffe air raids…*

Aunt Annie herds us into the little living room where we meet Uncle Dom, who looks strikingly like Dad (only older) with a debonair Niven-esque moustache. Pulling himself up from the orange couch (which looks like it's trying to eat him alive) he vigorously pumps our hands.

"Alright, lads," he beams. Uncle Dom smells a bit like mothballs and tobacco and the place smells a bit like the gas cooker that Annie just ignited under the kettle but the overall effect is strangely pleasant, soothing and just a little bit sleepy. Ruefully, I rub my wrist. Uncle Dom (God bless him) has a grip like a vice and a gleam in his yellowish eyes like he's seen a lot and done even more.

"Vera Lynn," he explains, waiving a hand at the woman singing on the screen of the 1970s model television in the corner. The resolution's fuzzy and the volume's at maximum, making the framed photos on the set's top buzz and rattle with the music. There's eight pictures in all, each of the same mischievous, freckly little boy and as I study them, I wonder what our cousin would have looked like today if the Royal Ulster Constabulary had just done their damned job all those years ago.

Aunt Annie returns from the kitchen with a plate of biscuits, singing along to the TV in a sweet, quavering voice. Uncle Dom joins in, grunting the final words of each line with a nod of the head and it's impossible to tell if they're gazing at the TV or the photos just above it.

Obviously, I never met Brennan and I've only just met Aunt Annie and Uncle Dom but there's something about this place, something about that old song that turns me inside out and I can't tell if the music's making me happy or horribly sad. Either way, it leaves me with an unfamiliar ache in my throat and the foreboding feeling that one day I'll be in a photo in someone's quaint parlour too.

Uncle Dom squeezes Aunt Annie's hand as another tear traces a line down her cheek like an afterthought. *Some wounds never heal, I guess.*

"Here's the thing, lads," says cousin Gav, as we huddle around three enormous, ice-cold Imperial pints. "This place is shite, yeah?"

Glancing around *The Cricketers*, I can't say I'd go that far. It's a pleasant enough pub: cool and shady with a large L-shaped bar, three slot machines, two dart boards and a chaotic clutter of fly fishing gear hanging from the ceiling.

"Somewhere in the county, I imagine there's a pub called *The Three Fishermen* with bats and wickets strung from the rafters," Uncle Dom had quipped for the eleventh time when he'd heard where we were meeting our cousin.

"Ooooh Gavin, he's trouble, he is," Aunt Annie had chimed disapprovingly. "You'd do well to stay clear of him. Likes his lager and his ladies, he does." Even after all these years, even in England, Aunt Annie gets nervous when anyone goes to the pub, especially when it's the men folk in her family. And you can hardly blame her. Her shining character reference for cousin Gav? Well, I couldn't speak to that, but Henry and I had contacted him regardless.

"I mean, it ain't shite," continues Gav, pulling a Marlboro Light from a pack with his teeth. "But it ain't The Old Smoke, innit." I can see how a woman Aunt Annie's age could find Gav troublesome looking, with his wiry frame and pockmarked cheeks and over-gelled hair and narrow jeans and pink Lacoste shirt.

"The Old Smoke?" echoes Henry, clearly as fascinated by our wily English relative as I am.

"The Old Smoke, The Great Wen, The City... London, mate." Gav punctuates his statement with three perfectly formed smoke-rings, leaning forward conspiratorially before continuing.

"Hand on my heart, gents. Brilliant clubs, wicked DJs and more fanny than you can shake your knob at. It's the bollocks."

By the time we get off the train, onto the Tube, off the Tube and resurface at Charing Cross, we're already half-cut but that's what happens when you're guzzling tall cans of Stella like you're being paid to. It's gone half-past eleven by the time we weave into Trafalgar Square but it might as well be noon for how busy it is. The square's impressive. Huge and flanked by the National Gallery and St. Martin-in-the-Fields, great grey structures that look like they grew out of the ground forever ago. Henry wants to get a photo in front of one of the massive, stone Landseer Lions and since it's early (by London nightlife standards) we oblige him. Gav points up at Nelson's column and makes some obscene joke about Winnie Mandela that neither of us get, but we're drunk enough by now that raucous laughter's an easier response than '*huh?*' Gav (like most lads here) doesn't laugh *with* you so much as he laughs *towards* you, leaning in for each cackle with the same upper-body motion that would precipitate a head-butt.

"Alright, where to?" I ask, anxious to get on with the *more-fanny-than-you-can-shake-your-knob-at* part of the evening.

"Hold on, mate," says Gav as he pulls a small cylinder of *Lynx Africa* from his jacket with a flourish. Aerosoling himself liberally with the cheap, gag-worthy body spray, he pulls his head to the left then right, rotates his neck once and satisfied with his pre-mating dance, points to a neon sign throbbing on the perimeter of the square.

"Gents, I present to you… The Hippo Club!"

Fuck, I'm under-dressed. And it's not just because this place is on the swankier side. Londoners go balls out wardrobe-wise whenever they go *anywhere* on *any* night of the week, I'm learning. It could be Tuesday Quiz Night at the *Plough and Checkers* but every guy's still going to be kitted out in leather loafers, dress pants and a Ben Sherman shirt and every girl's going to look like she's going to the Oscars; so you can imagine how I feel going out for a Saturday night in London when I'm dressed like a Thursday night in Vancouver. *Fuck it. Play the Canadian card. At least you stand out. I'm a lumberjack and I'm okay…*

It's packed in here and I don't mean busy, I mean wall-to-wall slammed and there's something feverish about the energy: something edgy and volatile and sexy and suddenly I realize what it is: everyone's drunk and I don't mean hammered, I mean fall-on-your-face drunk. *I like England*, I think, as I follow Gav and Henry through the pulsing, pissed-up crowd. *No one does anything half-ass here.* The Hippo club has a glowing dance floor but they may as well have saved the money because everyone's dancing everywhere. Even the line-up for the bar (or *queue*, as they call it) is a bouncing, bobbing mass of sweaty designer shirts and slender shiny shoulders. Gav follows suit as we fall into line, thrusting out his neck as he gyrates to the beat and surveys the crowd with a smug grin like he owns the club himself.

"I got this one, lads," he yells over the din, leaning across the bar and waving a twenty-pound note at the nearest barman.

Slowly, I rotate, taking in the dizzying melee of London nightlife: the ecstatic mob, the lights, the DJ high on his pulpit, gesticulating like a manic street preacher, the runway... *Runway? Why's there a runway in here?*

"Here we go, lads," says Gav, handing us each a glass.

"What's this?" I ask skeptically

"Rum and Coke," replies our host affably. Skeptically, I raise the barely cloudy liquid to my mouth, wincing and shaking my head as I gulp.

"Little light on the Coke, isn't it?" I ask.

"Well, you don't want to drown it, do you?" says Gav pragmatically, digging in his pocket and producing a tiny zip-lock bag of pills.

"What are those?" asks Henry.

"Just vitamins, mate. Hangover helper," replies Gav, shooting my brother a pronounced wink.

"Good call," replies Henry with a shrug, holding out his hand. *Oh for God's sake Henry. These are just vitamins about as much as those brownies in Denmark were just vegan.* Casually, I bat his hand away.

"Bob Marley," I mouth, giving him a meaningful look. Henry stares at me blankly for a moment as the synapses crackle and fire in his liquor-addled brain.

"Oh! Yeah, no thanks... mate," he replies. Gav shrugs indifferently, popping one of the tablets into his mouth, his Adam's apple bobbing in his throat as he knocks it back with the rest of the rum.

"I'll get this round," I suggest, seeing as we're still within yelling distance of the barman. "Then I want to check out that runway..."

We're crammed on the dance floor, sort of moving up and down with the crowd because it's easier than fighting it. The runway doglegs into the mob like a crooked, empty promise and no matter how many times I ask, Gav just gives me the same response, clapping my back, eyes twinkling as his pupils gradually grow larger and larger.

"Just you wait, my son. Just you wait…" Which I am, but I'm getting bored with expectation so yeah, I'm dancing and for now, the runway makes a great place to put my fifth rum while the DJ punches through one crowd-pleasing track after another. That's when something pokes my shoulder: the toe of a high heel shoe attached to a slender leg attached to a gorgeous girl with a blond bob-cut streaked with pink.

"Oy!" she says, looking down at me. "Wots that drink doin' on my runway, then?"

"Sorry," I manage, quickly removing the offending beverage.

"Sarry," she mimicks. "You a Yank, then?"

"Canadian," I correct. She squats in front of me, each of her knees inches from my shoulders.

"Alright, Mr. Canada," she coos saucily, catching my chin between her thumb and forefinger. "Enjoy the show." And with that, she struts to the end of the runway.

On cue, the music grinds to a halt and the lights go down and the crowd begins to roar. If you think a hot girl looks hot in the daylight and hotter still in candlelight, you can imagine how she looks silhouetted in a spotlight wearing next to nothing, dry ice swirling around her long, slender legs. Glittering, glimmering gorgeous. The techno track explodes and this angel's strutting past, tossing her hair and smacking her ass and thrusting her hips and as the strobe tracks across her flat stomach and muscular back and small knotted calves, I fall madly, deeply in lust.

"Oh, definitely, mate. I'd shag her arse off," slurs a club kid as he relieves himself at the end of the stainless steel trough.

"Nice bit of crumpet," nods another fella, fixing his hair in the mirror.

"Probably bite your knob off if you so much as made eye contact with her," comes a muffled warning from one of the stalls. A general murmur of resigned agreement from the population of the men's restroom. Pensively, I shake, tuck and zip. *They make her sound like a trophy*, I think, as I study my reflection in the mirror. With some relief I realize I don't look as drunk as I feel. *I like winning but I love trophies.*

Weaving back to our place by the side of the runway, I'm exhilarated to see the spunky little princess in question standing with Henry and Gav.

"It's *Lynx Africa*," explains Gav.

"Well it smells rank, mate," replies the girl. Turning to me, she smiles broadly. "Alright, Mr. Canada," she says, batting her eyelashes. *She's shorter than I thought, even in those heels. Love it.*

"This is Lucy," says Henry, who's the only other one actually present since apparently we're finally losing our cousin to his MDMA trip. Gav's eyes look like a Japanese anime character's and he's dripping with sweat and chewing gum like he's in a gum-chewing competition. Glancing at him then Henry, I quickly ascertain the difference between wingman and cock-blocker.

"Gav, wanna dance?" I ask.

"Yeah, bruv, brilliant, nice one, bruv," he nods emphatically, chawing away on his Wrigley's spearmint.

"Wicked," I reply, steering him into the crowd. "Right behind ya, buddy." Turning back to Lucy, I extend my hand, offering my winningest, most Canadian smile. "I'm Danny."

"Wot you think about her kid?" asks Hayley, the mocha-skinned beauty with the tight caramel curls. Poor Henry, the girl's accompanied us to this late night pie shop less because of any interest in him and more because she doesn't want Lucy hanging out alone with a pair of drunk Canadians. *Girl power. What a sensational pain in the ass.*

Henry really is a wicked wingman and through no fault of his own, things have been gradually degrading since we left The Hippo Club and parted ways with Gav (who'd gone wheeling into the night in a cloud of *Lynx Africa*, armed with an address for an after-party in Soho).

It was no one's fault but my own, really. I was the one with the three (up until now simple) rules:

1) No dating girls who work in bars
2) No dating smokers

3) No dating mothers

In light of Lucy's ridiculous hotness, I'm willing to ignore Rule 1. Besides, she's up on that catwalk, not down on the dim floor with its clammy, groping hands or behind the bar with those Adonis barman with their ripped, bronze douchebaggery. I can *even* get past Rule 2, providing she chews gum with Gav-like enthusiasm before coming at me with that pretty mouth (although she does make it look strangely sexy, the way those lips wrap around that filter). But a kid? Hayley, the bitch. She knows exactly what she's doing and she's waited until Lucy's gone to the restroom to do it. Despite the third strike scenario, the smirk on her best friend's full lips just makes me want to defy her even more.

"I haven't met her kid yet," I reply with forced nonchalance as I kick Henry under the table, who's staring down at his slice of lemon meringue and trying not to giggle.

"So I was thinking, yeah?" says Lucy, sliding back into the booth next to me. "I could show you around the city tomorrow if you like. Big Ben, Buckingham Palace, the lot."

"Love to," I reply, shooting Hayley my best *fuck you* smile. I get the chance to shoot her another one later when Lucy gives me a no-nonsense kiss goodnight.

"Bangers and mash," I announce to the waiter, full well knowing that there won't be any buyer's remorse with this lunch; not on my end, anyway. *The Clarence* is a pub in Westminster, in the centre of London, just off of Whitehall, en route to the swanky district of Mayfair. By four o'clock, it will be filled with pin-striped suit-wearing twenty-somethings, gripping their pints and smoking their Pall Malls and thrusting out their chins as they bang and banter about their bank jobs but right now, just past noon, it's all but empty, which suits me just fine.

"Ooh, someone's a hungry boy, then," remarks Lucy, who looks no less sexy the next day as she did the night before.

"Damned straight," I agree. We'd been all over the map: The Palace, the Houses of Parliament, Horse Guards Parade, Tower Bridge, Covent Garden, Leicester Square. On Lucy's recommendation, we'd done it on foot, because *you miss so much when you're riding the bloody Tube*, so my feet were as much in need of a rest as my stomach was in need of sausages AND potatoes AND cabbage AND gravy.

I'm two bangers in, having made a sizable dent in my mash and have just begun working on pint number two when three City boys wander in, sauntering up to the bar for a drink. Lucy leans forward.

"You're my brother's mate, yeah?"

"Huh?" I reply, the beer suspended halfway between my mouth and the table. Subtly, she nods her head toward the bar. "Who are they?" I ask.

"My boyfriend's best mates," she replies unapologetically, before carrying on like nothing's happened.

"After lunch," she continues, "I thought we could go to Soho, it's like the Red Light District in Amsterdam, then maybe up Oxford Street. Brilliant shopping…" *Holy fuck, she's the female version of me.* It's a realization that scares me as much as it turns me on. Actually no. It turns me on more. But not as much as the sex. This whole relationship is amazing, I've never experienced anything like it before. *Dynamite* doesn't begin to do it justice.

A HEALTHY HANDFUL OF LATE nights, afternoon sex and hangovers later, Henry and I are standing outside Paddington Station with a distraught Lucy beside us. The English leg of our trip is over and done and there's a Ryanair flight to Belfast with our names all over it. I've already told her she can't come to the airport, despite her moaning and I'm already feeling a bit frayed around the edges about the whole thing and I'm not sure if it's the emotion of the situation or the cigarette she's lighting that sets me off but something does.

"Piss off with that thing," I snap, plucking the smoke from her mouth and tossing it down a storm drain. "And fuck off with the long face and the *I'll miss you* bullshit. Just go back to your boyfriend already."

Even as I'm saying it, I'm realizing how harsh it sounds and I'm already wishing I could take it back but what makes it worse is that she doesn't get angry. Doesn't yell. Her face just drops—slowly, like a kid who has lost her ice cream—and when she blinks and those two tears race each other down her pretty cheeks, it's game over.

"Hey, hey, I'm sorry. C'mere," I say, pulling her in and as soon as her head hits my shoulder the sobs start in earnest. *Oh my God, this girl really loves me! Do I love her? Maybe?!* "Marry me." The words fall out of my face faster than I process them. Suddenly, she's laughing and crying and laughing and by the time my brother and I are on the train, I can honestly say I'm not quite sure what happened. Henry's sitting in the seat opposite me, an astonished look on his face.

"What?" I snap.

"You spectacular idiot," he says quietly, as the train lurches out of the station.

"Hey, at least I didn't ask her to come visit this time," I reply, as London slowly slides behind us.

"You were engaged."

"I was engaged."

"What about your rules? No barmaids, no smokers, no kids…"

"I was convinced I was going to change her. Stubbornly so, even with my brother doing his damnedest to convince me otherwise. I guess the writing was on the wall, though. We —Henry included— went out every single night, and not just out. We went out hard and we'd see the night through and stumble into the morning wincing and weaving and waning until heavy heads hit pillows. Then late afternoon, we'd wake up and do it all over again. That first day of sightseeing was the only time I ever experienced London in the daylight, really. But I'll tell you what: I know it at night like the back of my hand."

"What about her child?"

"Oh the kid? Never met him. He lived with her folks for some reason."

"Maybe because she was a promotional girl at a nightclub?"

"Hey, I said she was a wicked chick and loads of fun. Not Mother of the Year."

Matt McCoy

chapter 8

"Are we talking about the illness today?"

"Yeah, of course. Sorry if I was a little short last time."

"You have nothing to apologize to me for, but that's not why you're here is it?"

"No, I guess not."

"Things are progressing, I take it?"

"If you mean still in remission and still on treatment, then yeah, things are progressing. The spinal tap's out of the way for another three months, too, which is always a relief."

"I imagine it is. Anything new to report?"

"Yeah, actually. They've got me seeing this counsellor. So I can... how did he put it? 'Navigate the physical, psychosocial and neurocognitive challenges that often present themselves with this illness.'"

"Clinical euphemism for?"

"Clinical euphemism for, 'If you think cancer's a bitch, wait until you see how the chemo messes you up.'"

"Did you find the meeting beneficial?"

"Meetings. Plural and indefinite, every Friday morning at eleven. I guess 'beneficial' is one word you could use to describe them."

"What's another one?"

"Depressing. There's a risk of cardiomyopathy from the Doxorubicin, reduced bone density from the Methotrexate and Dexamethasone and tooth decay from everything else. And have you ever heard of

the kid who missed the bus

Secondary Leukemia? You can thank the Cyclophosphamide for that one. Even if you're one of the lucky ones, you still have yearly nerve-racking CBC's to look forward to and echocardiograms every five years. It's not fair."

"Tell me about the psychosocial challenges."

"You know, fear of telling people about the illness. Fear of it returning."

"Right."

"Can we talk about Ireland now?"

"Of course. This was your first visit to Ireland?"

"It was. Aunt Teresa still lived there. Great-Aunt really. Dad's mum's sister. She lived in the old Bogside neighbourhood of Derry where all the insanity had begun all those years back. By then, it had become a relatively quiet urban corner of a relatively quieter country. Rusty-red terraced houses lining narrow streets with murals of the Troubles covering the flat sides of three-story apartment blocks like giant cautionary tales, reminders of an ugly quarrel best forgotten but never truly gone."

WE HAVE A WEEK ON the bonnie green isle and apart from the music, the Guinness and the damp chill that creeps into your bones by teatime, it's more or less like England.

"How long are ya here, then, Daniel Liam and Henry James?" asks Aunt Teresa from her chair, punctuating her sentence with three enthusiastic puffs on her cigarette, none of which make it as far as her lungs. Aunt Teresa has a strange habit of coupling middle names to first names, at least when it comes to family members.

"Just about a week, Auntie," replies Henry, blinking through the acrid bluish cloud that hangs around the old lady like the ghost of a dead husband. She's a sight, Aunt Teresa: knobby knees obscenely jutting southwest and southeast respectively and arms akimbo and jaw thrust forward like a terrier.

"Looks like the weather's gonna be nice, anyway," I offer with a shrug, not sure what to do with this visit (which so far feels more like an audience with a mad queen).

"Too true, Daniel Liam. Too true," nods Aunt Teresa emphatically, doing another convincing impression of a chimneystack. "Tank da Lord!" she adds, less as an observation and more like she's daring us *not* to thank Him. The old woman's eyes bore through us in the smoky silence, her eyebrows doing a strange dance like they're attempting to mount an escape from her forehead. Teresa has some kind of mild palsy, which causes the north end of her face to do this little dance whenever she's chewing over a thought. "And what do you have to say then, Henry James?" she asks my brother, completely out of the blue.

"Um, I…" Henry stalls out, scrabbling for context and glancing at me sidelong for help but I'm as lost as he is. A crooked smile slowly spreads across her bony face.

"You're a pair of bobs, aren't you," she says appraising Henry approvingly before turning her cataracts my way. "Alright," she says, like we've passed some kind of test. "You'll stay here in the spare room upstairs, but if the Peelers lock you up for mischief, I don't know either of youse, right? Now I'll go wet the tea and make some cheese and sausenger baps."

"Sounds great. I'm starving," I reply, still not quite sure exactly what's happened or what I'm about to eat.

"Too true, Daniel Liam, too true," says Henry with a wink.

"AND YOU'RE BOTH LOOKING FOR contracts in England, now?" asks the gym owner who's interrupted us halfway through our bench press to introduce himself as Damien McGowan.

"Sure," I shrug, sliding another twenty-five pound plate onto the bar. *Lucy's in for a surprise if she thinks I'm going to keep carrying on like Keith Richards when I get back. She's only met off-season Danny so far.*

Henry and I had been more or less smoked out of Aunt Teresa's that morning and wheezing all the way to the bus stop, we'd decided to find a gym in Belfast in which to sweat out the secondhand nicotine before exploring the city. For us, working out is as normal a part of a morning as eating cornflakes, so finding *Fitspace* ten minutes after getting off the bus is a welcome stroke of luck.

"And you said your family's from here?" probes Damien.

"Mum grew up on Arran Street and Dad just across the river," confirms Henry. You can see the wheels turning as Damien looks at us, slowly nodding like a cartoon character with dollar signs for eyes. *Canadian pro hockey-playing brothers from the bad side of Belfast make good, then return to Northern Ireland to connect with their roots. That's the craic...*

As usual, my wheels are turning too.

"We'd be happy to endorse your gym in exchange for free access this week," I offer. Damien's eye's twinkle.

"I'll tell you what, mate," he counters. "I can do you one better than that..."

The next morning, we're standing in the centre of *FitSpace* in the glare of lights and cameras from UTV while a gaggle of reporters snap photo after photo of me and Henry.

"Danny, Mickey Doolin here from the *Belfast Telegraph*," begins one eager fella with a notebook poised under his nose.

"It's Danny Boy," I correct. "Danny Boy Doyle." Another flurry of flashes and snapping shutters.

"Jesus Christ," mutters Henry out the side of his mouth.

"Danny Boy," what's the one thing you like the most about Northern Ireland?"

"Oh that's easy," I reply with a winning smile. "It has to be the people."

"Dead on!" replies the beaming reporter. To be honest, I've only met Aunt Teresa and this Damien McGowan guy but I'm guessing this is the answer they're looking for.

"And you, Henry?" asks a man from the *South Belfast News*.

"This gym," replies my brother dutifully. "*FitSpace. Small Price... Big Results!*" *Impressive*, I think, watching Damien beam from the sidelines. He even pulled out the company slogan. After the press finally disperses, I blaze through my weight routine with a little bit more exhilaration than usual. One week's free gym membership and our faces all over the TV and newspapers tomorrow. Not bad for our first forty-eight hours in the Old Country!

"I KNOW," I SAY INTO the phone. "Of course, me too." Sighing, I look around the bar, making sure no one's in earshot. "Fine. I love you too." Hanging up, I thank the bartender at the *Crown Bar Liquor Salon* and head back to the table where by now, my beer is warm and my chips are cold.

"That the calling card Mum gave you?" asks Henry as I stuff the piece of plastic back into my wallet.

"Yup," I confirm, taking a long slog from my pint. Guinness tastes pretty good at room temperature anyway. Reminds me of stealing the dregs from the bottom of Granddad's cans when I was a kid. Henry's a lager man. Doesn't know what he's missing.

"She's gonna shit herself when she gets the bill," observes my brother and he's probably not wrong. Lucy had left for a fortnight in Cyprus the day after we'd left for Ireland and in the last two days alone we'd logged in about four hours of long-distance time. Factoring in countless nights of lusty conversations with Mona back in Vancouver as well (Mona and me, we have this understanding) and we're looking at a bill that's going to force Dad into a second mortgage if I'm not careful.

"Whaddya want me to say," I reply. "She's my fiancée." Henry tries to resuscitate the chips with liberal sloshes of malt vinegar.

"Yeah," he says. "Mum's gonna love that too."

Henry turns to me thoughtfully as we leave the famous pub and amble down Great Victoria Street.

"I wonder what Aunt Teresa will think when she sees us on TV tonight…"

"EEJITS!" SCREECHES AUNT TERESA THROUGH the door. Henry and I look at each other, jaws on the pavement. Bending down, I call through the mail slot.

"Auntie, we're not quite sure what we've done to upset you…"

"Are ya away in the head?" she yells. "Youse two faffin' about Belfast, getting on the telly like a pair of pop stars, tanking some knob-knocker at a bathhouse and tipping your hats to everyone in the bleeding city but not a word for your Auntie who's fed ya and put a roof over ya…"

"Um, it's a gym, not a bathhouse," I correct. Henry looks at me with exasperation. "What?" I hiss. "It's not!" Sighing, I stand back up.

"Is she drunk?" whispers Henry.

"I hope so," I reply, "otherwise she's bat-shit crazy. Auntie, we're so sorry," I call. "We… were just trying to respect your privacy."

"Bollocks!" comes the muffled reply. "D'you think I came up the Lagan in a bubble?"

"Auntie…" begins Henry.

"Get fecked!" she yells, shutting down the dialogue in two words. "And up your arses!" adds the old lady for good measure. Henry and I collapse on the stoop, overcome by barely containable mirth.

"She's totally my favourite auntie!" gasps my brother.

"Me too," I agree, wiping the tears of glee from my cheeks.

"Think she'll let us back in?" asks Henry.

"Oh eventually, I imagine," I reply.

By teatime, the deadbolt clicks unlocked and that night Aunt Teresa chain-smokes and stares out the window and by the next day, you'd never know anything had ever happened if not for the empty gin bottle on the coffee table.

"BALLS!" BLURTS OUT HENRY, WINCING into his hoodie as the needle buzzes across his thigh like a wasp. "I thought you said this didn't hurt…"

"It doesn't. Not much anyway. Don't be a pussy," I reply, pleasantly preoccupied with my own raised, rashy leg. The pointy-headed little ginger-haired Leprechaun glares up from my thigh, fists raised, angry and aggressive with his little green suit and his little yellow boots and hatband. *The colours will calm down a bit*, I've been told, *and it'll stop looking like it's embossed and it'll scab a bit and you'll need to keep it covered for a few days and moisturized.*

In one ear and out the other. I'm just amped that I've finally got one and this one in particular because what else are you going to get with your brother in Belfast? Henry's getting the Fighting Irish mascot too and damn, Dad's going be proud of his boys for this one. We'll be back in Prince Peaks in a week, but not before a final stop-over in London because I've got a contract to find if I'm going to come back and put a ring on Lucy's finger. She's going to be in

Cyprus for another week so at least she's out of my hair until I get next season sorted out.

"You tell your Ma and Da hello from me," commands Aunt Teresa in a voice that makes you almost certain she means, *do it or I'll fecking murder you.* If it weren't for her dancing eyebrows, she'd be genuinely intimidating. Spontaneously, Henry and I smother her in a huge hug whether she likes it or not, and I'm pretty sure she does because she gets this soft look on her battle-axe face, just for a moment before shoving us roughly away.

"Now feck off, the both of ye," she says gruffly, but those wild old eyes look a little shinier than usual as she stands in the doorway, waving like a wind-up toy until our bus turns the corner, out of sight.

OUR FINAL WEEK IN LONDON works out well, both of us landing contracts in England for the following season (not on the same team mind you, which disappoints us more than either's willing to admit) but at least we're going to be in the same country. Henry's going to a team up north and I'm heading to Romford, a suburban town in northeast London. By the time we're in the Departures Lounge at Heathrow, we're thrilled to be saying, *see you soon* to Old Blighty, not *goodbye.*

"HEY THAT HURT!" I COMPLAIN, ruefully rubbing my shoulder where Mum's just punched it.

"Not as much a paying your seventeen hundred dollar phone bill did!" she replies, following the admonishment with a parent-sized hug and parent-sized tears now that the business end of our reunion is over. It's something else seeing everyone. Nan is looking old in earnest and she's slowing down and not happy with it, you can just tell. Ash is more woman than girl now, but all sister and amazing as ever and so happy to see us. And the twin aunts? They're still the twin aunts and still smiling, despite their bare ring fingers and Dad's Dad and as expected, beaming over me and Henry's matching tattoos because somewhere inside, he still misses Ireland, even if he never admits it. Even if he says no when you ask him.

Henry and I aren't home long, though. After the UK, this place feels like a ghost town and even the prospect of our upcoming summer in Vancouver seems a little constricting, what with London calling in the Fall. But on the upside, at least I get to see Mona.

"ENGAGED?" SHE REPEATS, SUDDENLY SELF-CONSCIOUS, an arm covering her ampler-than-ever bosom. Slowly I nod, suddenly wondering if I should have even told her about it before our reunion sex. Mona and I, we've had this arrangement since the beginning of business school and I've never seen it as wrong because for some reason, I've never seen the rules applying to us. It's just sex and we're just friends and we respect each other way too much to mess it up with emotions. Besides, I love Lucy. *I'm not sure what's more ridiculous: my amorous claim about a bar-star single mum seven-and-a-half-thousand kilometres away or the fact that every time I try to convince myself of it, Desi Arnaz* pops into my head.

Something's different with Mona this time though, and the next time we have dinner, I don't mention Lucy and I don't invite her back to my apartment and I don't ask her why she looks so sad. Like I said, Mona and I are friends.

"YOU'RE WHAT?" I SAY INTO the receiver, as annoyed that Lucy's bringing this up on the tail end of the conversation as I am that we're having the conversation at all. My final order of business prior to relinquishing the calling card to Mum had been to ring Lucy one last time and let her know that it was off. All of it. The engagement, us, everything. I mean, what was the point? I'm over here screwing Mona again, and she's back there, undoubtedly banging her boy-friend—who she's never *actually* broken up with—not to mention God-knows-whoever else she meets at the Hippo Club. *She met me there, didn't she?* That conversation was a week ago and that was the last I'd expected to hear from her but here we are, talking again.

"I'm coming out next month, aren't I," repeats Lucy. *I don't know, are you? Why do they always have to end statements like they're asking questions?* Truth be told, she doesn't sound any more thrilled sharing this news than I feel hearing it but I think we both know we have to see this through to its inevitable end; whatever the reason, maybe just so we can both walk away knowing that we *really* tried. Naturally, time and space had slowly diminished the heat of the moment, turning the red-hot romance of London into a cool, pragmatic grey, leaving the reality of what I'd proposed seeming ridiculous and futile. Mona's new sad eyes aren't making it any easier, either. *Like it or not, a visit from Lucy is going to sort things out, one way or another.*

"That's great," I respond with Oscar-winning enthusiasm. Turns out her dad's taking her and her kid to California (even English kids have this thing with Disneyland, apparently) and at some point she's planning on leaving them there (surprise, surprise) and coming up the coast for a few days of R&R with yours truly.

"Alright, ring you next week with the details. Ta-ta for now. Bye… bye… bye… bye…" CLICK. I return the receiver to the cradle, not sure why I'm so annoyed. *And that's another thing: why do they always have to say bye, like six times?*

"FUCK!" I YELL, SLAMMING MY palm against the steering wheel as the Vancouver traffic crawls across the Oak Street Bridge in the shimmering evening heat of a hotter-than-average summer evening. Lucy had managed to catch an earlier flight out of Los Angeles, which would have been fine had it not been for the fact that I'd managed to swing some training sessions with the Vancouver Canucks. Hitting the ice with the city's NHL franchise was an opportunity I didn't expect her to understand, and arriving at Vancouver International in time to meet her at Arrivals was something I didn't expect I'd pull off, but I didn't expect her to hitch a ride into town with some chick she'd met on her flight, either. I'd expected her to stay put. But who was I talking about? The longest Lucy was motionless for was the five hours (on average) that she was passed out each night. She had this inertia. That's what I'd loved about her but right now it's what I hated.

> *Caught a ride into town with a girl I met on the plane.*
> *(She has a Mercedes!) At 1029 Hamilton, Apt. 303.*
> L.

By the time the Air Transat service desk had handed me the hurriedly scrawled note, I was already exhausted from today's practice, bemoaning tomorrow's 6am practice and pretty sure I was coming down with a stomach bug. I'm in no mood for the arduous drive back into the city let alone an evening with the blonde, brakeless freight train who I had to keep reminding myself was here to *give it another go* or at least talk about it. *That's what I love about Mona. No bullshit. Just sex and good times and good company. On my terms. On a normal clock. No bar job, no smoking, no kids.*

Rolling into the trendy city neighbourhood of Yaletown, I realize that the British Invasion has already left a bad taste in my mouth, and I haven't even seen her yet. *Not a great start...*

"ALRIGHT," SHE SAYS WITH A guarded smile and a quick peck on the cheek and an awkward half-hug. She smells like Burberry Brit and chardonnay.

An empty wine bottle sits on the spacious loft apartment's glass coffee table and behind it in a weird, IKEA-esque chair sits the tenant: an attractive Asian woman with an unattractive look on her face.

"You're late," says the girl, leaning back and re-crossing her legs like a James Bond villain. Lucy's suitcase is already in my hand.

"I'm sorry, and you are?" I ask, feeling the saliva evaporate from my mouth like the dry wind before an angry storm. *Seriously. Who the hell are you?*

"Um, Emily?" she responds, like somehow I was supposed to magically know this.

"She drove me from the airport in her Mercedes," explains Lucy, as she pulls on her boots.

"Yeah, you said that in your note," I mutter. "C'mon let's go."

"I have a question," says Emily, standing up to her full height of five-foot-nothing. "What kind of guy stands a girl up at the airport?" Lucy's suitcase thuds to the concrete floor.

"Are you fucking kidding me?" I snarl.

"Come on, leave it," says Lucy, tugging on my arm, and it's a good thing because I'm ready to snap this bitch in half like a fortune cookie.

"Call me," Emily mouths to Lucy, holding her thumb and pinky up to the side of her head. With a glare that I hope says every angry, obscene thing I'm thinking, I slam the door behind us, loud enough, I hope, for the folks on the second and fourth floors to hear as well. Lucy walks ahead of me down the narrow hall running her hands along the walls as she goes. Just tipsy enough for her gait to take on a cute coltishness; just enough to make her hips (her tiny little hips) sway just that little bit more. By the time the elevator's brushed steel doors close behind us, I've forgotten about all the bullshit and all I can think about is getting her naked. Lucy looks at me in the loaded silence.

"You gonna ask me how my flight was, then?" she asks quietly, leaning against the mirrored elevator wall, lips slightly parted on the end of the question as her chest rises and falls. I can't actually remember how I cover the space between us because the next second, I'm slammed against her and it's like we're trying to devour the lower half of each other's face. Breathlessly, she's wrestling with my belt and I'm slamming one hand against the red *stop* button and hooking the other one into her panties. Cupping my face, she looks me in the eyes with that filthy little look on her face and that's when everything goes primal: her against the wall, legs wrapped around me and I'm pistoning away like it's my last night on earth and it's hot and hungry and hard and I almost pass out when the end comes.

Lucy clears her throat, as the elevator doors swish open, straightening her skirt and averting her eyes as we push past a pair of impatient tenants.

Cramming her suitcase into the trunk, I come around the car then stop.

"I thought you quit," I observe flatly. Lucy shrugs, exhaling a cloud, and suddenly I'm standing in the cold company of post-coital common sense. *It's just Lucy,* I realize as my hormone levels recede and my focus re-sharpens. *Just Lucy. And her kid and her nightclub job (said she'd quit that too) and apparently her cigarettes too. Just Lucy. Nothing's changed.* With a sigh, I slide into the driver's seat as she butts out and gets in. Leaning across the shifter, she gives me a kiss but the wine

the kid who missed the bus

145

has gone sour on her tongue and the acrid stench of tobacco hangs in her hair.

"Emily says *Bar None's* good tonight or maybe *the Roxy,*" she suggests. *Jesus Christ, here we go…*

"Luce, I can't tonight," I explain. "Hockey in the morning. And I'm coming down with something." The rest of the ride is silent and sullen. *Leopards and their spots,* I think. *You just can't change 'em.*

"Lucy stayed with you, then?"

"She was supposed to, but I pulled the plug on that the minute I realized that there was nothing to fight for here. She was always going to be too much work. Too high maintenance, like Astrid, only Astrid couldn't help it."

"How did you manage that?"

"Told her my landlord would evict me if I had anyone over. It's a Canadian thing, I said."

"So you put her in a hotel?"

"Yeah, but I paid for it, at least."

"How benevolent of you. And you saw her the next day, I imagine?"

"Actually no. This is where I feel a little badly. I told her I was sick, which was true, but I didn't answer her calls the next couple of days either. And since she was only in town four days total, I didn't speak to her again until her last evening."

"You gonna at least take me out for my birthday?" she asks coldly.

"Sure, I reply, banging the phone against my forehead. *Shit, that's right. It's her birthday. What an asshole.* "Should I pick you up from the hotel?"

"I'm not staying at the hotel," she replies evenly. Pick me up from 1029 Hamilton." *Of course you are. Fuck you, Emily. And your stupid chair and your mirrored elevator.*

"Okay," I sigh, hanging up.

"You're what!" says Mona, gawking at me in disbelief. Palms

Matt McCoy

up, I continue.

"It's just…" I trail off shaking my head. "I think I've made a mistake."

"And?" my faithful friend prompts.

"And nothing. I just think I've made a mistake." Mona and I sit on the couch in silence, pretending to watch the infomercial. *Just like with Astrid, but Mona can skip a meal without croaking…*

"I don't think I've ever heard you say that before," she observes quietly.

"That's because I've never made a mistake before," I reply solemnly before attacking her, gnawing on her neck. Mona shrieks, squirming away as my hands begin to wander.

"No," she says firmly, "You get un-engaged and we'll talk."

We watch three more infomercials that night and through the entire evening, there's this little smile playing at the corners of her mouth.

"You look great," I acknowledge, as I pick Lucy up on the shady Yaletown street corner. And I actually mean it too, but my compliment garners nothing. No, *thank-you* or *oh you're so sweet,* because we both know why she looks so stunning tonight and the best thing I can do is accept the, *fuck you, this is what you're missing,* as gracefully as possible. *Whatever,* I think. *Still gonna parade you around.* Maybe we're done but nobody else knows that and if this is the last time I'm going to have her on my arm like a Rolex, you better believe I'm rolling my sleeves up.

Dinner on Robson Street seems like the obvious choice; the restaurants are great, plus downtown Vancouver's trendiest, most populated retail stretch seems like a good place to go out with a bang, as far as showing her off goes. Three days into a four-day flu bug, I'm still not feeling stellar but I'm not about to squander the opportunity for a high-exposure pre-meal saunter. Sure, I have an open bottle of Pepto in one hand which I'm casually knocking back like it's Gatorade, but who's going to laugh? *Have you seen what's on my other arm?*

Cyprus had been kind to Lucy, turning her blonde hair platinum and her skin golden. She's wearing a denim skirt that's about four inches long and that bellybutton ring looks like the little silver door-knocker to a tight, toned party for two. Forget the husbands and boyfriends, even the wives and girlfriends are glancing at her: some with appreciation, others with envy. Just for a moment, I feel like this must be similar to (albeit smaller than) the feeling of holding the silverware above your head, beaming from the top of the open top double-decker in a Stanley Cup champions' parade. I glance admiringly at Lucy. There's no doubting I love trophies. I just don't want to marry this one.

We go to *Cin Cin*, this Italian place with a killer second story al fresco patio. Dinner's more of the same, but now the wandering-eyed husbands and boyfriends have been joined by blushing bus boys and waiters strutting about in their long aprons, grasping their great wooden pepper mills like giant brown cocks. It's funny how alcohol works, because by the time we're on to the tiramisu, I'm im-patiently glancing at my watch and hoping Mona's up when I even-tually get in. Meanwhile, Lucy—who's been knocking back cocktails like she's in London—has achieved that slightly wall-eyed state that accompanies thick-lipped innuendo and poor decision-making.

"Wot you gonna give me for my birthday," she asks, waving her drink at head height and kicking me in the shins in a failed attempt at playing footsies.

"Dinner," I reply tiredly. "I'm not going to screw you, Lucy."

The ride home is as anticlimactic as everything else and by the time I drop her back off in Yaletown, there's really nothing left to say. And that's exactly how we leave it as she clacks up to the apart-ment door and rings her new friend's buzzer. *Well that's over. Emily's going to be thrilled*, I think. *And so is that scary broad, Hayley, back in London.* I wonder what Mona will think?

"You okay?" asks Mona as she opens the door and lets me in.

"Couldn't be better," I assure her. And that's all the talking that needs to be done right now because Mona and I have better things to do. *No bar job, no cigarettes, no kids*, I think, as I tear off her clothes and happily ravage that oh-so-familiar body. *THIS is more like it!*

"And she'd wanted this for a while?"

"Oh, who knows? She didn't at the start, that's for sure."

"But I imagine she had feelings for you some time prior to you developing feelings for her..."

"I'd never really thought of it in those terms. We'd always shared a fondness, though. I mean we could hang out. And the chemistry was consistent, like a slow burn. Not fireworks, maybe, but it wasn't about to burn out either. It felt like I was thinking with the right head finally."

"Did things change between you?"

"Sure, but not in the way you think. She didn't make a big deal about it. She just carried on...like it was the most normal thing ever, which, whether she realized it or not, was exactly what I needed her to do."

"And you lived happily ever after?"

"Until preseason, anyway. Had a contract waiting for me in England..."

THIS IS THE EASIEST GOODBYE yet and not because Mona matters less. She matters more in fact, because she doesn't ask me where I've been when I come in late and she doesn't grab my hand automatically every time we're out in public and she doesn't say *I love you* and then puppy-dog-eye me until I parrot it back. Hell, she doesn't say *I love you* at all. She just makes everything easier. That's why I love Mona. Anyway, this is an easy goodbye because she's smiling and I'm smiling and she's coming out at Christmas so there's no wartime maybe-ness about the when and where of our reunion and subsequently no tears.

"Behave," she says. That's all. And with a big soft kiss and a big warm smile, she's gone and I'm trudging through the obnoxiously West Coast themed concourse of Vancouver International Airport looking for Gate 125 and digging in my pocket for my passport. *I won't have time for a woman anyway*, I think, imagining that between the rink, the gym, and the new reputation I'm planning on building, a monkish month or two might do me good. Passing a large fountain, I stop and watch as numerous tubes along its rim spew ropes of crystal-blue water that surge up then splash against the totem pole centrepiece. *I miss British Columbia the most when I'm leaving it behind.*

THERE'S A WARM FAMILIARITY ABOUT Heathrow; something anyone who has gone through this airport more than once experiences the minute they return, like they've done it a thousand times before. There's a little more confidence in my stride as I navigate Terminal Two's maddening multicultural crowd, a little more purpose as I weave away from the Express, instead riding the steep escalator down to the Tube; the Piccadilly Line into London East (Cockfosters, and I'm not making that name up). Twenty stops later I'm changing trains at Holborn, switching to the Central Line, eastbound another five stops to Liverpool Street Station. Now we're over-ground at least, which makes little difference since the afternoon is a close, heavy grey like the sky on the HP Sauce bottle. Somewhere between platforms 8-18 is the train I'm looking for, but it's not until I'm skeptically passing Platform 11 that I finally find my National Express connection and almost three hours after leaving the airport, I'm finally rolling into Romford.

CONTRACT-WISE, ROMFORD'S A SIMILAR SITUATION to Rungsted, just with crappier weather, no parades and no sports car but no worries. I'm here to play hockey and to be faithful to my girlfriend back home and Jesus, sixteen weeks is going to be a long time without sex but it's probably going to be good for me.

It's a strange adjustment. Visiting is different. It's when you're living here that's when you notice the little things: differences subtle enough not to require a complete gearshift but foreign enough to induce a strange sense of vertigo like you're living in a dream, like the cars are on the left, and they're smaller. And some of them have three wheels. And milk's in glass bottles and Cornflakes are in different boxes and it's Lucozade not Gatorade with added *vitamins* not vitamins, and half the names on the Top Forty Charts are unrecognizable and the accents? Well, sometimes they might as well be speaking Danish. Apart from the little things, though? It's just like Canada.

The team's a bit of an adjustment. The Chieftains are a somewhat storied franchise in the ENL (English National Ice Hockey League) with a bee in their bonnet about bygone glory days, a continuing taste for silverware and a wish-list for the upcoming season that includes *The Autumn Trophy* and the *Essex Cup* and the *Kent Cup*. Expectations are high and as always, higher still on an import like me, but that's how I like it. The fan base isn't anything close to huge—The Havering Ice Centre has a capacity of 1,200—but it's a fervent crowd with passionate people whose lager-fuelled love of footie happily spills over into the ice rink every time we lace up our skates for a home game. Funny that a team from northeast London has a logo depicting a North American Indian in full headdress. I'd always pictured something more along the lines of *Braveheart...*

ROMFORD CHIEFTAINS 3, MEDWAY BEARS 0
Cardiff Devils 1, Romford Chieftains 4
Romford Chiefs 1, Milton Keynes Thunder 1
Romford Chieftains 2, Bracknell Hornets 1
That's one helluva start.

I'M LIVING IN A TWO-BEDROOM apartment with a teammate: a big, ugly lad with an even bigger cranium who had at one point been a draft pick for the Vancouver Canucks. Hands like Gretzky but the problem was he skated like a Clydesdale and drank like Shane MacGowan and that's the abridged version of what he was doing on the Romford depth chart.

Pumpkinhead and I go together like fish-and-chips roommates-wise but any illusions I've fostered about being faithful are fast evaporating. I'm not cut out for this celibacy business. Three weeks without Mona has me crawling up the walls, desperately trying to fit my rationale around my urges. *It wouldn't really be cheating, would it? I mean I don't want to break up with her. I just have a need. A cold, clinical, emotionless need, which is nothing like what her and I have...* By the time I've formulated my defence and watered it with a few cold pints, I've all but convinced myself that a quick roll in the hay is the moral equivalent of a much-needed piss.

I'm feeling strangely defiant once my mind is made up because I guess it beats feeling guilty. Besides, we all have our crosses to bear. Take Pumpkinhead, for instance: his is boozing, but that suits English drinking culture to a tee. I'm not saying England's full of social alcoholics. I'm just saying that it's the ideal place for a real sauce-hound to fly in under the radar. My new roommate? He's turning every spare moment into a drunken, debauched shit-show. But I'm no steely-livered 19-year-old anymore and it's not long before I'm fading on this out-every-night nonsense. Hockey's not like bricklaying. It's not like I can wander in a half-hour late, half-cut from the night before, offer the foreman a half-baked excuse, mortar half a row until half-past eleven then half-heartedly choke down half a sandwich. There's nothing half-ass about hockey, even in England.

But there's nothing half-ass about Pumpkinhead's drinking, either. When I dial back a little on the craziness, his solution is to bring the craziness home. I don't stand a chance, not with the buzzed babes bundling in behind him three or four nights a week with their long legs and loud voices and tall cans of Strongbow. *It's not really cheating, is it? I mean I don't want to break up with her. I just have a need. A cold, clinical, emotionless need, which is nothing like what her and I have...*

"We'll let *them* decide," he slurs a little too loudly, with a blatant wink. I appraise the two *birds* (that's what they call them here) who he's brought home, who now perch on the far end of the couch chirping loudly and playing with their hair. *They're always so drunk, these birds. That's the M.O. when you're as pretty as Monsieur P.*

Anyway, Pumpkinhead's room is upstairs and mine's right below it and there's not much left to do (after the birds picked their branches) but to drink up and split the party into two bedrooms.

Things are going pretty good with mine; we're stumbling down the hall, clacking teeth accidentally, reeling and laughing and eventually we're grinding into the bed. But I'm fed up because I'm in the middle of it with this girl and Pumpkinhead, he's really thumping around upstairs and drunk or not, it's really distracting when you're trying to *get your leg over* (that's what they call it here). I'm about ready to thump on the ceiling with a broom when a BANG much bigger than a thump stops me mid-makeout.

"Fuganell," mutters what's-her-name as I roll off, throw on some boxers and pad down the hall to investigate. Pumpkinhead was pretty blitzed when he'd headed upstairs with bird number two and I'm having these visions of him passed out on the floor with a sprained dick or maybe he dropped her on her head trying to do something tantric... Either way, things have gone horribly quiet and I'm getting this uneasy feeling when suddenly, there's a clatter of feet on the staircase and the girl in question comes flying down, banging past me and limps out the front door. One more BANG as the front door slams behind her.

"Danny Boy!" comes Pumpkinhead's urgent voice from the bedroom. "Danny Boy, get up here!"

He's sitting on the floor, totally naked, a stunned look on his face and that's something, seeing the big man visibly shaken.

"What the hell, man?" I ask, helping him to the side of the bed and doing my best to avoid eye contact (or any other kind of contact for that matter) with his slowly deflating hammer. He just sits there blinking like he's trying to process something unimaginable. "What'd you do?" I try again. Pumpkinhead just shakes his pumpkin head.

"Nothing, man. I was just lifting her into bed. Like a knight."

"Like a knight?" I echo.

"You know. Gallantly."

"Oh," I reply, still confused. "And?"

"And her leg fell off," he whispers.

"Her leg fell off?" I echo again, like saying it a second time is going to make it sound less strange. *Nope.*

"She had a fake leg. It fell off when I picked her up," he explains. *So that was the bang. Still doesn't explain why she stormed out...*

"What did you say?" I demand. Another long silence as Pumpkinhead shakes his head, sighing heavily before continuing.

"I said, 'Gross, where's your fucking leg?'" *Real gallant there, Sir Pumpkinhead...*

"Oh," I reply, for lack of something better to say. It's not often I'm speechless, but this takes the cake.

"What the hell did she expect me to say?" he laments. "I mean, that's just messed up."

The double-standard is laughable because looking at Pumpkin-head, it's a wonder he gets laid at all, period. His head's not just huge, it's hideous. Something like Sloth from *The Goonies*. Apart from being down one limb, his bird was pretty alright-looking, really. He should have just sucked it up and put half-a-notch on his bedpost and called it a good story for the boys, but no. That was Pumpkinhead. Never really aware of his own shortcomings but enthusiastically blunt about everyone else's.

We're in the locker room one pre-game, silently taping our sticks and lacing our skates and getting our war-faces on and out of the blue, Pumpkinhead looks up, interjecting like he's halfway through a conversation in his own head.

"…and what the hell, De Araujo," he says to one of our team-mates who apart from a snaggled mouthful of overly-English teeth is actually fairly handsome. "What's with the buck-teeth, buddy? Do you throw in a mouth-guard before you screw your girlfriend?" The place collapses in laughter but less because of De Araujo's mouth and more because this inbred-looking ogre is the one pointing it out and to one of the toughest guys in the league as well.

The English love a good ironic laugh.

"Back in England then, yeah?" says a familiar voice on the other end of the phone. *What the fuck! How did Lucy get my number?*

Turns out that when she's not partying or smoking or having a hangover or buying more smokes, she finds a little time for TV.

A teammate and I had recently appeared on an episode of *Channel 4's Big Breakfast*. We were there to promote the league, shooting weird and wonderful things into a goal set up on a Glice (fake ice) surface while presenter Mark Little aped about in his obnoxious lime-green jacket and pink shirt, asking utterly asinine questions about hockey and Canada. Regardless, it was a riot travelling down to the canal-side studios in East London to shoot the popular morning show.

"Ready?" asks a tubby production assistant, sticking my purple sweatshirt with a lapel microphone and little red AIDS awareness ribbon. I nod, watching the intro on the monitor as the three pre-senters find their marks in front of the camera. CUE OPENING SEQUENCE: Toast popping from a toaster as brassy kid's show music blares over an aerial shot of a red brick house with a blue door. Zooming through it, we wind along a full breakfast table, past jam and oranges and tea, straight up to a great silver cloche, which opens revealing the show's title in big, obnoxious rose-coloured let-ters: THE BIG BREAKFAST. (A chorus of canned cheers.) A red light goes on above the set and suddenly, the presenter trio springs to life like they've just been shot with caffeine guns.

"Good morning and g'day, I AM Mark Little!"

"I'm Danni Minogue!"

"And I'm Paula Yates!"

"It is F-F-Fridaaaaaaay!" finishes Little. *I wonder why England's most popular early a.m. broadcast is two-thirds Australian?* More canned cheers as Little continues in his Oceanic twang. "Yes, the weekend is nearly here, it's December first and you are watching The Big Breakfast on Channel Four!"

"Yes!" confirms Danni Minogue. "Coming up today, Prince Nas-eem Hamed gets some gloves-off romance advice in Zig and Zag's Love Clinic…"

"Fair enough," intones Little, a little insanely.

"And later, the incomparable Madonna!" crows Paula Yates, (canned cheers, again).

"Cool!" asserts Little as he looms in the camera with a thumb's up. "And *stick* around as we *chill* with two of the Romford Chieftains to talk hockey and see what they're made of on some ice of our own!" The presenter presses two fingers to his ear like he's receiv-ing late-breaking news. "But now with the time at eight-o-three! It's across to Pete Smith with Big Breakfast news and weather!"

"This is live you know," reminds the tubby production assistant importantly. *Maybe that's why everyone's so fucking excited.*

"You was really good…" says Lucy.

"Thanks," I reply. Apparently, she'd got my number off cousin Gav. *Cheers, Gav.*

"Met Prince Naseem, then?"

"Yep," I confirm.

"And Madge?"

"Uh-huh," I sigh.

"Dead lucky, you are," she observes. You know that kind of telephone silence where you can tell that the person on the other end wishes they'd never called but can't for the life of them figure out a self-respecting exit strategy? Bingo.

"Bye, Lucy," I sigh, letting her off easy.

"Bye, Danny," she replies in a small voice. And that's the last time we ever speak.

Danny 1, Marriage 0.

chapter 9

"How's everything?"

"Her hair's falling out. Handfuls of it. Her eyebrows too."

PUMPKINHEAD ISN'T A LAUGHING MATTER anymore. He's not gal-loping loose-saddled across the rocky plateau of his addiction like some functional alcoholics. He's still on the downward spiral and the orbit is getting tighter and faster as the empty whiskey bottles start stacking up around the place and if you think living with him is be-coming impossible, playing with him is even worse. By mid-season, the Chieftains cut him loose and that's the end of Pumpkinhead.

"YOU'D LIKE A WOT?" ASKS Coach Steven, like I'd just asked for a sex-change.

"A host family," I reply evenly.

"And what exactly is a host family?" he asks incredulously. Coach Steven's a player-coach with a huge moustache, a huger heart but two left feet. Great guy for sure (miles better than Dick Head), but not exactly in the running for *Coach of the Year.*

"You know, a family that you live with who cook your meals and do your laundry and generally clean up after you…" *After years of sub-standard billet situations, I'm not about to pass up the chance to turn Coach's ignorance to my advantage. Why not put in a special order and see what happens?* Exhausted from my stint with Pumpkinhead and missing the fill-in-the-gaps comforts of more or less co-existing with Mona, I'm ready to trade in a few shares of my freedom and privacy for the daily guarantee of a hot meal and the nightly guarantee of a proper sleep.

Coach Steven and team owner Russell pull some strings and find me a family called the Gilbraiths, who are miles away from perfect but just down the road from the rink, so that's something anyway. They're a messy lot. Not dirty (that's where I draw the line) but untidy in a rushed, chaotic sort of way. I have my own bathroom though, and the food's not bad either and these people are HUGE fans (even by Canadian standards). Like I said, less than perfect, but a change nonetheless. A good opportunity to turn over a new leaf and get back on track. I had a month until Mona was arriving for Christmas; long enough to go on a much-needed sabbatical from myself, anyway.

"I have a girlfriend back home," I told Mrs. Gilbraith, because shooting myself in the foot was the only way I was going to be able to stop myself from running around.

"Oh, he's a lovely Canadian boy with a girlfriend back home," she'd told her pepper-pot friends down at the shop that morning as she filled her basket with mushy peas and sausage links and marmite and cheese and a copy of *OK Magazine*. And if the old girls knew something, everyone knew it. I'd made it next to impossible for me to cheat. But not impossible…

"SHHHHH. READY?" I ASK. I can feel her nod in the darkness, feel her breath inches from my face, smell the leather of the standard issue boots that are tied together and slung over her shoulder. Carefully, I take a step, pausing as the groaning floorboard does its damnedest to rat me out to my unsuspecting host family upstairs. I take a second step, heavier than usual quite naturally, with the second pair of feet standing on mine but it's one set of footfalls nonetheless and as long as that's all Mrs. Gilbraith hears, we're home free. The girl and I continue across the room in this fashion, both giggling under our breath. Me because it's amazing the lengths I'll go to for sex and her because this reminds her of dancing with her granddad at a wedding reception when she was eight. As we tumble quietly onto the mattress I wiggle my toes, the feeling returning to them as she wiggles out of her pants.

"Did I hurt your feet?" she whispers. I dismiss her concern with a wave.

"You only weigh about eight-and-a-half stone." (That's what they call one-hundred-and-twenty pounds over here.) "Keep your uniform on," I add. *Naked, she's just another girl. If I'm going to screw a cop, I'm going to screw a cop...*

A wise man once said, 'The slipperiest slopes are lined with lacy knickers.' He wasn't wrong. Within a week I've added a secretary and a masseuse to the roster, everyone taking turns walking on my feet and sneaking out the back door and no one knowing about each other and it's a mess, a dangerous mess. But at least I feel like me again.

"Did you like who you were?"

"Honestly, I'd never really thought about it."

"Didn't you feel guilty?"

"I would have felt guilty if I got caught."

"What about remorse for what you were doing while you were doing it?"

"What's the point if you're going to do it anyway? Besides, that's what the guilty box is for and there's a big-ass lock on that one."

"But why? Why didn't you just stop this behaviour?"

"Because I couldn't. I'd never been able to. So it was either compartmentalize or..."

"Or hate yourself?"

"Okay, easy there!"

"Did I misspeak?"

"It's just, I'm not a bad person."

"I know."

"I just... It wasn't about not being guilty. It was about not feeling guilty."

"Do you feel guilty now?"

"Of course."

"What happened to that big-ass lock of yours?"

"You tell me."

I LET THINGS FALL APART with the three girls before Christmas. The masseuse and the secretary take it in stride, (probably because they're slags and have other guys on the go). It's the pretty little policewoman who takes it the hardest and I feel badly for her because she's sweet but the local boys won't touch her with a barge pole because the badge is just too much for them. Their loss because she really is a sweet girl, not just a cop. That's just what she does.

HEATHROW'S A DIFFERENT PLACE WHEN you're just picking someone up. When you're not hauling half your life behind you on wheels, sore and sour and gummy-eyed and grumpy. It's pleasant, especially so right before Christmas. No one does Christmas quite like the English and no one does airports quite like Heathrow and nowhere is quite as exhilarating this time of year as International Arrivals: a busy, buzzing collision of tired smiles, hugs and happy tears. Mona's flight is right on schedule because a light dusting of blowing North Sea snow isn't going to deter a Boeing 727 and suddenly she's here; waving, wonderful, a familiar face in a sea of faces and just for a moment I wish I could just erase everything else and make this as perfect as it should be.

I heard once you can tell if someone's cheated by the way they kiss (it changes after the fact, apparently). Mona's mouth feels normal on mine: soft, warm, sincere. And I'm not sure how mine feels but I'm playing it safe, transitioning into a hug and grabbing her suitcase before she has time to notice if anything's different.

It's amazing how easily we fall back into our rhythm. There's no catching up or tentative small talk or anything. We just pick up where we left off (whenever and wherever that was) and our hands find each other's effortlessly and our fingers lace, and in that pristine moment I'm feeling about as content as I've ever felt. Mona stops me so we can take a photograph in front of the twinkling, two-story conical wireframe Christmas tree that soars up through the Terminal One atrium like something from Whoville. It takes three attempts. The first photo cuts half my face out of the frame and the second features an oblivious Romanian family in the background but the third is perfect; just me and Mona and the Christmas tree. *We look like a really happy couple. It's funny how photos can't capture bullshit or back-story.*

It's with some pride that I nonchalantly navigate the Tube and the trains and I'm pretty sure Mona notices how in stride I take everything now, even the teeming holiday crowds. But jetlag is a cruel mistress. By the time *Greater Anglia 2205* wheezes and hisses into Romford station, Mona's fast asleep on my shoulder. I look down at her and there's that feeling again. Something like tenderness couched in remorse. Either way, it weighs something. *I wish I could stop cheating on her.*

"Hey," I say quietly, gently shaking her shoulder. "We're here."

"IT'S CHRISTMAAAAAAAAAAAAAS!" CROWS COUSIN GAV, singing along to the tail-end of Slade's seminal 1973 holiday hit as he returns to the table with a fresh round of pints. Judging by the enthusiastic way that everyone in the pub roars along to the chorus, it's clear that this tune's more popular than Jingle Bells. Every other country in the world stopped writing Christmas carols a hundred years ago but not England. Each winter, a new crop of hopefuls climb the British pop charts and the good ones stick like glue, joining an ever-growing canon that includes the likes of WHAM!'s 'Last Christmas', Wizzard's 'I Wish it Could be Christmas Every Day' and Band Aid's 'Do They Know it's Christmas'. Like I said, no one does Christmas quite like the English.

Gav slides the tray onto the table, sloshing stout across the streaky surface. No one seems to care except Henry's girlfriend (an uptight skirt with an attitude that Brits call posh but Canadians call bitchy and aloof) and by the look of it she's a hit with absolutely no one. Mona on the other hand? She's as comfortable a fit as usual. She doesn't even try, which isn't to say that she doesn't make an effort, but more that she doesn't really need to. Mona's awesome and every-one loves her. She'd been a huge hit with Auntie Annie and Uncle Dom and now, cutting loose in the *Last Shamrock* (the most Irish of

London's Irish pubs) she was winning Gav's heart too, who despite his best efforts is fawning over her like a gangly, spastic child.

"There you are, my luv," he croons, sliding a pint of Guinness in front of Mona, who thinks he's harmless and lovely, despite Aunt Annie's earlier warning.

"Thanks, Gav!" she says, flashing that big, open smile she reserves for people she *really* likes.

"I wish you wouldn't smoke," complains Henry's girlfriend, giving Gav a withering stare. *Miserable cow.*

"And I wish the Hammers would pull themselves off the bottom of the table and start playing some quality football but we can't always get what we want, can we, mate?" replies Gav, exhaling with what can only be described as a *fuck-off* smile.

I'd first met Gav in the summer, remember. And summer-Gav was off-season-Gav but come September, he was showing his true colours, which happened to be claret and blue. Come December, he (like most other West Ham United supporters) was battling bouts of bitter pessimism about his underperforming East London club, expressing his angst with something between fierce love and fierce loathing. But that's what football looks like.

"What the hell's this?" I ask Henry, pinching and pulling the chest hair that's visible just above his v-neck.

"Shit!" exclaims my little brother. "That hurt, asshole!" Henry had never been a hairy guy and suddenly, he's sprouting chest hair like Magnum P.I. Coincidentally, he'd finally given Guinness a chance two weeks earlier. Just saying…

"I know this one!" he exclaims, shifting gears, his ears perking up as Shane MacGowan slurs through the second verse of 'Fairytale of New York'.

As the chorus swells, pints are raised aloft and drunk, Celtic voices roar with a deafening, festive cheer. I look over at Mona and her eyes are shining too, because I think she realizes that we're sharing something here that come-what-may, will go down as one hell of a memory. I don't think I ever loved her more than at that moment. I don't think I was ever prouder to be Irish, either.

"GODDAMMIT!" I EXCLAIM, SLAMMING MY hand against the front door.

Christmas had come and gone like it does, and New Year's Eve too and then Mona, and in the grey, heart-burned, hung over aftermath that is January, I'd lasted all of a week and a half before slipping back into my old ways. Maybe absence makes the heart grow fonder for some but like it or not, I seemed a slave to the school of: *out of sight, out of mind.*

I'd met this one at the local bar. Got off with her (that's what they call kissing) on the dance floor and heard myself inviting her back to my place before I had a chance to think about it. She wasn't even that pretty (despite the excessive makeup) and even less so under the unforgiving glare of my kitchen lights but I was on that old autopilot by now so there I was in nothing but my boxers, offering her a drink.

"I've got juice or water," I'd stated flatly.

"Milk," she replied. *Who drinks milk at 1:00am?* I was starting to wish I'd kept my jeans on.

"Cheers," she'd said, knocking back the glass of *Tesco Choice* two-percent like it was Champagne. "Now c'mere big boy…" I was horrified, rooted to the cold linoleum as she flounced towards me like an oversexed clown; all crimson lips and milk moustache and mascara-clotted eyelashes, and before I could react she was in my face, fuzzy-tongued and sour.

"I'm feeling a little ill," I'd told her, which suddenly wasn't a lie. I was in such a rush to jettison this mess, I threw on my shoes and walked her to her car in my boxers, watching with no small amount of relief as she drove away. That's when I realized I didn't have my house keys.

"Goddammit!" I repeat, instinctively checking my boxers again, despite their lack of pockets. When the deadpan 16-year-old Gilbraith girl *finally* opens the door, I'm shivering and swearing and feeling annoyingly guilty, even though I didn't even screw the Dairy Clown.

"What are you doing?" asks the kid.

"Oh just hanging out, you know," I reply sullenly, my tone as cold as the icy vapour billowing from my mouth. There are two kinds of 16-year-old girls: those who make a huge deal out of absolutely everything and those who don't give two shits about absolutely anything and thankfully, little Miss Gilbraith is of the latter variety. For now, I've maintained the illusion of the *lovely* Canadian boy with a girlfriend back home.

"FUCK." SOMETIMES THE WORD IS more than just an expletive; more than just filler, or punctuation or emphasis. Sometimes it sums up a situation, its implications, and the entire range of emotions attached to both. Those fucks aren't crass fucks. They're meaningful, eloquent and all encompassing fucks. This fuck was one of those.

"You alright, Doyle?" asks a fellow D-man as I peel myself from the sideboards and slowly skate off the ice, cradling my right arm in my left, wrestling with waves of nausea as my body tries to make sense of the white-hot pain searing through my shoulder.

"No," I grunt through gritted teeth. I must look like I mean it, judging by the concerned row of helmeted heads on the bench.

There's something awful about an empty locker room mid-game. It's like standing in an empty bus stop or on a deserted train station platform. It's an empty, hollow stillness. The feeling that you're not where you're supposed to be and everyone else is.

"Let's have a look then," says Terry Evans, the team doctor, who's trundling in behind me. Tel (as he's called) is a melancholy character at the best of times with eyes that slope down forlornly at the corners. When he talks, his words seem to come with great labour, on the shoulders of heavy sighs and sad, sidelong glances. The good thing about Tel? He always makes you feel like he's one sigh away from confirming a career-ending injury, which makes most of his actual prognoses seem pleasantly un-daunting by comparison. Not this one, though. "I'm sorry, mate," he says, slowly shaking his head after carefully examining my shoulder. "Separation. That's your season done, I'm afraid." With only eight weeks left of my one-year contract, he might as well just come out and say it. *That's England done, mate.*

Heathrow's a different place when you're hopped up on painkillers and heading for the departure lounge. It's a great, soulless glass exit door and no one's there to bid you farewell.

VANCOUVER HASN'T CHANGED A BIT. Mona hasn't changed a bit either, but that's a good thing. She can barely hide her excitement when she sees me, which makes it hard feeling sorry for myself for long. Especially as we come to a stop in the airport's pay parking lot.

"Are you kidding me?" I ask incredulously, as we stop in front of a black BMW 5-Series. *My favourite car in my favourite colour.* And judging by her grin, that's exactly why she bought it.

"You can drive it whenever you want. When your shoulder heals, of course," she adds, giving me a peck on the cheek before skipping around to the driver's side like a girl in love. Staring at that shiny machine, those wicked rims and tinted windows and midnight black paint job, I think I might be in love too. We never talked about me moving in. Never had the chat and the excited hug and the, *what a big step this is for us* bullshit. We just presumed, both of us. And we fell into it comfortably, like a routine we'd already rehearsed in our heads. Turns out, it's easy (which is a good sign because as far as I'm concerned, if it's right it's going to be easy, right?) We'd never talked about going to Hawaii either, but there it was one day when I came back from my appointment at the physio.

"Yep. Kauai," she says with the same grin that accompanied the BMW. "Twelve days." *I've always wanted to go to Hawaii. Somebody's gunning for the Girlfriend of the Year trophy.*

"How are we going to pay for this?" I ask, painfully aware that I'm not working yet, even if she is.

"Don't worry about it," replies Mona. And I don't. Mona's got a comfortable marketing job and enough credit to build a card castle, so yeah… Hawaii.

LIHUE AIRPORT IS A DIFFERENT place altogether. Low and lush and friendly smiles and diffused light filtering in. Heathrow loudly, proudly celebrates its status as an airport, but Lihue feels like it's doing its best to convince you that it's something entirely different. I'm not sure what exactly, but it makes you want to take a nap.

It's a matter of moments before this caramel skinned, full-lipped beauty approaches, draping a heady bouquet of fake-looking flowers around my neck.

"Aloha," she says, all shiny white teeth and big brown eyes and just for a moment, I wonder how much of a welcome I could wrangle out of her.

"What?" asks Mona, as we roll our suitcases across the concourse.

"I like Hawaii," I grin, tugging on the flora around my neck. "Not here five minutes and I've already been laid." Mona rolls her eyes.

"Original," she says.

It's a chest-clearing cough, but it sounds more like *yark!* Rubbing the salt from my eyes, I get my bearings. The small bikini-clad figure of Mona waves from the beach. She's a lot further to the left than she was half-an-hour ago when I struck out into the waves, slapping along in my flippers with the naïve confidence of a mainlander. *Good,* I think. *She's probably too far away to see how badly the Pacific Ocean just handed me my own ass.* The rental boogie board gently taps my leg as it glides up on the wash; my faithful companion on a tether that's lashed to my wrist with Velcro. The molded Styrofoam-fiberglass seems sea-worthy enough and I can't figure out why it should be any different with me on it but as yet, I haven't resembled anything close to the *GoHawaii* promo video.

"You're fighting it, bra," says a small voice at my side. This 12-year-old kid on his own board washes up alongside me with maddening ease. Pulling himself up, he flashes an open, easy smile, which I return once I realize he's sincere, not snotty.

"Am I?" I reply.

"Yeah, bra!" nods the kid emphatically. "That's why you're getting axed out there. It's the ocean, bra. Respect it and you'll be boss."

"Boss?" I reply faintly, my throat still itching with saltwater.

"Boss," he replies. "Bitchin. Primo. Rad. Excellent."

"Ah," I reply, feeling more like a mainlander than ever. "And how do I become boss, exactly?"

"Keep your body higher up the board, bra. Like this," he replies, demonstrating in four inches of water. "And start kicking before the wave."

"Thanks, bra," I reply, test-driving the local lingo as I turn and head back into the surf, but my inquisitive little friend isn't quite done yet.

"So, what do you do?" he asks, paddling alongside me.

"I'm a hockey player," I reply, a statement which effectively turns his eyes into round, brown saucers.

"No shit!" he says excitedly. "I love hockey, bra. San Jose Sharks, all the way! Who you play for?"

"The Romford Chieftains," I reply, because saying I'm between teams sounds alarmingly similar to when unemployed losers say they're between jobs.

"They in the NHL?" asks my excited inquisitor, and God, I wish I could say yes and just for a second that familiar black cloud passes in front of the Hawaiian sun: the one that reminds me that I never played in the NHL and never will. It's a small cloud now, but it still shows up occasionally and even small clouds can cast shade, trust me.

"You know England?" I ask.

"Sure," replies the kid.

"It's like the NHL for England."

"Sweet," he replies enthusiastically, looking at me with a new admiration, and suddenly, the little cloud passes and it's sunny again. "I wish I could skate."

"I wish I could boogie board," I reply. By now, we're quite a way from the shore, further than I'd ventured before and the swells are large and rolling and gentle.

"It's easy," says the kid, positioning his board so it faces back at the beach. Patiently, he waits as I follow suit. "Ready?" he asks. I nod, not entirely sure what to expect. "Move up your board a little bit," he suggests, which I do.

"What now?" I ask.

"Now, we wait," he replies. "Next set's rolling in shortly." *Waiting. I hate fucking waiting.* I glance over at the kid curiously. He's got this serene look on his face as he gazes across the water, chin resting on his hands and there's a look in his eye that for a moment makes me wonder if I'm missing something and that somehow, he's got it all figured out.

"That's gnarly, bra," he says almost sleepily.

"Huh?" I reply.

"You're a hockey player. SO gnarly." I look up at the impossibly blue sky, across the rolling, rollicking swells, at the strip of white beach in the distance, at the pink dot that is Mona.

"Yeah, I guess it is," I reply. Suddenly, the kid's nose twitches like he smells something; quickly, he glances over his shoulder.

"Okay, here we go," he says, and suddenly I'm feeling this nervous excitement like I'm ten again. I follow his gaze. Slowly, the ocean behind us begins rising and the ocean in front of us begins dropping like someone tipping a glass and we're in it. "Paddle!" he yells and goddamn, I do! Arms are sawing and legs are kicking and suddenly, it's like a massive hand just lifts us and throws us and I'm roaring along, skipping along the water like a stone, tearing along this wave so fast, I have to white-knuckle the fiberglass lip just to stay on.

"Yeeeeeeaaaah!" comes a long, loud yell rising above the roar of the crashing surf and it's only when I'm staggering out of the white foam backwash that I realize it's me. My pint-sized instructor's beaming ear-to-ear as he wades over for a high-five.

"I'm doing that again!" I state emphatically.

"Wait," he says, as he runs up the beach, grabbing something from (presumably) his mother's purse before running back.

"Here," he says, handing me a felt-tipped marker and holding out his boogie board. "You gotta sign my board, bra. My friends will be crazy jealous."

I like to imagine that somewhere on the North Shore of Kauai today, there's a boogie board out there waiting for a wave, with Danny Boy Doyle scrawled across the nose.

"You enjoyed Hawaii?"

"Oh yeah. Waves, volcanoes, luaus... It was something else. The condo was a bit of a joke, though. No beachfront to speak of, just rocks, gulls, and a few old men with metal detectors but we drove

Matt McCoy

over to the South Side and scammed towels from the fancy hotels."

"I don't understand."

"Back then, a hotel towel was as good as an all-inclusive wristband. We spent most of our time sipping illicit Mai Tais beside pools we had no business enjoying. That's another thing I loved about Mona. She was always up for it."

"Not afraid to have a craic?"

"There you go! Exactly."

"YOU OKAY?" I ASK FROM the couch.

"Yeah," replies Mona from the kitchen table. When Mona's stressed, she gets quiet and when she's paying the bills, she gets stressed. Since Hawaii, things had been a bit quieter around here. I wasn't sure what was going on with her, things used to be so easy. Ring... Ring... Ring...

"I'll get it," I offer, glad for anything to break the stillness. Mona doesn't even look up from her bills. Sighing, I pick up the phone. "Hello?"

It's not a long call but as I hang up, I'm realizing I might have a solution to Mona's debt doldrums.

"Who was that?" she asks.

"My agent," I reply, pulling up chair at the table. Mona takes a deep breath as she takes off her reading glasses. *Poor girl, she knows exactly what that usually means.*

"And?" she asks tiredly, rubbing her eyes.

"The Milan deal fell through. Henry's not going there now either, so no huge loss."

"Oh," she says; one simple syllable filled with so much hope.

"But there's a team in Germany..."

"Oh." This time the word sounds hollow and flat, like something empty hitting the floor. Leaning forward, I grasp her hands.

"Mona?"

"Yeah?" she replies in a small voice, avoiding my gaze.

"Look at me," I say quietly. If a picture's worth a thousand words, an expression's worth a million because there's something in those shiny, pleading eyes and that quivering bottom lip, something that says everything she's felt since business school. Everything she's never truly admitted. Things that even the car and the trip and the years of dogged, tolerant friendship have never actually articulated, not until now. And somehow, she's said it all without saying anything. In that moment, at that kitchen table, I tell her something and when I say it, I mean it more than anything I've said in my entire life. "I'm tired of this long-distance garbage—seeing each other on holidays. It's bullshit. This contract, it's good money. I could look after us. You wouldn't even need to work. Mona, I want you to come with me." She's silent for a moment before answering.

"Okay." That's all she says.

"Mona came to Germany with you?"

"Not immediately. Marketing jobs require a bit more than two week's notice. I left in August and she followed me out two months later."

"What happened to your brother after the Milan deal fell through?"

"He was still dating the cold chick back in England."

"They were getting pretty serious?"

"Serious enough for him to sign a contract with a team in Guilford."

"And you chose Germany."

"I chose Germany. Their First Division. One of the best leagues in Europe and definitely the best league I'd ever played in."

BAD NAUHEIM LIES ON THE banks of the Moselle, in a valley between low vine-laden sandstone hills, near the Luxembourg border. If you've seen a Rhineland wine country postcard, you're getting the idea. It's an old city. The oldest in the country, allegedly, and its town centre is so perfectly picturesque, the buildings' facades so quaint and fascinatingly medieval, it looked like something off of a Hollywood movie lot. Bad Nauheim has a population of one hundred thousand. One hundred and two if you count Mona and me.

Bad Nauheim also has a First Division hockey team: The Lions. And on the heels of my relatively successful stint with the Rungsted Tigers, I figure keeping with the cat theme might be a good omen

for my fur-lined European career. Like most teams on this conti-
nent, the Lions are a mixed-bag of up-and-comers and post-glory
near-retirees; some local boys, a couple of Albertans, an ex-Montreal
Canadien, an ex-Toronto Maple Leaf and the goalie, an ex-Detroit
Redwing who never seems to tire of reminding everyone that he
used to play in the NHL. *Like anyone gives two shits, pal.*

Our coach is an old Soviet relic named Victor Something-ov who
allegedly got the job thanks to his connections with the Russian
mob. The guy smells like vodka and sounds like a Slavonic curler,
always yelling, *Hustle hard! Hustle hard!* because that's pretty much all
the English he knows. Between him, the Anglo-Germanic player
roster and the French guys who are running the organization, things
make about as much sense as a United Nations summit most of
the time. Regardless, the hockey's good. Turns out that the rink's as
unique as the team: a circus tent sort of scenario with a roof but
no sides. On the downside, we often have blowing rain and snow
to contend with but it beats choking on the cigarette fumes. Did I
mention that everyone in Germany smokes? Everyone.

I have mixed feelings about my new contract. On one hand, I'm
a 27-year-old veteran coming in with a clean slate and an impressive
history. On the other, I'm in a new country with a new language,
new system, new teammates, no alliances, a Bratva affiliate for a
coach and a bunch of Monsieurs running the show.

Mona and I have an apartment downtown, in the heart of the
city, in a neighbourhood that looks like a Playmobil village. The
roads are barely a lane wide and the cars (albeit tiny) are parked
bumper-to-bumper along every cobbled curb, making walking the
fastest form of transportation for anyone who's actually serious
about getting from A to B. On the upside, our apartment's pretty
large. Two bedrooms, in fact, which is exactly twice as many as we
need; but hey, we'll take it.

"What the hell?" I yell, racing into the kitchen expecting to find
Mona in the middle of a home invasion. Instead, she's standing on a
chair, white as a ghost, gesticulating at the fridge like it's just grabbed
her ass.

"Underneath," she manages to gasp. "It was huge!" Another

shriek as the offending party scuttles out from beneath the appliance like it's facing off with me mid-linoleum. "Oh, God," moans Mona, as it crunches under my foot. "Do you think there are more of them?"

"Doubt it," I say nonchalantly, helping her down from the chair. *Of course there's more. They might be German cockroaches but they're still cockroaches. They're probably goose-stepping through the walls as we speak.*

The sightings become a daily occurrence but something I'm willing to work around (it's just cockroaches) but Mona's on chairs more than she's on solid ground and clearly one or two screams away from a psychotic break. It's early December when I take it up with the team staff and those damned French guys, they look at each other with this guilty look like they knew all along and it's only a matter of weeks before we're being relocated.

"It feels Christmasy," I offer.

"It's December twenty-second. Everything feels Christmasy," replies Mona flatly, as we stand hand-in-hand staring at our new home. The house (if you can call it that) is in the middle of a muddy pasture. The driveway is nothing but two tire ruts running through the grass. And to add insult to injury, it's taken the better part of an hour to get here from Cockroach Haus.

"Are we even in Bad Nauheim anymore?" asks Mona as we trudge towards the hovel.

"Ask her," I suggest, gesturing to the cow, who placidly blinks at us for lack of something better to do.

"Oh no!" whispers Mona. We're three handfuls of popcorn in when it happens, and not even through the opening credits. It's just one of those unlucky sloshes: the kind that happens in those fishbowl wineglasses. The kind that always ends up on a white blouse or a new book or in this case, a beige couch.

"*Ich habe durst,*" says the little blond boy, rubbing his eyes as he wanders from his bedroom.

"It's okay, Lucas. Go back to bed," says Mona, leading the little fella out of the living room and away from the scene of the crime.

I trace the burgundy stain with my finger, knowing full well that it's there to stay. *Fucked. Completely fucked.* I was going to have to buy Heinrich a new couch. This wasn't going to bode well for Mona, either. The Lions' WAGS (wives and girlfriends) were an insulated, exclusive little bunch. Babysitting for Heinrich and Angela was a step in the right direction socially speaking. Dousing their couch in Merlot, on the other hand, was not.

"I'm so sorry," mumbles Mona, returning from the kid's bedroom. I throw an arm over her shoulder.

"Shit happens?" I suggest.

Poor Mona. Recently, the shit that had been happening had been happening with distressing regularity. The farmhouse (which as it turns out, was nearly in Luxembourg) was an unmitigated disaster: leaky roof, drafty and worst of all, mice infested (Merry-fucking-Christmas). They were tiny, harmless Disney mice of course, but they may as well have been rabies-infested New York sewer rats, judging by her reaction. We shared the place with two cats too: tenured tenants who clearly didn't give two shits about Mona's mild dander allergy nor (ironically) about mice, although they did seem to have a thing for cheese, judging by the mangled wedge of Cambozola on the counter.

All things considered, it's not surprising that Mona spent so much time in the city. But it wasn't easy for her, switching gears from marketing exec to hockey mistress. There are only so many cathedrals and museums you can see, only so many cafes you can sip coffee at, before boredom sets in. And there's only so long you can live somewhere and not speak the language before loneliness sets in. And there's no consoling someone who is bored and lonely, especially when they're homesick.

The day that her purse is stolen on a cathedral tour is the day it all comes to a head and not because of the three hundred Deutsche Marks. Mona's done. Exhausted. At the end of her rope. *Fertig*, as they say over here.

Things hadn't been exactly a cakewalk for me either. Hockey's a double-edged sword. It's a great lifestyle if you're doing well but a bad streak, even a small one, can see you packing your bags just as easily. You're only as good as your last game. That's hockey. That's hockey anywhere, really. Even though I'm on form, I'm in my mid twenties, now. I'm not healing like a teenager anymore.

At first, Mona and I would spend our Mondays sightseeing, even taking excursions to Bruges and Brussels and Paris. But as the season took its toll, my days off turned into recovery days, lying on the couch buried in icepacks. When the season (and my contract) ends, it's not a minute too soon because I'm sure Mona wouldn't have lasted another week.

"How did you do?"

"We finished fourth overall. Made the Playoffs. Had an awesome run in the first round but fizzled in Game 7. Regardless, I put in a great performance and they were eager to re-sign me for the following season."

"And then you returned to Canada?"

"No, not immediately. We went to England for a week. Saw Aunt Annie and Uncle Dom and Gav, of course. But there was nothing pressing in Vancouver and I wanted to do something nice for Mona, for everything, you know? Especially since Germany had turned out to be such a pile of scheissen. I left her with Gav for the day (safer than it sounds) and hit High Street looking for a travel agency."

"What's the European equivalent to Hawaii?" I ask the *Lunn Poly* agent, a large girl in an ill-fitting red company suit jacket.

"Let's see," she says, tapping the computer keys so rapidly, I wonder if she's actually typing anything or faking it for my benefit.

"Tenerife," she announces, clearly pleased with herself.

"Alright," I reply. "I'll book two at your best all-inclusive."

"Yeah, no. Sorryyyyyy," she offers, drawing out the last word so it sounds like an air raid siren.

"Huh?" I reply.

"All booked." She laments shaking her head.

"What about Ibiza?" Another flurry of keys.

"Booked."

"Barcelona?"

"Booked."

"Santorini?"

"Sorryyyyyy." *Jesus Christ, is she serious?* Leaning forward, I enunciate slowly, clearly, trying to mask my frustration.

"Look, I understand that it's June but I just want to take my girlfriend somewhere warm and sunny. Whatever you've got." A final flurry of keystrokes.

"Ooh, here we go," she says, spinning the computer monitor around so I can see the screen.

"Alright! Where are you sending us?" I ask. A grin spreads across the girl's face.

"Tunisia!"

ALLAHU AKBAR, ALLAHU AKBAR, ALLAHU AKBAR, Allahu Akbar…

At first the sound is a part of my dream: an unfamiliar drone that slowly cuts through my fitful, sweaty slumber.

Ash-hadu alla ilaha illallah, Ash-hadu alla ilaha illallah…

I'm awake now, but the sound continues, staccato and distant but strangely close, like someone talking through a megaphone. Grabbing my pillow, I crush it over my head, trying to smother myself back into the dream I was so rudely awoken from.

Ash-hadu anna Muhammadar Rasulullah…

"Jesus Christ!" I exclaim, rolling over in exasperation.

"He's got nothing to do with it, sweetie," says Mona, yawning.

"What is it?" I ask.

"It's the Muslim call to prayer," she replies, stretching like a cat. "Must be a mosque nearby."

"I don't want to pray," I grumble.

Ash-hadu anna Muhammadar Rasulullah…

"Then go back to sleep?" suggests my ever-pragmatic girlfriend. But it's too late for that. The room's uncomfortably chilly (thanks to the over-enthusiastic air conditioning) and my bladder's bursting for a piss, (thanks to the two litres of water I necked the night prior).

Hayya alassalah, Hayya alassalah…

Suddenly, there's a second sound: a screeching, crowing racket that counterpoints the drone from the minaret like some strange exotic duet. *A rooster? Are you fucking kidding me?* Welcome to North Africa, I guess.

We're staying at the Delphin Habib, a gleaming white Moorish-themed resort in Monastir, a city in the Sahel area of Tunisia's central Mediterranean coast. Day one was spent on the private beach, which really could have been anywhere hot. I'd spent the better part of the afternoon wading around in the water while my shoulders burnt, ruefully staring out to sea and wondering if you could see Sicily on a clear day. *Should have gone to Italy, dammit.* Today was going to be different, though. Today, we were venturing outside the compound.

"YOU WILL LOVE IT, MY friends," grins Youssef, flashing a crooked mess of yellow teeth. Youssef is the hotel's self-styled gardener/ cook/masseuse, although how qualified he is for any of these positions is anyone's guess. His directions to Forte El Ribat, seem simple enough though, and blistering heat aside, I'm actually pretty stoked to see some castle ruins.

The route takes us through the city proper and that's when reality slaps you in the face, because it's not just glimmering, gorgeous oasis-like, it's real life too. We pass a beggar (clearly on the same dental plan as Youssef) who sits on the side of the road, arms outstretched, palms up, begging alongside his three-legged mutt.

"Please!" he calls in awful English, as we pass. "Hungry!"

Why don't you eat the rest of your dog?, I think, immediately feeling guilty for even thinking it then immediately finding the thought horrifically funny then immediately feeling guilty for finding it funny, which only makes me want to giggle more. *God, I've got to get out of this heat…* According to the New York Times, Tunisia is known for its golden beaches, sunny weather and affordable luxuries. Apparently, it's also known for its poverty and pissy stench, but they don't tell you that, do they? But it is a beautiful country in its own right. And the castle ruins are amazing. And the moon that night is, bar none, the biggest moon I've ever seen.

But Tunisia's not all kebabs and shits and giggles. I'm having some issues with Bad Nauheim. The Lions, it turns out, are as broke as the guy with the tripod dog and they're doing their best to screw me out of my last month's salary. That's ninety-five hundred bucks that I'm not about to walk away from and if they think they can mess with Danny Boy Doyle, they've got a great big Canadian surprise coming.

"Not a fucking chance," I say adamantly into the hotel phone. "You pay up, *then* I'll come back and we can talk about next season," which is a load of horseshit, because Mona and I meant it when we said *auf wiedersehen* to Germany.

"Did they pay up?"

"Eventually, but I had to sue them to get it. Turns out they were stiffing everyone on paycheques. The only way they could clear their debt was to drop from Tier A to Tier B."

"And they did?"

"And they did. And good riddance."

"And you and Mona returned to Canada?"

"Yeah. Back in cockroach-free, mice-free, beautiful Vancouver."

"Wow. You should work for Tourism British Columbia."

chapter 10

"How's everything?"

"You always say that."

"I do?"

"Yeah. Or 'How are things?' but there aren't things. There used to be things but now there's only one thing. It's there when I wake up and there when I go to bed and it's right there waiting underneath everything else, all day, every day. Shaving in the morning (your daughter has cancer), meeting with a client (your daughter has cancer), driving home (your daughter has cancer), watching the game (your daughter has cancer, your daughter has cancer, your daughter has cancer)…"

"How is she?"

"By the time we're done with this awful shit, she'll have been exposed to ARA-C, Cyclophosphamide at a dose of 1 gram/m2, Dexamethasone, L-Asparaginase, Methotrexate, Vincristine, 6MP, 6TG and Doxorubicin for a total does of 75mg/m2. She also received intrathecal chemotherapy with Methotrexate on sixteen separate occasions. She's been jabbed, probed, poked, cut open…"

"How are you?"

"How do you think I am? Do you know what it's like waking up in the night hearing her sobs, rubbing her back as the chemicals rip through her body as she retches up her poor little guts and all you want to do is hold her hair back and tell her it's going to be okay; only all her hair's fallen out and you don't know if everything's going to be okay at all. You don't know anything because you're not a

doctor. You're just a desperate, useless man."

"There's no shame in crying, you know."

"I'm not crying."

"Here. Use the serviette."

"Thanks."

"It's not fair, is it?"

"No, it's not fair! She's just a little girl!"

WE'VE BEEN BACK IN VANCOUVER three months and officially speaking, Mona and I have been together for a year. I'm not certain of the exact date but she assures me it's today, which works out beautifully since we're out for dinner anyway. The German ordeal had knocked Mona sideways and I wanted her to be happy; after all she'd put up with a lot of shit from me. Somewhere in Europe, she'd stopped being Mona: the independent marketing maven and became Mona: Danny's de facto housewife/tourist/girlfriend. Of course, it didn't help that she'd been ringside for my previous dalliances as far back as business school.

"What's the matter with your lasagna?" she finally asks.

"Nothing. Why?"

"You've been pushing it around your plate for ten minutes."

"Oh."

"You look sullen."

"Pensive," I correct. Because I'm taking stock and realizing that this is the first proper adult relationship I've had and all said-and-done, it's actually going pretty well. Not fireworks maybe, but maybe that's the point. Well, if I'm being honest, I'd been feeling her insecurity sneaking in for a while and somewhere in the back of my mind, I figure that getting engaged would kill the pesky paranoia too. Whatever the case, Mona's folks love me and I love her and we really are best friends and seeing as it's our anniversary, what the hell am I waiting for?

"Let's get married," I announce. Mona's forkful of manicotti hangs suspended between her plate and her mouth.

"Okay," she says quietly. "Now eat your pasta."

And just like that, we're engaged.

"I WAS OUT WITH THE boys! Seriously, call them if you want!" I declare defiantly, standing my ground in the kitchen. My mouth is dry and there's this awful bitter taste on my tongue but that's not from the booze. I get like that when we fight.

Six months into this engagement thing, I'm hitting a brick wall and if history has taught me anything (thanks, Lucy), it's that nuptial promises are more like iodine than *Band Aids*: they have a way of cleaning things out, not covering them up. Stepping into the ring is proving harder than she'd anticipated, even if I have promised her the title.

"I know what you're like!" she snaps. "I know how you are with other women."

"Jesus, Mona, I'm not cheating on you!" I repeat, swaying slightly and wishing I'd maybe said no to that last shot of Jameson or maybe even the last two or three. The whiskey's fueling my self-righteous indignation though because I've been true-blue since Deutschland.

"Well, I know you're at least thinking about it." *Of course I'm thinking about it. I'm a guy. Doesn't mean I'm doing it.*

But becoming my fiancée has only raised the stakes, apparently. The one and only thing that makes Mona and I work is how effortless she makes everything. I'm supposed to be the storm and she's supposed to be the calm before it (and after it, for that matter) and when she takes that away, we have nothing but a big fucking tempest. Six months into the engagement, I'm feeling cornered. Trapped. Again.

I'll never forget the look on her face when I broke up with her. Hate and hurt and disbelief. We never would have lasted, anyway.

Danny 0, Mona 0

"That was it?"

"It's not as callous as it sounds. We fought and talked and talked and fought for another couple of weeks, but that was the night I knew we were done."

"It never crossed your mind to make it work?"

"Sure, but how could it? Marry your best friend? That's bullshit. Marry someone who's not and if you're lucky, they'll become your best friend, but not the other way around."

"This must have been a difficult time. You were living together, after all."

"It was. And sad. I missed what we used to be."

AFTER THE BREAK-UP, I MOVE into my aunt's place. Remember the twin aunts? One of them married a dentist. They still live in Prince Peaks but have an apartment in Vancouver, which works out well for me. It's a few stories up with a glamourous view of the adjoining high rise apartments and a *peek-a-boo* view of the North Shore, which is real estate agent jargon for, *if you crane your neck far enough around the balcony, you can see about five inches of nondescript green shit which is allegedly a mountain.* But it does have a stationary bike, so that's something. I should be happy here but I'm not. I'm contract-less and down a best friend, which equates to bored. Bored and lonely. And broke.

Timing's everything though, because I'm barely three days into feeling sorry for myself when the phone rings.

"You free tomorrow morning?" asks my agent.

"Dunno," I say, dripping with sweat as I pedal into my second hour, for lack of something better to do.

"Be at the Richmond Ice Centre at nine."

"If you think I'm going to try out for some local Old Timers' team…" I start in hotly.

"Cool your jets, rock star," he soothes. "This isn't a tryout. It's an audition. Bring your gear."

If I was curious then, I'm even more curious now, pushing through the double doors of the R.I.C. The place is packed with fellas (all players presumably) and the only thing that outnumbers hockey haircuts is the Nagano 1998 Winter Olympics logo which is splashed everywhere like some kind of prolapsed rainbow asshole. The atmosphere in the locker room is different too: cramped and crowded but without the cagey coolness that comes with tryouts or the quiet intensity of pregame nerves. This feels more like some kind of social: guys laughing, clapping each other on the back, casually catching up and buckling on pads and generally not taking themselves too seriously. I'm still not entirely sure what this is all about but at least I'm doing it with some familiar faces.

"Hello, hello, hello!" begins a diminutive man with a clipboard, who breezes into the locker room like a theatre director followed by an assistant lugging a cardboard box that's almost as tall as he is. "Welcome to the VISA commercial audition! Today, you'll be playing real Olympic hockey players. Won't that be exciting?" *Fuck you, Peter Pan.* There's a moment of confusion for some of the dimmer stars in the room who think we're actually playing *against* Olympians, not playing (acting as) them, but that's soon sorted as the assistant cracks open the box and pulls out national team jersey after national team jersey. German, Russian, Canadian, Switzerland, the whole lot. One at a time, he hands them off to Peter Pan, who tosses them to each of us.

"German for you, Ukraine for you, Canada for you…" I'm staring ruefully at the guy with the Team Canada jersey, recalling how close I came to donning something similar with Team Pacific all those years back, when the odd little man-boy clocks me. "Well hello, bright-eyes! I think you'll make a beautiful Belarussian." I catch the jersey on my chest. *Belarus? Seriously?* I'm about ready to walk out when he continues. "There's one hundred of you here today but only sixteen will make the cut. From those sixteen we'll be picking eight for our Winter Olympics commercial which will be broadcast all over North America." *That's more like it! Shitty odds, high competition and notoriety at stake. I speak that language. Maybe I'll stick around…*

"What do we have to do?" asks a gruff voice from the back of the room.

"Well, manly hockey stuff, silly!" replies the little prick, hands on his hips. "Now, we're going to do this alphabetically." There's a general exodus of shuffling skates as he continues in a shrill voice. "I need Austria through Estonia on Rink 1, France through Japan on Rink 2, Kazakhstan through Poland on Rink 3 and Romania through Yugoslavia on Rink 4…"

Apparently, *manly hockey stuff* consists of cross checking each other because that's exactly what we do. All day for twelve hours. And since I make the cut, that's what we do for two more days too. Take after take after take, and by the end of it I'm battered and bored and my jersey just stinks (no laundry money in the production budget, I guess) but I make the commercial. Forget fifteen minutes of fame. I get approximately two seconds. But it's seven thousand bucks. And everyone sees it. I mean everyone.

"You must have been elated after the commercial."

"Not really. Everyone knew about it but you could tell by the nods and smiles that they wouldn't have recognized me if I hadn't pointed it out."

"But the money was a nice bonus, I imagine."

"The money was a one-off. It sorted me out for the short-term, but Vancouver's a pricey place to hang your hat, even when you're house-sitting an aunt's empty condo. Thank God that the Landsdowne Country Club came along when it did."

"The Landsdowne Country Club?"

LANDSDOWNE IS A PRESTIGIOUS COUNTRY club in West Vancouver: forty-two acres of gorgeous British Properties mountainside looking down its nose at the city below. A home away from home where the privileged set meet, dine, socialize, and otherwise frolic. Included in this expansive award-winning facility is an ice rink with scheduled hockey lessons. Right now they're down an instructor, but by the end of summer, they're not.

Brooke…

I meet Brooke shortly after starting at Landsdowne. She's my de facto boss since she's running the entire hockey program which doesn't officially put her in charge of me *per se*, but definitely gives her a general type of seniority, which doesn't sit right with me from Day One. Apparently, I don't sit right with her either. The hockey community's a pretty tightly knit bunch and I know a lot of these guys already so the reception from the boys is a warm one. According to her, there's a level of humility with which you're supposed to begin a new job and I'm displaying zero. All she sees is a cocky guy who needs to be brought down a few notches. Whatever. I'm a professional hockey player and she should be glad to have me. But she's not, apparently, and it really bothers me how much that bothers me. No girl, I mean, *no girl* has ever not been at least a little interested in me. This is seriously getting to me.

Brooke's stunning, and I don't mean Nicola-pretty or Astrid-innocent or hot-mess-Lucy or down-home-Mona-cute. I mean quite literally stunning. She's the kind of girl that leaves you tongue-tied and weak-kneed and flushed and that's just when she walks by. She's flawless, with killer curves and shiny chestnut hair and Eastern European eyes. And she's sweet too (to everyone else at least) and she loves hockey. It's demoralizing how high a girl like Brooke sets the bar because you either get to be with her or you get to spend the rest of your life wishing you were and comparing every other poor girl to an ideal that you'll never attain. That's Brooke. Stunning. Devastatingly so. The whole package. And so far, she's not buying the Danny Boy show at all.

"I'm pretty sure we pay you until noon," she had observed coldly at eleven-thirty at the start of Week Three as I swaggered through the Landsdowne offices, my hair still wet from the showers.

"See this?" I say, pulling a paycheque from my pocket, thrusting it in her face and pointing at the name scrawled across the bottom. "I'm pretty sure it's not yours. When it is, you can start telling me what to do. Got it?" *What the hell, lady. I'm a pro hockey player.*

I'm not sure whether it's because no one's ever spoken to her like that before—because she's just a really sweet girl that can see the good in every obnoxious asshole—but things get tentatively warmer after that. Over the next couple of weeks I arrive at the club early (so I can get my daily workout in) and coincidentally, she starts arriving early too (so she can catch up on her paperwork) but we both know that's a crock. If this was a middle school dance, we'd be at arms-length, elbows locked, hands firmly planted on shoulders, eyes awkwardly diverted. But that still qualifies as dancing…

"You bringing your girlfriend tonight, Doyle?" asks Richard Didier after work one day. Dickie Diddler (as everyone calls him) is the head honcho at Landsdowne. He's a large-framed live wire of a guy, in his fifties with a dark tan, a huge smile and an even bigger personality. You know those forever-young types who still manage to pull off a lifestyle the rest of us fondly call our twenties? That was Dickie. No one was going to tell him the glory days were over, no way. Dickie had lost three fingers on his right hand in a car accident years earlier. Left them in a neat row in the ashtray apparently, which made it next to impossible for him to hold a stick, which sadly spelled an early end to his professional ice hockey career even though he was easily good enough for the big leagues. *Fuck it,* he'd often say after a few drinks. *Still got enough digits to hold a beer.*

"Oh, we broke up a while back," I reply, glancing over at Brooke. I'm sure I can see her stiffen at her desk as she stares at her monitor with way more concentration than her job demands, and I swear some pink has crept into her cheeks.

"Excellent!" replies Dickie. "You can be my wingman." *What the hell, man. Aren't you married?* Tonight's the Landsdowne office party at Yaletown Brewpub, a steak and craft beer favourite just one block away from Lucy's bitchy friend, Emily, and her posh apartment and her Mercedes. I steal a look at Brooke and all that drama seems so long ago and unimportant now.

This is getting ridiculous, I think as Brooke and I make eye contact down the long table for the hundredth time that night. We've been doing this all evening—over popcorn shrimp and champagne, over steak and Caesar salad and pale ale—no matter how much I stare, I just can't stop because she looks intoxicating. Dickie, on the other hand? He's just looking intoxicated.

"Doyle!" he hollers as the plates are being cleared away and the alcohol begins working its charms and everyone starts playing musical chairs. "C'mere Doyle, this is where all the babes are!" And he's not wrong. I'm just not sure Brooke and her friend Lila appreciate the sentiment as much coming from a man their dads' age.

"Hey," I nod, sliding into the chair next to Brooke, with a look that says, *Dickie, class act, right?* Brooke smiles a smile back that says, *Oh my God, I know!* and a pleasant little flutter in my gut tells me that we just bonded a little more.

"So, Lila," continues Dickie, undaunted by something as irrelevant as a thirty-year age gap. "What do you like in a guy? *Probably someone who didn't start dating during the Nixon administration,* I think.

"Um... I don't know," falters the poor girl, which gives me all the opportunity I need.

"What about you?" I ask, rounding on Brooke. "What do you like in a guy?" Brooke bites her bottom lip as she looks at me, which almost makes me forget the question all together.

"Oh, let's see. I like tall guys, dark hair preferably... they've got to play hockey, of course. Oh, and have a tattoo or two."

"So you like me?" I ask squarely. For a moment, Brooke's on her heels, but she recovers with admirable speed. *I guess a girl who looks like that knows how to handle a come-on.*

"You don't have a tattoo," she responds coolly, less as a statement and more as a challenge. I stand up and I swear we don't break eye contact as I unbuckle my belt and yank down my jeans. Never have I been so proud of the pointy-headed little ginger-haired Leprechaun glaring up from my thigh. "I stand corrected," she replies quietly, looking up at me with those heart-stopping, Eastern European eyes. *Game over.*

Alcohol's one hell of a social lubricant. By the time the bill arrives, I've dropped the macho bullshit and Brooke's dropped her guard and Lila's dropping hints that she's *heard all about me* (which can't be a bad thing coming from a best friend) and I can't remember when dropping my pants has ever been this good an ice-breaker.

"Where we going now?" asks Dickie, signing the entire table's credit card slip with a flourish.

"The Roxy?" suggests Brooke.

"Excellent!" declares Dickie, glasses rattling as he bangs the table for emphasis. "I haven't been to the Roxy in weeks!" which is amazing in itself since most guys his age haven't been to the Roxy in decades.

"He's serious?" asks Brooke quietly.

"Oh yeah," I reply. "Dickie's got an extra gear. Just watch."

Dickie Diddler doesn't just have an extra gear. He has nitrous tanks too, apparently. And connections out the wazzoo, judging by the way the line outside the Roxy parts like the Red Sea when we arrive. The rest of the evening is a blur of shots and drinks and sweaty high-fives and yelling indecipherable words in each others' ears and by the time the lights go up, we're all unapologetically hammered.

"Hey!" says Dickie as the last few of us who are still standing cluster on the Granville Street curb. "You got a smoke?"

"I don't smoke, Dickie and neither do you," I reply patiently. The big man nods, his brow furrowing deeply until he finds another thought in his Cognac-induced fog.

"Hey!" he starts again. "You wanna take 'em back to my place for a sauna?"

"Who?" I ask. Dickie points a completely non-subtle finger at Brooke and Lila, who stand only feet away.

"Don't you have a wife?" I ask.

"She's visiting her sister in Halifax. The cow!" His last statement is laced with such unbridled venom, it's clear that *being married* tops the list of his marital complaints.

"We're going to grab a cab," says Brooke, gently rubbing the back of Lila, who looks like her last two shots of Cuervo may have been a bad idea.

"Yeah, no problem," I say with what I hope sounds more like compassion and less like disappointment. "See you on Monday." *Shit-fuck-shit-goddamned-mother...*

"You wanna go pick up some chicks?" asks Dickie, as I watch Brooke and Lila's cab disappear in a sea of other cabs.

"No boss," I reply. "I don't."

"How was Brooke with you on Monday?"

"There never was a Monday. Not for us, anyway. The next morning my agent called. There was a team in Texas with a hole on their back end and their season had started a month ago."

"WHERE?" I ASK AGAIN, FEELING my pulse hammer a little harder as I clutch the phone a little tighter.

"Colorado City," repeats my agent. "Texas."

"And they're called the what?" I ask again.

"The Dust Devils," repeats my agent.

"I thought that was a vacuum cleaner."

"I thought Colorado City was in Colorado but I guess today's just full of surprises, isn't it," he replies brusquely. "You want to go then or what?"

"What are they offering?" I ask.

"One year," he replies. One year. It's as good an offer as I'm going to get at my age. I'm in limbo here, anyway. Ah, goddamn, there's Brooke, but I'm finally getting to the point where I'm not making life decisions with my crotch and goddamn, I'm going to keep it that way. It's only a year, right?

"You still there?" My agent's voice cuts through my thoughts.

"Let's do this," I say. Hanging up, I stare out the window at the grey, concrete depression that is Vancouver from October to God-knows-when. I don't feel like celebrating this one. I feel relieved. And relief can sometimes be as draining as stress. Slowly, I sink onto the couch and close my eyes. As I drift off to sleep, I can see the tail-lights of Brooke's taxi disappearing down the street.

Hockey 1, Love 0.

COLORADO CITY'S A TWO-HORSE WEST Texas town located in the Sun Belt on the southwestern edge of the Staked Plains. It's flat and dusty and famous for its *Heart of West Texas Museum*, not its budding professional hockey franchise.

This is American Football country, make no mistake: Proper Friday Night Lights sort of stuff and with regional high school gridiron clashes drawing crowds of thirty thousand plus; hockey seems more like an afterthought for most folk. Regardless, we get treated like rock stars (free haircuts, swag) and although the good citizens of Colorado City treat us with the cautious fascination usually reserved for snake oil salesmen, we're in Texas and Texans can't help but love their teams. Maybe we're only getting a modest paragraph on the ass-end of the *Colorado City Mail* instead of the ten page spread reserved for the overgrown high school quarterback and his over-active pituitary posse but at least we're getting something. This is the

Dust Devils' inaugural season after all.

Like I said, I'm the late registration and the team is fifteen games to the breeze before I even lace up a pair of skates, but no worries. I'm still in the fashionably late window as far as I'm concerned and from where I'm sitting, this dusty outpost is fertile ground for a veteran defenceman. But maybe not quite as fertile as I imagined...

The team hasn't won many games yet and morale's more nonexistent than low in the locker room. It's a weird lack of intensity, like everyone's afraid to commit emotionally to this campaign and no real surprise, with the revolving door attitude the organization has already adopted toward its players.

"What's your contract?" asks a fellow defenceman.

"A year," I reply, which garners sarcastic looks from the guys within earshot.

"Good luck with that," chimes the goalie. "A couple of bad games and you'll have a pink slip on your locker and that's that. These guys are ruthless down here." *Whatever,* I think. *I've seen worse.*

SOMETHING'S STIRRING IN THE VISITORS' locker room in Albuquerque and it's not pre-game nerves although it should be. The New Mexico Scorpions had handed us our asses last time we met, and that had been on home ice.

"He's from *Sports Illustrated!*" whispers one of our wingers excitedly, pointing to the suit who leans on a locker flipping through his notepad. That's about all the encouragement I need.

"Hi," I begin, offering my hand. "I'm Danny Boy Doyle and I'm The Real McCoy." It's a line I've successfully employed on several occasions and today's no exception.

"Hi, Danny Boy Doyle," he replies, working my arm like it's the handle on a hand-pump. "I'm Mark Hampshire, Sports Illustrated," and ten minutes later I'm firing on all pistons and my new teammates are enjoying the latest installment of *The Danny Show.*

"The way I see it, there will be two significant days in my life: the day I leave hockey and the day my obituary hits the papers and frankly I have no idea what's going to happen after either." A chuckle around the locker room as Hampshire furiously scribbles in his notepad, which is a green light as far as I'm concerned. "I tried to quit hockey once," I continue. "I'd played three years in Europe and after some trouble with compensation, I said to hell with it. I'm through. Hockey screwed me so I'm going to screw hockey. Which was ridiculous. You don't screw hockey." *Damn, that sounded good!* Hampshire seems to like it too, because that pen's going a-mile-a-minute. Pausing, I let him catch up.

"Go on," he says, pen twitching for more.

"I went home to Vancouver but I was miserable. Frustrated. Pacing. Ended things with my girlfriend at about the same time too. I had to go back to hockey. It's what I do. It's what I love. When I'm playing hockey, I'm me. I'm Danny Boy Doyle. That's when I feel like a whole person." *And... CUT!* Hampshire flips the notebook closed.

"Thanks Danny," he says. With an obliging grin I shake his hand again, then one more time for good measure as he leaves.

"That's Doyle," I remind him with a wink. "D-O-Y-L-E."

"How was the game?"

"An unmitigated disaster. New Mexico went up three goals in as many minutes and by the midpoint of the second period it was 6-0. We pulled our rattled veteran goalie and put our backup between the pipes but he lasted all of five minutes before getting a game misconduct for attempting to fillet a Scorpion's thigh with his stick. Back came the veteran (who at this point had completely lost the will to live) and by the final horn, we'd lost 9-0. There were four fights that game and we lost all of them too."

"Doesn't sound like one for the books."

"No, it sure wasn't. But to be fair, we'd played twelve games in seventeen days and half our squad was out with injuries."

"Where were you living at this point?"

"The team had snapped up a bunch of units in an apartment complex so I got one of those. Each player had their own suite and there was a communal aquatic and sauna facility behind the lobby, above the parkade. They gave me a car too. The whole package was pretty sweet: almost an Athletes' Village sort of scenario. The boys

and I spent most of our free time inhaling appetizers at the twenty-four hour restaurant in the mall down the road or knocking back beers by the pool. The chlorine content was a little high, leaving you itchy and red-eyed after a few laps but the hot tub and the sauna were just fine, so no complaints."

"No more billets either I guess?"

"Not in the conventional sense. But there were host families."

"The difference being?"

"The difference being that no one lived with them. They were locals; huge fans who opened their homes on weekends to the player they'd been designated to entertain. Barbeques, ballgames, that sort of thing. Something to make us feel more at home."

"A community liaison sort of scenario?"

"Exactly. The pair assigned to me were amazing people. Margaret and Duane, or Heavy D as he liked to be called. Heavy D wasn't actually heavy at all. He got the nickname for his knack of getting things done. Heavy D was an oil man who worked for some huge outfit headquartered out of Dallas. The only thing heavy on him was his shiny, dessert plate-sized belt buckle: a relic from his rodeo days, allegedly.

"Heavy D and Margaret had three little lower case D's too. Davie (5), Dalton (7) and Duke (11), sincere kids with blonde hair, freckles and 1950's crew cuts that gave them the look of characters from a Norman Rockwell illustration. Heavy D was an enthusiastic gun collector and kept about thirty of varying makes and calibers scattered throughout his sprawling home. You'd think it would be hazardous what with the kids, but those little D's could shoot almost as well as Daddy (even the youngest) and firearm safety was treated with the same reverence as grace before meals and prayers before bed. Heavy D was passionate about four things: God, family, sports and the Second Amendment. Welcome to Texas."

IT ONLY TAKES TWO WEEKENDS, four top sirloins and a bucket of potato salad for me to really feel at home at Heavy D's. The kids are great, Margaret makes the best peach cobbler this side of the Rio Grande and Heavy D and I get along like beer and nachos.

"Ya'll come back every Saturday if you want," offers Margaret and give or take a few hangovers, I do.

I'm beginning to feel at home with the team too, enjoying my role as one half of the second defensive pairing in a squad that's finally picking up a few W's and slowly clawing its way up the league standings. Maybe I'm imagining it, but the crowds have been feeling a bit bigger too. *Bona fide Dust Devil,* I think to myself as I drive home from the rink after practice. *Still sounds like a vacuum cleaner. Maybe it sounds differently out loud.*

"Bona fide Dust Devil." *Nope, definitely a vacuum. Ridiculous. But not as ridiculous as this shitty music. Gotta figure out how to change these radio presets...*

I'm poking the four incriminating buttons on the dash, quietly swearing to myself as I get assaulted by Travis Tritt then Garth Brooks then Faith Hill then some twangy garbage I don't even recognize then Travis Tritt again, and that's when I miss my exit ramp. Turns out, it's the last turn for a few miles and by the time I realize that I'm well and truly lost, I'm sitting at a red light between a low-rider El Camino and a Cadillac with a half-naked senorita airbrushed on the hood. *Fuck. They're getting out...*

"*Que pasa,* homes?" asks the bandana-wearing guy leaning in my window, his lips curling menacingly around a metallic grill of a smile. Seven of them surround my car; most mustachioed, all bare-chested and each covered in tattoos that snake right up their necks onto their faces. One guy even has an angry-looking Virgin Mary on the side of his head.

"I said what's up, *homes?*" repeats the guy again in a tone that makes it clear he probably isn't a part of the Dust Devil's host family scheme.

None of these guys look happy. In fact, if medals were awarded for synchronized brow furrowing they'd collectively take home the gold. Usually, I'm good at reading faces and responding accordingly but the faces I'd previously encountered didn't look like they'd been attacked by a manic two-year-old with a felt-tipped marker. I can't recall what tattooed teardrops mean but I'm remembering what Heavy D told me just last weekend. *Every Texan loves his sports teams.*

Hope to God this goes for Texicans as well...

"Hey, fellas!" I say with a grin. "I'm Danny Boy Doyle and I'm The Real McCoy." Like one, they take a step forward—just one step—but suddenly, inexplicably, I feel ten times closer to meeting my Maker. *Oh God, is this guy actually growling at me?*

"I'm a Dust Devil!" I exclaim hastily, realizing with growing dismay that the name sounds more like a rival gang than a vacuum cleaner *or* a hockey team. Metal-mouth's eyes bore into mine like gimlets. Without breaking gaze, he raises his voice for the benefit of his compadres.

"He says he's a Dust Devil." The gangbangers chuckle, but from where I'm sitting they sound more like hungry hyenas and I feel more like a zebra than a vacuum. Suddenly, Metal-mouth is lunging through the window, snarling in my face. "I'll tell you what you are bitch, you're bat-shit loco." He throws open the door. "Get out of the car!"

"I'm a hockey player!" I explain. "I'm a Colorado City Dust Devil!" Silence.

"Get out of the car," repeats metal-mouth quietly. I can already see the Vancouver Sun headline. *IDIOT CANADIAN HOCKEY PLAYER SLAIN IN WEST TEXAS GANGLAND EXECUTION. FAMOUS LAST WORDS: I'M A DUST DEVIL.*

Cotton-mouthed, I get out of the car, raise myself to my full height and prepare for whatever comes next, which I'm pretty sure will be somewhere between fairly unpleasant to horrific. That's when Metal-mouth cups my face in his hands, (Jesus, even his fingers are tattooed).

"I fucking love hockey, homes," he says gently. "What position do you play?"

"I'm a defencemen," I reply.

"Shit, I fucking love defence. Who you playing next?"

"Um, the Austin Ice Bats," I reply weakly.

"I fucking hate Austin!" he yells. "You do something for me, mang." Metal-mouth tilts his head, staring at me with brown-eyed sincerity.

"Anything," I reply, and at that point I pretty much mean it.

"When you play Austin, you get out there and you murder them. You hear me? You fucking murder them!" I nod vigorously, negating the need for the *or else* which I feel certain is coming.

"Absolutely! All of them, murdered. Murdered to death. You have my word."

"Good," he replies, roughly patting the side of my head. "Now get out of here. This place is crawling with assholes."

The next weekend, I tell Heavy D about my ordeal.

"Damn, Danny!" he says, shaking his head in disbelief. "That's Barrio Latino turf. Could've got yourself shot." He looks left then right before leaning in and quietly continuing. "You want to borrow a piece? I've got a .39 Special you could keep in the glove box…"

"No thanks, D," I reply. "But I'll take another beer. And maybe a street map if you have one."

THAT MONDAY WHEN I ARRIVE for practice, half the team is huddled around our veteran goalie who's huddled over a copy of the latest Sports Illustrated. On its glossy cover is a picture of Tiger Woods making a birdie on a hole that won him a green jacket but I couldn't care less.

"Let me see that," I say, grabbing the magazine and frantically leafing through. There it is, in big bold letters! *'LONE STAR'S IN THE MAKING—The Sun Belt is experiencing a minor hockey league boom, but for the Colorado Dust Devils the operative word is bust.'*

Scanning, scanning… there I am! Sitting on the team bus, sipping a cold one! Holy mother of God, I'm in Sports Illustrated! *'Twenty-six-year-old defenceman Danny Doyle, his handsome face marred slightly by an indentation beneath his right cheekbone that is approximately the width of a puck…'*

I'm grinning so much, my *handsome face* hurts. The article itself is dripping with sarcasm and less than complimentary as far as the team goes, and no surprise really, but who cares? I'm in Sports Illustrated! *His handsome face…* Awesome.

On the way home, I stop by the gas station and buy every Sports Illustrated on the rack.

"Really?" she says, even more interested than before. The other guys left *The Smoking Gun* ten minutes ago, but I've got half a drink left and I'm really enjoying toying with her. Why else would I be flirting with a 50-year-old bank manager in a second rate Texas bar masquerading as a Wild West saloon? Swiveling sideways on her stool, she shows off a pair of legs that look like they've been around the block more than once.

"Really," I confirm, sliding the magazine across the bar. "Page sixty-eight." The clumped mascara pulls apart like spider legs as her eyes widen.

"Y'all from Canada?" she asks incredulously.

"No, just me," I reply, but my dig at the Texan vernacular goes sailing right over her bottle-blonde head.

"Oh you poor baby! You don't even have Christmas up there, do ya?" she laments softly. But what she lacks in education she makes up for in makeup. I'm not saying she looks like a rodeo clown but if there was a Miss Colorado City pageant for middle-aged financiers—you get the picture.

"What's Christmas?" I ask, affecting a pretty convincing veneer of innocence.

"Why, Christmas is the time when we celebrate the birth of our Lord and Saviour Jesus Chrast," she explains. "It happens in the winter."

"It's always winter in Canada," I reply dolefully. "Snow as far as the eye can see."

"Well, what do y'all do for fun?" she asks.

I shrug. "I dunno. Collect fire wood, shoot moose, scalp Indians... you know."

"That's amazing," she gasps. *Not as amazing as your weapons-grade ignorance,* I think. "How do y'all get around in all that snow?" she inquires.

"Snowmobiles mostly," I reply. "And if you don't have one, then usually horses. I don't have either so I have to skate everywhere. That's why I'm such a good hockey player." At this point, I'm almost cracking *myself* up and I'm finding it hard to believe that she's still biting, but she is. Hook, line and sinker.

"What's your name again?" she asks.

"Danny Boy Doyle," I reply, but at this point, I'm pretty sure I could say Santa Claus and it wouldn't arouse suspicion. Unfortunately though, it's not suspicion that's getting aroused this evening.

"Well, I have an idea Danny Doyle," she murmurs, leaning in. "Why don't y'all come back to my place and we can talk more about Canada there?" Suddenly, there's a veiny hand on my knee.

"That's not very Christian is it?" I gulp, watching in horror as her acrylic talons slowly trace circles up my jeans…

"The way I see it," she breathes, "Jesus made my body and he made it so it tingles when it's touched just right too." *Lady, your body has less to do with God and more to do with Mary Kay…*

"Gotta go, sorry." I say, hastily banging back the rest of my drink and slapping some money on the bar. "Hockey."

It takes two minutes of driving with the windows down before I finally get the noxious smell of her perfume out of my nostrils. Times like this used to make me miss having a girlfriend. Any girlfriend. Now, they just make me miss Brooke. *Brooke.* A girl I haven't even kissed.

"You said the Sports Illustrated article had been less than flattering as far as its take on the team…"

"Yeah, it was awful. But to be fair, we had spent the better part of our inaugural year propping up the league so you can hardly blame them for not focusing on our tentative three game streak."

"How much of an effect did your arrival have on the team's success?"

"A fair bit, but less because of my skill and more due to my clean bill of health. The Dust Devils had been decimated by injuries and were gasping for a healthy D-man in particular. In my thirty-plus games, we'd done quite well, grinding out enough wins to sit sandwiched in the middle of the Western Professional Hockey League (WPHL) table. Although wins didn't come easy down there and the margins were generally pretty slim."

"Things were beginning to go well then?"

"Things were beginning to go well. Then I blew out my knee."

Matt McCoy

I CAN FEEL IT WHEN it goes. I can almost hear it. We're on a road trip in Lake Charles and we're tied with the Ice Pilots going into the third and we're enjoying most of the possession and that's when it happens. It's not a nasty hit. I'd been dealt far worse in Germany and even Denmark. It's the landing that gets me—the way my leg folds underneath me as this guy falls on top—and that's more or less that. Knees are knees.

You know that scene in the movies where the skinheads crowd into the jail showers and the inmates clear out because one lonely patsy (usually the new guy) is about to pick up the soap whether he likes it or not? That's how I feel as the visitors' locker room clears after the game and the Dust Devils coaching staff corner me.

"What do you mean you're releasing me?" I ask incredulously, looking up from my ice pack. "I'm injured!" I'm not one to read a contract's small print (that's what my agent's for) but I do know the basics and I know there's not a team on the planet that can kick a downed defenceman out of bed because he got injured. That's why there's a physio clause. The Chairman waits until the retreating feet of the last of my teammates recede down the corridor before continuing.

"It's barely a bump. You're fine," he grins thinly.

"We just need to make space on the squad," explains Coach, who's even lousier at bullshitting than the Chairman. The rest of the administration are staring around the room uncomfortably, doing their best to avoid the elephant in the room, which in this case happens to be my right knee that has ballooned to the size of a football. There are hollow apologetic formalities and requisite shaking of heads before they finally exit the locker room and by the time they leave, each of them deserves an Oscar. Not one of them even offers to help me to the bus, either. I have to use a hockey stick for a crutch as I hobble across the parking lot to the waiting team bus.

A couple of bad games and you'll have a pink slip on your locker and that's that. These guys are ruthless down here. I'd been warned. I just didn't expect that it would apply to legitimate injuries as well. They probably think I'll go to the apartment and pack my bags as soon as we get back to Colorado City. That I'll bugger off with my tail between my legs and my knee on ice and that'll be the end of that. They're wrong. I'm Danny Boy Doyle. They haven't seen me angry yet.

As soon as I'm back in Colorado City, I drive straight to the university which is home base for the Dust Devils' team doctor, a guy who's as decent as he is candid. The doc's not in when I show up and I end up sitting in the car for three hours, drumming my fingers on the steering wheel and intermittently glancing at my watch before he finally arrives. But when he does, it's worth the wait.

"It's your ACL," he confirms, gently extending my leg until my sharp intake of breath tells him to stop. "You're going to need sixteen to eighteen weeks of rehab." *Ha! That's what I thought.*

"Could you put that in writing?" I ask.

"Certainly," he replies. I watch with Machiavellian satisfaction as he peers down his bifocals and scrawls on a sheet of official Colorado City Dust Devils stationery.

"This needs to be faxed directly to the league," I inform him in a tone that sounds like I'm relaying a message from someone higher. Holding my breath, I watch as he finishes writing, scribbles his signature at the bottom of the page and looks up.

"Of course," he says with a knowing smile. *Attaboy*, I think. *Hippocrates would be proud of you.*

"*The Dust Devils' staff must have been terribly put out.*"

"*Put out doesn't even touch it. They were furious. The WPHL ordered them to follow through with my rehab.*"

"*And they did?*"

"*They had no choice. But they did have one last card to play. A week later, I got a call from Coach and I knew something was up immediately because he wasn't ripping my head off or describing exactly where in the desert he was planning on burying me. Instead, he was calm. Pleasant even. Things had changed, apparently, fresh injuries on the back end. He was hoping we could put all this behind us and get me back in the lineup by next game...*"

"So what you're telling me," repeats Heavy D, handing me a beer and banging the cap off his own using the veranda railing.

Matt McCoy

"What you're telling me is that they want you back on the roster, despite your stunt with the doctor and despite your legitimately messed up knee?"

"That's the gist of it," I confirm, necking my first icy gulp, appreciating the pleasant carbonated back-throat burn of my Bud Lite.

"Can you skate?" he asks.

"I guess," I reply. "With enough tensor bandages and painkillers." Heavy D shakes his head.

"They're taking you for a ride, buddy," he states matter-of-factly. "Do you know what it says if you step on that ice, even for one minute? It says you're one hundred percent healthy, even if you're not. And if you're healthy, you don't need rehab and if you don't need rehab, they're legally off the hook to provide it for you."

"Sons of bitches," I mutter, leaning back as the big picture comes into focus.

"Still want to play?" he asks. I shrug.

"I always want to play. Not if it screws me out of rehab, though."

"And you're sure you're good to go on that thing?" he asks again, nodding to my knee.

"Sure," I reply. "Probably shouldn't but what the hell."

"Okay then," says Heavy D, draining the last of his beer. "Then I think you should play."

"And do what when they terminate my physio?" I ask.

"Don't you worry about that, Danny Boy," he says with a grin. "I've got someone I want you to meet…"

DORAN INGALLS ISN'T EXACTLY WHAT I expected when I walked through the door with the words *Ingalls and Associates* painted in block Century Gothic letters on the frosted window. Somehow, I was picturing a thin, sharp-tongued character in an ill-fitting black suit: something more along the lines of Dickensian barrister. This guy looked more like JR from *Dallas.*

"What's the problem, son?" says the lawyer in a lazy drawl, loosening his bola tie, kicking his snakeskin cowboy boots up onto the desk and tipping back the brim of his ten-gallon Stetson with one finger. He's motionless and silent as I recount the events of the last week and his posture doesn't change once I'm done.

"Well, what do you think?" I ask. Doran Ingalls, Attorney at Law stares at me bemusedly, before finally responding.

"Do y'all like lemonade, Mr. Doyle?"

"Sure," I reply, completely confused. He presses the button on a desktop intercom that looks like it was purchased the same year desktop intercoms were invented.

"Flo, why don't you bring in two tall glasses of lemonade for myself and Mr. Doyle." The beverage-toting assistant appears so quickly it's almost creepy. "Mmmm-MM!" says Doran Ingalls, smacking his lips. "Makes you wish life handed you more lemons, doesn't it." There's a long, appreciative pause before he continues. "Here's what you're gonna do, Mr. Doyle. You're gonna get out there and you're gonna play some hockey."

"And what are you going to do?" I ask.

"Me?" says Doran Ingalls, taking another appreciative sip from his glass. "Well, sir, I'm gonna do everything else."

Things are dodgy the minute I arrive in the dressing room. They changed my jersey number and my stall and my teammates are looking everywhere but at me. Suddenly I'm feeling pretty relieved that I lawyered up.

Scanning the crowd during the warm-up skate, I spot the un-holy Trinity: Coach, the Chairman and between them, the league Commissioner; vultures waiting for their prey. The Commissioner isn't the only guest of honour, though. There's my salvation: Doran Ingalls and his ten-gallon Stetson and right next to him is Heavy D giving me a reassuring thumbs-up. Game on!

A few minutes in, I'm suddenly benched for ten unprecedented minutes then magically find myself serving a five-minute major in place of the team goon. No surprise, I don't step on the ice again. As far as the unholy Trinity is concerned, Mr. Canada just stepped in a bear trap. Boy, do they have a surprise coming...

The call doesn't come in until eight o'clock the next morning and when I get to the rink, Coach and the Chairman are waiting for me.

"You want to talk about this?" I ask nonchalantly. *Look at these assholes and their shit-eating grins.*

"You know what, Doyle?" responds Coach. "We don't. Just clean out your locker and go." As I turn to leave, one more volley sails over the bow of the HMS Danny Boy. "Can we expect you to leave town tonight or tomorrow?" This time, I'm the one grinning.

"Oh, I'm not going anywhere, Coach," I reply evenly. "Sure, you can legally release me, but the league's already ruled on my physio. Sixteen more weeks of it, in fact. You know what you can expect? A bill from my lawyer."

With that, I saunter out of the office as best as someone can saunter with a buggered knee. And if looks could kill, I would have needed much, much more than physio right then.

"COLLECT," I MUTTER INTO THE receiver and suddenly I'm ruing how much I abused Mum's calling card while I was in Ireland. Huddling into the phone booth, I try to quell the shudders that are gradually turning into shivers as the Colorado City night sets in. That's the messed up thing about West Texas. You can fry an egg on the hood of your car during the day and probably freeze a tray of ice on it that same night. Sun Belt my ass. Someone should sue the state for false advertising. RING, RING, RING…

"Hello?" says an almost forgotten, but familiar voice. I forget myself and start to respond but the crackling drawl of the operator cuts me off.

"Will you accept a collect call from Danny Doyle?" *God this is embarrassing…*

"Uh, yeah," replies Henry. "What's going on, Danny?"

"Hey, brother," I reply, forcing faux-enthusiasm through my chattering teeth. Like his call to me so many years ago, Henry knows that we don't phone each other unless we're at the end of our ropes. We don't talk much, but we're still each other's best friend.

Henry is all ears as I give him the Readers' Digest version of the last couple of weeks: How Coach (the evil bastard) responded by sticking a new player in my apartment with me, a Native guy who lasted two weeks because he was as unhappy with sleeping on my couch as I was about having him there. How the Bailiff and the

Sheriff had locked me out of my own apartment, forcing me to re-rent it at the non-player rate of eight hundred and fifty bucks instead of two-fifty. How the organization had taken my car. How they'd threatened the rest of the team with fines and even expulsion if they so much as said one word to me.

"Man, that's singularly fucked up!" says Henry as I finish. "They're treating you like a piece of shit."

"I may as well be," I sigh.

"How are you getting by?" he asks.

"This guy I know, Heavy D, he's floating me the cash for rent and physio. Hooked me up with his lawyer too."

"Good thing," says Henry. "But you're pretty broke apart from that?"

"Broke or broken?" I reply.

IT's A TEN-BLOCK TREK BETWEEN the pay phone and the complex and that's a long time to be alone with your thoughts. That's the hardest part: the isolation. Not playing hockey is awful, being broke is frustrating and being car-less is a pain in the ass. But the loneliness? The loneliness actually hurts. *Keep your chin up.* That's what Henry had said before hanging up. And I am, but I'm starting to wonder why. The payout? The pride? Love of the game? This game's handing me my ass at the moment. As far as the gamble goes, I've gone all in with Heavy D's bankroll with a couple of high cards so I have to see the flop, the turn and the river whether I like it or not. But win or lose, then what? That's what's niggling at me worse than the cold as I round the corner and wince into the unforgiving desert wind. *Maybe hockey's not enough to fill the hole anymore and even if it is, I'm roaring towards thirty with a buggered knee. Maybe there's more to life than playing hockey and playing the field. Maybe all this free time has given me too much opportunity to look in the mirror. Maybe I'm wondering if I like what I've become and who I've run over to get here.* And in the middle of this, as these thoughts tumble and clatter around in my head, there's that face again, crystal-clear like she's right in front of me: Brooke.

A car load of teammates drive past, not stopping even though there's no way they don't see me. As I watch their tail lights recede, a

Matt McCoy

ball of tumbleweed the size of a motorbike skips across the asphalt and disappears into the darkness of the frigid Texas night. I quell another full-body shiver. *Just like Henry said, singularly fucked up.*

"Had you spoken to Brooke since you left Vancouver?"

"Not once. I didn't even have her number."

"But you thought about her often?"

"Continually. Even though I didn't have a sexual stake in the situation. I'm not saying I didn't think about sex with her, the mere idea made my knees pleasantly watery. But something else was keeping the flame smoldering this time."

"Genuine feelings, possibly?"

"Sure. It was new to me, whatever it was."

"You were still single, though. Were there any other women?"

"Well... yeah."

WEEKS OF PHYSIO CAN FEEL like years when no one's speaking to you. It's not something you get used to, not when you live on the same floor as the guys you once called teammates. Not when you're snubbed anew every morning and treated like a complete stranger. Not when you're dealing daily with diverted gazes and stony silence. Wounds don't heal when the scab keeps getting ripped off. In English private schools, there's a name for this kind of cruel enforced social ostracization. It's called *being sent to Coventry. Being sent to Colorado City* must be the North American equivalent. Thank God I've got Heavy D for company on the weekends and thank God that Monday to Friday I've got Gabby.

Gabby's my physiotherapist. At first I'm just thankful for the company. Any company. But Gabby's hot. Hot in that curvy, compact, golden skinned, blonde haired Texan sort of way. And seeing her in those tiny little shorts and spandex tank tops and those impossibly white sneakers five days a week is getting unbearable. I've tried everything. I've even told her about Brooke. But Gabby's as uncomplicated as the plastic clasp on her sports bra and that's exactly what I need right now. And since sex for me carries the emotional significance of an overdue pee, it's only a matter of weeks before our friendship develops benefits.

"Like this," she says breathlessly, flipping up the bottom half of the physio table so it looks like an 'L' and positioning herself on it in a way you wouldn't believe even if I tried to explain it. As I happily crawl up behind her, I can't help imagining the look on Coach's face if he could only see just how well my physiotherapy was actually going.

"You sure talk about this Brooke girl a lot," she observes once we're done and she's wiggling back into her tiny shorts. And it really is just an observation since Gabby and I are really, truly just friends.

"Do I?" I respond, which garners a good-natured look that says, *oh come on, you know you do.*

"Well, you'd better do something about it when you get back to Vancouver," she says, folding the physio table back to its horizontal position.

"I will," I assure her. But the real question is *when?* I have four more weeks of physio before my consultation with the medical examiner from Dallas. If the ruling goes against me, I'll be out three thousand, six hundred in rent and a staggering twenty-four thousand in physio. I've been having this recurring nightmare where I'm stuck in Colorado City forever tending bar at *The Smoking Gun* while a revolving door of middle-aged bank managers ask me asinine questions about Canada. But if I win...

"You okay, partner?" asks Heavy D as we drive to the medical judiciary.

"Yep," I reply shortly, although the reality is that my stomach's in my throat and my knees feel like jelly, even the good one.

There's a twenty-minute wait before the ruling and a ridiculous amount of preamble before we actually get down to business and I'm doing my best to read the faces of Coach, the Chairman and the Commissioner but I'm not the only one who brought my poker face. The presiding judge begins.

"Having heard the testimonies of both parties and reviewed the Medical Examiner's report, this court is ready to make a ruling..."

The judge hands a document to the court clerk to read aloud. I glance sidelong at Heavy D and Doran Ingalls. My allies look at me as if to say, *you've got pocket Ace-King, Danny. It's all down to the deck now.* The clerk clears his throat.

"On behalf of the State of Texas, we would like to offer our sincere apologies to Mr. Doyle who has, at the hands of the Colorado City Dust Devils, endured abuse which can only be described as appalling…"

Ace…

"This court hereby rules that Mr. Doyle shall receive thirty-eight weeks of pay…"

Ace…

"…as well as five years of comprehensive medical coverage to be covered by the Colorado City Dust Devils organization."

King.

Full house off the flop! Don't even have to see the turn and the river. Texas Hold'em: one helluva game.

Dust Devils 0, Danny 10.

"THANKS FOR EVERYTHING," I SAY, grasping Heavy D's hand as we part ways at the Colorado City bus depot where I'll catch the bus to Permenian Air Park then board a plane to Vancouver.

"My pleasure, Danny Boy!" he replies with a grin. "You always have a home in Texas." But home is where the heart is and something tells me mine's in Vancouver. I watch as my new friend drives away from the depot until his car becomes a silver speck that disappears in the dusty Texan haze. Turning, I notice with dismay that Bay 3 is empty.

"Excuse me," I say to the large, black woman behind the ticket counter. I'm looking for the Permenian Air Park connector. Did I miss the bus?"

"No, child," replies the woman. "You missed *a* bus. But there'll be another one along shortly. What's your name?"

"Danny Doyle," I reply.

The woman pauses, peering over her glasses. "Danny Boy Doyle, the hockey player?"

"Just Danny Doyle," I say with a smile, strangely okay with how that sounds. Saying it heralded the end of a chapter in my life. A chapter that made me grow up too fast, yet insulated me from encroaching adulthood. It was a bittersweet ending.

"And the bus will take me to the airport?" I ask.

"The bus will take you exactly where you need to go," she replies with a wink.

chapter 11

I CONTEMPLATE THE SECOND HAND on my watch as I lean in the entranceway of the Landsdowne Country Club. She's late, but I'm not bothered. I've waited this long, I can handle a few more minutes.

She's not my first girl—and no surprise to anyone who knows me—but she's the first I've ever felt this way about. Brooke's different than the rest, though. Trusting. Not a jealous bone in her body, even with my history.

"Everyone deserves the benefit of the doubt," she'd sometimes say, punctuating her sincerity with a peck on my cheek. If she isn't my fresh start, I don't know what is.

I'd met her at a restaurant one rainy autumn night shortly after returning to Vancouver.

"I didn't think you'd come back," she said.

"I didn't know I had something to come back for," I replied, but that's what love looks like sometimes.

Autumn turned to winter, and we moved in together. Brooke would tell me about the girl who ran the country club hockey program and I would regale her with the exploits of the handsome hockey player that went to Texas and conquered America. I'm not afraid to take a gamble, I told her emphatically. And I wasn't afraid to have a *craic*. And I wasn't afraid, full stop.

"Good," she replied. "Because I'm pregnant."

We broke the news to Brooke's family the following Sunday and they were as delighted with the news as we were and when we left, her father shook my hand twice.

But now, as I wait outside the Landsdowne Country Club, I don't feel quite so invincible. Fishing in my pocket for the hundredth time, I check for the ring. It's a tiny band with a diamond scarcely bigger than the gleam in my eye but it's the best I can do at the moment. No, she's not my first girl by a long shot, but I'm hoping she'll agree to be my last.

Brooke arrives and everything clever evaporates from my head. I'm lost, completely lost in those big, beautiful eyes and I'm digging in my coat and I'm down on one knee and all I can hear is my heartbeat and the rumble of an approaching thunder storm. I tell her I adore her. Tell her I need her and can't imagine a life without her, and the wind begins picking up and licking at her hair. Brooke's laughing and crying and saying yes and flying into my arms and the program director and the hockey player's lips collide as the rain begins to fall.

Had anyone else been present, they would have witnessed one of the West Coast's happiest moments.

epilogue

"Happy New Year."

"Happy New Year. Sorry it's been a while. I've been dealing with everything..."

"I imagine. How's Levi doing?"

"She's still in remission. We're down to maintenance therapy now. Daily doses of Mercaptopurine."

"And how are you doing?"

"Brooke says that life never throws us curve balls that we can't handle."

"Do you believe her?"

"So far."

"I hope you appreciate the irony of your wife comforting you with a baseball analogy..."

"Can I ask you something, Father?"

"I thought we'd agreed you wouldn't call me that."

"That's what I wanted to ask you about... Dylan."

"That's better."

"Why the informality? No confessional booth, no collar, this first name business..."

"Do you think our conversations would have been as candid if I was just a silhouette behind a cherrywood lattice?"

"No, probably not."

"Exactly. Collar or no collar, I'm a regular guy. From what I can tell,

you need a friend more than you need a priest, anyway."

"Is that why you put up with my coarse language and sordid stories?"

"Damned straight."

"That was my friend talking, not my priest, right?"

"Now you're catching on. Do you believe the cancer will remain in remission?"

"Who's asking?"

"Your priest now."

"I want to believe."

"But you're scared to."

"I don't get scared."

"Come now, we both know that's not true."

"Desperate maybe."

"When you first started coming to me, you were terrified. Your daughter had been diagnosed with leukemia and you had nowhere left to turn."

"I came to absolve myself. I thought if it could make even the smallest difference..."

"You came for the wrong reasons."

"I don't understand."

"You and how you lived your life are not the reasons your daughter is sick! But this guilt you're feeling? These confessions? Your daughter isn't the only one healing here."

"We don't even know if she is."

"You have to believe that she is."

"Blindly?"

"It wouldn't be called faith otherwise would it? The truth is, all the 'Hail Mary's' and 'Our Fathers' in the world aren't going to change the circumstances."

"Then what will?"

"Nothing that's inside our control, I'm afraid."

Matt McCoy

"What's the point in paying penance, then?"

"Exactly."

"I don't understand."

"Penance isn't the point. Admittance is. Confession doesn't change the circumstances, Danny. It changes you."

"Well, suppose that I am sorry, for certain things. Certain parts of my life. How am I supposed to receive forgiveness without penance?"

"That's simple. Start by forgiving yourself."

"Hmm, never thought of that."

"So, when's the last time you were on the ice?"

"Yesterday. With Levi. It was awesome."

Levi Doyle 1, Cancer 0.

Acknowledgements

To Mum and Dad, my eternal support through good times and bad. To my sister, Mary Pat, and my brother, Mark, my very first best friends.

To J.A.W., whose persistence, encouragement and support made this project a reality.

To Nicole Dosenberg and Helena Costa, whose countless critiquing hours gave this project perspective.

To Carlo Sferra and Doran Ingalls for their commitment to my journey.

To Dylan, whose patience and genius made this project what it is.

To my publisher, Michelle Halket, thank you for believing in me and bringing my story to life.

To Corey Spring, Scoop Cooper, David Pratt and Christine Simpson; thank you all for supporting me.

To all the naysayers who believed I would never make it. I thank you wholeheartedly because you motivated me more than you could ever imagine.

A special thank you to Brett Kuntz who was my first real hockey coach, he always supported me and pushed me to be the best player I could be. MACKADOO will never forget you.

To Tom Renney, my former Junior coach. Thanks for teaching me the game and allowing me to be a part of your family. You taught me what it takes to win a championship.

To Mike De Araujo, Sam Dawson, David Vaughan, Fernando Costa: thanks, boys, for always being there as true friends.

To all my friends and family who have supported me throughout the years: thank you.